A Leader's Guide to Leveraging Diversity

New Frontiers in Learning

The **New Frontiers in Learning Series** features books presenting cutting edge developments in learning practices that drive performance in organizations. Particular attention is given to strategically focused linkages between learning and performance. However, the focal point of each book in the series is on learning processes and performance outcomes at the individual, team, and/or organizational level. The theme that unifies the books in the series is learning solutions that add value in highly competitive environments, including both the non-profit and for-profit sectors.

Titles in the series:

Learning to Think Strategically

A LEADER'S GUIDE TO LEVERAGING DIVERSITY

Strategic Learning Capabilities for
Breakthrough Performance

Terrence E. Maltbia
Anne T. Power

AMSTERDAM • BOSTON • HEIDELBERG • LONDON
NEW YORK • OXFORD • PARIS • SAN DIEGO
SAN FRANCISCO • SINGAPORE • SYDNEY • TOKYO
Butterworth-Heinemann is an imprint of Elsevier

ELSEVIER

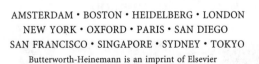

Butterworth-Heinemann is an imprint of Elsevier

Linacre House, Jordan Hill, Oxford OX2 8DP, UK
30 Corporate Drive, Suite 400, Burlington, MA 01803, USA

First edition 2009

Notice
No responsibility is assumed by the publisher for any injury and/or damage to
persons or property as a matter of products liability, negligence or otherwise, or
from any use or operation of any methods, products, instructions or ideas contained
in the material herein

Library of Congress Cataloging-in-Publication Data
A catalog record for this book is available from the Library of Congress

British Library Cataloguing-in-Publication Data
A catalogue record for this book is available from the British Library

ISBN: 978-0-7506-7892-6
ISSN: 1876-1852

For information on all Butterworth–Heinemann
publications visit our web site at elsevierdirect.com

Printed and bound in the United States of America
09 10 11 12 13   10 9 8 7 6 5 4 3 2 1

Working together to grow
libraries in developing countries

www.elsevier.com | www.bookaid.org | www.sabre.org

ELSEVIER   BOOK AID International   Sabre Foundation

Contents

Preface

The *Frontiers in Learning Series* was initiated for the purpose of presenting cutting edge learning practices for driving performance in organizations. In practice this meant paying particular attention to strategically focused linkages between learning and performance — looking at learning processes and practices that are critical for dealing with contexts and environments that are dynamic and complex. It has become commonplace to acknowledge that organizations have to function in contexts that are highly unpredictable and characterized by innovation. Strategic learning and adaptive leadership are widely accepted as critical competencies for managers and executives. Cultivating a learning organization is now a widely stated intention, if often an unrealized one. Thanks to the increasing pace of globalization and technological innovation, for many organizations learning at the individual, team, and organizational levels is no longer a source of competitive advantage, it is critical for survival.

That being said, positioning learning as a continuous process is increasingly challenging. The same dynamics that make learning an imperative also create pressures that tend to drive time for learning, at least in terms of traditional delivery systems, out of the organization. Informal, incidental, project or work-based learning, are increasingly used terms in conversations that focus on learning in organizations. So too is the web, increasingly used to establish communities of practice and to connect social networks. Another consequence of the increasing rate of change and dynamism is a task-focused environment that creates the need for strategically positioning learning. Strategic learning itself is part of the capacity challenge facing organizations.

The literature conceptualizing and studying the learning challenges implied by the above is growing and vast. At the same time the gap between research and practice is widening. As this is being written the issue of the engaged researcher and the value of academic and practitioner co-inquiry is a theme of debate in the upcoming Academy of Management Meetings. The contributors to this series have all done scholarly work, while applying to and learning lessons from practice. The inaugural book in this series, Julia Sloan's *Learning to Think Strategically* examines how executives widely regarded as having responsibility and capacity for strategic thinking developed their capabilities. Beginning with a foundation in the classic strategy literature Julia systemically studied how these individual's learned over time to develop their competencies in strategic thinking. Implications for practice and research are presented, implications Julia uses in her own practice. Also in this series is a volume by Stephen John, *Strategic Learning and Leading Change: How Global Organizations are Reinventing HR*, shares the lived experiences of an organization seeking to strategically reposition itself, engage in organizational learning, and derive implications for developing people all to enhance performance.

This book by Terrence E. Maltbia and Anne T. Power, *A Leader's Guide to Leveraging Diversity*, provides a practical framework, based on extensive research, on how diversity is a strategic asset from a learning perspective. Their work provides an avenue for putting into practice the evidence that demonstrates that diversity is critical to innovation. The book presents a clear direction for building the strategic learning capabilities needed to create and sustain adaptive organizations that effectively respond to today's competitive demands. The result is a valuable contribution to the strategic leadership literature, offering specifics around creating intentional and performance driven learning linked to strategy. *A Leader's Guide to Leveraging Diversity* clearly defines the core competencies necessary for current and future organizational success.

Carol Gorelick
Management and Management Science,
Pace University, New York

Lyle Yorks
Adult Learning and Leadership,
Columbia University, New York

Acknowledgements

There are 22 voices, representing 20 cases, speaking throughout the chapters of this book — voices of experience, wisdom, insight, and inspiration. These voices come from diversity practitioners and leaders, who over the last three decades guided diversity strategies from inside and outside of organizations. These brave pioneers shared their life stories with us and provided the ground on which this book stands. We are grateful to them for being courageous in their diversity journey as well as communicating with us their lessons learned. Our deepest gratitude is for them. They truly changed the landscape of organizational life.

We would also like to express to our editors, Lyle Yorks and Carol Gorelick, for asking us to contribute to this series, believing in the value a book on leveraging diversity would make to a strategic learning series. They were generous in their feedback, insights, and encouragement, as well as long-standing patience. The Butterworth-Heinemann professional team including Alisa Marks, Hayley Salter and Xiaoyang You provided their expert assistance along the way. Their patience, confidence and commitment to us beginning with our first proposal through to the final page are greatly appreciated.

Special thanks to our thought partners, who were at our sides from the time this original work began, or entered during the writing process generously providing time and support: First, Victoria Marsick, Terry's academic advisor during his doctoral studies, provided both support and challenge that resulted in him producing an award-winning dissertation (The Academy of Human Resource Development's Malcolm S. Knowles Dissertation of the Year). Terry also expresses his sincere appreciation to Caryn Block, a wonderful teacher, gifted researcher, and new professional colleague, whose work on discrimination in the workplace triggered his early interests in diversity. Anne also expresses her gratitude to the many colleagues and friends who provided support of all sorts along the way, especially Dale Brown, Kevin Corrigan, Priscilla Gorman, Joy Leach, Mayumi Oda, Patricia Potter, John Schuster, Jane Taylor, Norma Walker, Kathleen Ware and Fatima Weathers, to name a few.

Our sincere appreciation also goes to our clients who have been and continue to be great teachers. They supported us along the way sharing their unique perspectives about why it is important to leverage diversity providing content, and telling us stories we've used as examples throughout the book. Many thanks to our families and friends for their ongoing support and love. A special thanks to our grandmothers, Tressa Gannon (Anne's) and Willie Hayes (Terry's), for their generous hearts and joyous expression of life in spite of the struggles they endured; and, to Anne's husband, Ralph, who sat through many meals listening to us as we analyzed the data that is the ground of this book, adding his intelligent two cents, cheering us on and throwing humor into the game.

Finally, two minds have a cadence when they come together to create. It is that rhythm that forms a partnership. We have been studying, researching, teaching, and writing together for over a decade. We know how to work and play together, and it is our collective energy that pushed this book to its finish. Without our collaborative efforts this book would remain but a dream. Thanks to our partnership!

Introduction

Early in our careers — the 70s for Anne and the 80s for Terry — we experienced our personal versions of a "rude awakening." Anne's occurred when a fellow researcher suggested to their boss that he alone attend a key meeting to present the results of Anne's research because he did not think it was a good idea to send a "girl." Terry's happened during his first field assignment after completing a Fortune 500 company's management training program when he overheard the plant manager refer to a problematic customer as a "stupid nigger." A colleague gestured to the manager that Terry could hear him, to which the plant manager abruptly replied, "So what? I'm not talking about him." A few years later a senior executive in the same company became a mentor to Terry - the powerful lesson here is how different people respond to diversity.

Those were the early days of the diversity movement. It was a time when women, African Americans, and other "minorities" entered the front doors of office buildings, but were not welcome in the conference rooms. Thirty years later, we both sit in conference rooms and work with leaders who choose to make diversity a strategic priority on their corporate agenda. In these meetings we literally see the face of change and feel the heartbeat of a new reality. We share our stories to remind all of us of the passing of an era — perhaps a simpler time for some, but for us, and people similar to us, it was a time intensified by our place in a society where we were excluded without question from the epicenter of the workplace. We entered the world of work at one point in time and find ourselves today light years away from those early encounters.

If you are reading this book it may be because you are leading an organization, business unit, educational institution, government agency, function, or team that has become increasingly more diverse, or perhaps you have agreed to take on a major diversity initiative. Whatever the reason, we hope this book inspires you to become aware of and appreciate the benefits of leveraging diversity.

Leveraging Diversity: Leadership Opportunities and Challenges

The dynamics of the emerging global marketplace and related workspaces resulted in what some have called the diversity industry or the diversity machine (Lynch, 1997). Driven largely by the continued diversification of the workforce, leaders recognized the need to strategically address this sea-change. It is worth noting that the diversity movement, with all its continuously shifting paradigms happened at the same time that the world of business was changing from the old economy to the new economy (Corporate Leadership Council, 2001).

The Changing Game of Business

The old and the new economies differ along four dimensions: information, source of wealth, path toward organizational success, and the set of scarce resources driving each. The winners in old economy firms were asset brokers who operated in an environment where information was scarce, expensive, and closely held by a few powerful individuals. Land, factories, and raw materials were the primary sources of wealth for old economy companies, and the path to success depended on the ability to leverage physical assets. As a result, competition over the scarce resources of capital and physical assets was a key area of focus.

In contrast, winners of the emerging new economy are knowledge brokers who operate in an environment where information is increasingly abundant, cheap, and rapidly transferable. As a result knowledge and ideas take center stage as new sources of wealth in addition to, or in some cases instead of land, factories, and raw materials. This new reality places a premium on the ability to leverage intellectual capital as a path to organizational success. Imagination, creativity, and the ability to quickly transform information overload into useful knowledge and competitive insight has emerged as the scarce resources of today's rapidly changing business environment. Competitive insight is a transformational process that involves collecting and converting information about customers, markets, and competitors into value-added products and services in a way that is faster and better than others are able to do it. Clearly, the competitive game of business has changed (Hamel, 2000; Goleman et al., 2002).

A Leader's Guide to Asking Strategic Diversity Questions

Columbia Business School Professor Willie Pietersen (2002), in his book Reinventing Strategy, draws the reader's attention to three critical leadership questions every leader must be able to answer to succeed in the new economy of the 21st century (pp. 9–10). Each of these questions has a set of corresponding questions related to diversity, listed in Table 1 (Simons & Abramms, 1996). These questions align with three strategic learning capabilities needed to leverage diversity: (1) achieving and sustaining contextual awareness, (2) creating conceptual clarity, and (3) taking informed action. We ask that you reflect on your responses and think about additional diversity related questions specific to your current organizational reality.

This book aims to help readers reflect on these critical leadership questions while adding a diversity perspective.

TABLE 1 Reflecting on Critical Leadership and Diversity Questions

Leadership Questions	Diversity Questions
What is the environment in which our organization must compete and win? ⇩ (Contextual Awareness)	What influence does and will diversity have on this operating environment? What specific demographic, government, social and market forces must we understand to be successful in the new, knowledge-based economy? What is the organization's diversity profile? What does it tell us about the various aspects of our culture that serve as enablers or barriers to leverage diversity for business success? What is the cultural impact of the new economy both in terms of how we do things inside the organization and in the marketplace? What diverse perspectives within the organization can we tap to gain a broad and realistic picture of our business environment? Other questions?
What are those "vital" few things our organization must do exceptionally well to win and continue winning in this environment? ⇩ (Conceptual Clarity)	What are our strategic priorities related to diversity, and what are the expected outcomes or results? What are the success measures/indicators? What specific organizational and individual skills and capabilities must be in place to leverage diversity for business success? What can we do to minimize potential legal exposure or risks while striving to leverage diversity? What other business initiatives can be linked to diversity to leverage its impact? What specific systems and processes must we link to diversity in order to make measurable progress? Other questions?
How will we mobilize our organization to implement these things faster and better than our competitors? ⇩ (Informed Action)	How do I prepare myself to lead and sponsor diversity initiatives? How do I sustain and expand my personal leadership effectiveness in situations involving diversity? How do we call to action leaders and others in the organization to leverage diversity for business success? How do I ensure that everyone in the organization is motivated and accountable for leveraging diversity in the face of competing priorities? Other Questions?

Source: Adapted from Willie Pietersen's, *Reinventing Strategy: Using strategic learning to create and sustain breakthrough performance* (2002, pp. 9–10) and Dr. George F. Simmons and Dr. Bob Abramms', *The Questions of Diversity* (1996).

TABLE 2 Leveraging Diversity: Potential Outcomes

Individual Level	Group Level	Organizational Level
▪ Job/Career Satisfaction ▪ Engagement ▪ Commitment ▪ Performance ▪ Personal Reward	▪ Cohesiveness/teamwork ▪ Communication ▪ Problem Solving ▪ Decision Making ▪ Creativity/Innovation	▪ Attendance/Turnover Rates ▪ Productivity & Quality ▪ Talent Pool/Resources ▪ Diverse Market Penetration ▪ Overall Effectiveness

Source: Adapted from Terrence E. Maltbia's, *The Journey of Becoming a Diversity Practitioner* (2001, p. 41) and Taylor Cox's, Jr., *Cultural Diversity In Organizations: Theory, Research and Practice* (1993, pp. 6–10).

Leveraging Diversity: A Leadership Choice

Leveraging diversity does not happen organically, it takes direct and deliberate engagement by leaders and by a critical mass of individuals at all levels in the organization. Through our work with leaders we have learned that well executed diversity initiatives result in a range of positive outcomes at the individual, group and enterprise level of organizations. These outcomes are listed in Table 2 (Cox, 1993).

Conversely, when diversity initiatives are not well executed, or no strategic focus for leveraging diversity exists, increased diversity in an organization results in lower group cohesion, increased conflict among associates, lower productivity, and higher turnover (Jehn, 1999). As chief architects of organizational culture, your daily actions and decisions as a leader directly influence the climate of your company and the related outcomes. How are you doing?

Study of Leading Diversity Experts and Award Winning Companies

The focus of our book is on the lessons learned from the experiences of twenty leaders guiding diversity strategies inside and outside of organizations. Fourteen are leading diversity experts (captured in 12 cases), who as a group have played a major role is shaping the theory and practice of workplace diversity. The remaining eight are internal diversity leaders accountable for making these processes work in organizations. These leaders generously shared their extensive know-how with us. We crafted case study descriptions for each participant and pass along what we learned in the chapters that follow. Table 3 summarizes the criteria used for inclusion in the study for both external and internal diversity leaders (Maltbia, 2001).

The 12 cases included in the external "expert" sample of the study were identified in the literature review as diversity "thought leaders" as a result of being cited frequently in theoretical, research, and business literature on workplace diversity. Collectively, the 12 external cases are impressive and distinctive. At the time of the study, as a group they had published over 30 major books focused on diversity (including a winner of The Society of Human Resource Management's Book of the Year Award), and literally hundreds of articles in various publications and newsletters. A number of the experts who participated in the study are owners of consulting firms that publish newsletters and journals dedicated to the field of diversity. The study's external respondents manage recognized diversity consulting firms with annual engagements exceeding $500,000 per client.

TABLE 3 Critieria for Inclusion in the Study

External Diversity Leaders	Internal Diversity Leaders
■ Degree to which others writing about diversity referred to the leader's ideas and concepts ■ Presence as keynote speakers at major diversity conferences and workshops ■ Evidence of demand for leader's assistance to help organizations address workplace diversity (client lists/business press)	■ Referrals from external sample participants ■ Senior diversity person of companies recognized for "award-winning" diversity initiatives ■ Leaders engaged in "turnaround" situations that achieved measurable success (e.g., class-action suits) ■ Leaders experienced with diversity initiatives in more than one organization

Source: Adapted from Terrence E. Maltbia's, *The Journey of Becoming a Diversity Practitioner* (2001, pp. 84–86).

In addition, the external diversity leaders developed numerous diversity products including award winning videos, interactive CD's, DVD's, tool kits, and other training materials; developed trainer and other certification programs for diversity practitioners from the novice to the seasoned professional; two are founders of accredited academic programs in intercultural communication and organizational development; several are, or have been, professors or adjuncts at major universities; and have appeared in various media including being featured on the cover of the *LA Times Magazine*, and articles in the *New York Times, Newsweek, USA Today, The Wall Street Journal*, and the *Washington Post*; and on television programs such as *The Today Show*, and being interviewed by Diane Sawyer. (See Appendix A for external case profiles.)

The diversity leaders in the internal cases represent companies that received extensive external recognition for various award winning diversity initiatives. For example, two companies received both the Catalyst and Opportunity 2000 Awards and four are Catalyst Award winners; while an additional two internal diversity cases successfully led turn around situations related to class action discrimination law suits and received recognition for significant change within a short period of time.

The U.S. Department of Labor Secretary's Opportunity 2000 Award (now the Opportunity Award), initiated in 1988, is one of the nation's most prestigious workplace diversity honors. It is presented annually to a corporation that established and instituted comprehensive workforce strategies to ensure equal employment opportunity and showed measurable results. Since 1987, Catalyst has honored leading companies for their creative initiatives to recruit, retain, and advance women, and is also viewed amongst the most recognized workplace diversity honors. (See Appendix B for profiles of the 8 internal cases using pseudonyms for both participants and their organizations). For the purposes of the study we used the following definitions of diversity, workplace diversity and diversity leaders (see Table 4).

TABLE 4 Definitions of Key Terms

Term	Description
Diversity	Diversity refers to any mixture of items characterized by differences and similarities (Thomas, 1996).
Workplace diversity	The various strategies, initiatives and tactics employed by organizations and their leaders to unleash the talent and potential of the changing workforce.
Diversity experts and leaders (external and internal practitioners)	The senior most persons responsible for providing strategic direction for diversity initiatives within an organization. External leaders are advisors who provided consultation to both internal diversity practitioners and their executives, mainly line-of-business presidents, CEOs or corporate functional heads.

Source: Adapted from Terrence E. Maltbia's, *The Journey of Becoming a Diversity Practitioner* (2001 pp. 33–34) and R. Roosevelt Thomas', *Redefining Diversity* (1996, pp. 4–8).

As a result of the selection criteria listed in Table 4, the gender profile of the sample included 60 percent women and 40 percent men; the racial profile of the participants was 50 percent White and 50 percent Black. The study participants were highly educated with 95 percent holding Masters Degrees and 45 percent holding Doctorate Degrees. The strategic learning model and related diversity leadership practices for driving performance breakthroughs in organizations discussed throughout this book are the result of insights gained from this research.

Prior to conducting the field work for the study, we completed an extensive literature review focused on diversity in the workplace. This review helped us better understand the history of the diversity movement in the United States, as well as the state of the practice in terms of workplace diversity issues and approaches. After completing the field study, including the analysis of the data, we returned to the literature to explore a number of key themes that grew from our findings. For example, both the preliminary literature review and study framed diversity in the workplace as a process of learning and change often resulting in personal and organizational transformation.

Another of the study's findings revealed the importance of a dual "coaching/mentoring" relationship between organizational leaders and trusted internal and external advisors on matters related to diversity. With these observations in mind, we explored the organizational transformation, transformative learning and executive coaching literature to gain additional insight. We integrated the insights gained from the post field study period into the diversity leadership framework which we describe in Chapter 1.

Lessons Learned

This book presents the results of our research using a diversity leadership framework. We designed this framework to help organizational leaders identify and build the strategic learning capabilities necessary for performance breakthroughs while leveraging diversity in the process. In the chapters that follow, we share with you the know-how of individuals who lead best in class companies, and understand and take advantage of the connection between leveraging diversity and business success. These leaders recognize diversity as an asset, a potential strength, not a problem to be minimized. Specifically they know:

- Diversity is a life work, a journey, not a destination.
- Diversity is not simply a formula or set of tools and protocols.
- Diversity work is both art and science and is highly contextual.
- Diversity work is successful when applied to meet the needs of the specific situation. There is no one size fits all.

In short, each of the leaders in our research said that diversity work requires deep change in everyone engaged in drawing out and productively working with diversity in organizations. When diversity is truly leveraged, employees do not feel compelled to "check their differences" at the door, but instead are encouraged to engage their full range of talent, perspectives and experience to achieve personal and organizational goals. Each leader's diversity journey included a process of learning and change that often involved a personal as well as an organizational transformation. It seems that their various individual and organizational responses to difference resulted in both individual growth and organizational renewal. And, the leaders expressed their belief that this growth and renewal is a key factor to winning in the competitive, global and fast changing business environment of the 21st century.

We are grateful to these leaders for being courageous in their diversity journey as well as communicating with us their lessons learned. Because of their willingness to share their journeys with us, we were able to develop the diversity leadership framework, which we introduce later in this chapter. First we frame the model by responding to three critical questions. What is meant by strategic learning capabilities? What is meant by leveraging diversity? What is meant by breakthrough performance? The ideas presented in this book build on these three questions.

References

Corporate Leadership Council. *Transitioning Corporate Culture from Old Economy to New Economy*. Washington, DC: The Corporate Executive Board, 2001.

Cox, T. *Cultural Diversity in Organizations: Theory, Research and Practice*. San Franscisco, CA: Berrett-Koehler Publishers, 1993.

Goleman, D., Boyatzis, R., and McKee, A. *Primal Leadership: Realizing the Power of Emotional Intelligence*. Boston, MA: Harvard Business School Press, 2002.

Hamel, G. *Leading The Revolution*. Boston, MA: Harvard Business School Press, 2000.

Jehn, K. A. "Diversity, Conflict, and Team Performance." *Performance Improvement Quarterly* 12(1) (1999): 6–19.

Lynch, F. R. *The Diversity Machine: The Drive to Change the "White Male" Workplace*. New York: Free Press, 1997.

Maltbia, T. E. *The Journey of Becoming A Diversity Practitioner: The Connection Between Experience, Learning and Competence*. Unpublished Dissertation, UMI Dissertation Services, Ann Arbor, MI, 2001.

Pietersen, W. *Reinventing Strategy: Using Strategic Learning to Create and Sustain Breakthrough Performance.* New York, NY: Wiley, 2002.

Simons, G. F., and Abramms, B. *The Questions of Diversity: Reproducible Assessment Tools for Organizations and Individuals,* 2nd ed. Atlanta, GA: The American Institute for Managing Diversity & ODT Inc, 1996.

Thomas, R. R. *Redefining Diversity.* New York: AMACOM, 1996.

SETTING THE STAGE FOR LEADERSHIP THROUGH LEVERAGING DIVERSITY

Is it possible to actually learn to leverage diversity? We think so. Throughout this book, leveraging diversity is positioned as a process of learning and change whereby an organization uses diversity as a vehicle to realize positive performance outcomes. It is a cyclical process — an ongoing self-renewing cycle — with no start to finish blueprint. It is a process that requires ongoing strategic learning and adaptation to respond productively to changes in the internal and external business environments.

In Part I we present our *Strategic Learning Model*, which will serve as your roadmap linking strategic learning to leveraging diversity. We continue with an historical perspective on diversity and suggest that leveraging diversity is the emerging diversity paradigm for the 21st century — the current wave of change — of our present reality. We propose that your success in leading this change initiative depends on clearly understanding and defining your organizational and personal rationale for engaging in efforts to leverage diversity. We help you answer several important questions:

- Why should I make leveraging diversity a strategic priority for my organization — what is my personal rationale? What is the organizational rationale?

- What will it take to make leveraging diversity a daily reality — what do we need to learn and change to be successful?
- How do we take action — what steps must we take to make our vision a reality?

And, finally we emphasize the importance of being clear about your organization's definition of diversity as a foundation for taking authentic, aligned, and informed action.

Strategic Learning:
A Leadership Framework
for Leveraging Diversity

Strategy means deciding how to use each of your resources for maximum impact in the competitive arena.

— *William G. Pietersen, Reinventing Strategy*

Our daily lives are full of opportunities for learning and growth. As Learning Organization experts Victoria Marsick and Karen Watkins (1990) point out, much of what we learn in adulthood is largely informal or incidental in nature. In contrast to formal learning, which is often institutionally sponsored and highly structured, we learn informally through our interactions with others or by seeking out books or other resources to gain knowledge or skill in an area of interest. Incidental learning is a form of informal learning that is often unintentional, is usually "a byproduct of some other activity," and includes learning from our mistakes or learning by doing (such as trial-and-error experimentation).

Much of what we know about diversity is a result of having what intercultural expert Milton Bennett (1998) calls "significant other cultural living experiences." Examples include living or traveling abroad, living in diverse communities (not simply driving by), and working intimately with diverse others on assignments in the workplace. Through the many reflective processes and tools we present in this book, you can draw out many lessons embedded in your existing repertoire of experience interacting with diverse others. While formal diversity training may represent a multibillion-dollar industry, it is the more informal, often incidental forms of learning that contribute to the sustainable capacity to leverage diversity.

As a leader you likely have numerous opportunities for learning to leverage diversity for strategic advantage present in your daily inter-action with employees, clients, and other stakeholders. In this chapter we introduce a framework to enhance your capacity for being mindful of these opportunities as you go through your daily activities.

Strategic Learning Capabilities

Strategic learning is emerging as a specific form of learning with a clear set of characteristics. Strategic learning is intentional, purposeful, and results oriented guided by the strategic objectives of the business and integrated with important business priorities and related initiatives. Pietersen (2002) defines strategic learning as having "four key steps — learn, focus, align, and execute — which form a self-reinforcing cycle that combines learning, strategy, and leadership into one organic process" (p. 4). Strategic forms of learn-ing aim to foster individual and organizational growth, adaptation, innovation, and renewal to keep pace with changes in the external and internal business environment.

Strategic learning is holistic with thinking, emotional, and behavioral dimensions. This holistic nature of learning brings focus to the importance of creating learning interventions designed to leverage diversity while engaging the "whole person," that is the head work (or cognitive), hand work (or behavioral), and heart work (or affective/emotional/motivational). Building on these ideas, we define the meaning of strategic learning capabilities as:

Intentional and performance driven learning linked to strategy that clearly defines the knowledge, skills and mindset necessary for current and future organizational success;

Involves establishing planning and accountabilities systems to ensure that learning is embedded in the actual work and major business processes of the enterprise.

Leveraging Diversity

Leveraging diversity is the collective impact of individual and organizational responses to difference in both the workplace and the external environment in pursuit of personal and organizational objectives. It is a process whereby an organization uses diversity as a vehicle to realize positive performance outcomes. These range from attracting and retaining a diverse talent pool, to successfully penetrating diverse markets. To leverage diversity, leaders must understand the various ways in which the "what" and "how" of diversity come into play, and increasingly in cultural terms. First, we are interested in leveraging the talents of our diverse workforce — leveraging difference for insight, innovation, and performance. A basic premise of strategic learning is that insight is a precursor to innovation. Second, in terms of action we place strategic learning at the core of leveraging diversity and the related performance outcomes. In short, we address the process and outcome dimensions of performance explicitly.

Breakthrough Performance

Performance is at the very core of organizational effectiveness. In organizations, whether at the individual, unit, or system-wide level, performance is about intentionality, that is, the ability to act deliberately to achieve results and desired outcomes. Performance can be assessed using five broad categories of metrics or measures including quantity, quality, time, resources and impact.

At a very basic level performance in organizations is about "increasing" something (e.g., sales, profits, market share, productivity, etc.) or "decreasing" (e.g., costs, error, customer complaints, employee turnover, etc.) in short, quantity related metrics. Quality metrics reflect the overall effectiveness of performance (e.g., exceeding product and service delivery expectations). Time metrics focus on the duration of performance and are often combined with quantity metrics, such as reducing cycle time or improving customer response time. Resource metrics relate to the required investment needed to generate a given level of performance in terms of people and operating costs. Lastly, impact measures focus on the collective effect of a given set of actions at the individual level (e.g., sense of belonging), group level (e.g., workgroup cohesiveness and effective communication), and the systems level (e.g., shareholder value) of the organization.

In today's rapidly changing and unforgiving global markets, the incremental gains resulting from continuous improvement are necessary. However these gains are not sufficient to meet the increasing demands of customers and other key organizational stakeholders, nor are they enough to respond effectively to fierce competitors. Continuous improvement is appropriate for a number of operational challenges leaders face, but adaptive challenges call for a break from the past and the generation of completely new business concepts. Gary Hamel (2000) notes in his book *Leading the Revolution*, the business concept innovation that results in a breakthrough performance relies on the "capability to reconceive existing business models — this is done in ways that create new value for customers, rude surprises from competitors, and builds new wealth for investors" (p. 18). Such performance breakthroughs often require, and are the result of, organizational transformation.

Transformational change in organizations involves discontinuous, adaptive and radical changes in how members perceive, think and behave at work. Leveraging diversity for breakthrough performance demands organizational transformation. Leaders who commit to building strategic learning capabilities to leverage diversity will transform their perceptions, thinking and resulting behaviors. It is only through this personal and organizational change process that breakthrough performance emerges.

In the next section we integrate important concepts drawn from organizational transformation theory, transformative learning theory, and the field of workplace diversity to provide a comprehensive blueprint to help organizational leaders conquer the complexity of today's markets and take advantage of the opportunities associated with using diversity as a source of competitive advantage.

Strategic Learning Model

The *Strategic Learning Model* (Figure 1.1) is based on the assumption that leveraging diversity is a process of learning and change intended

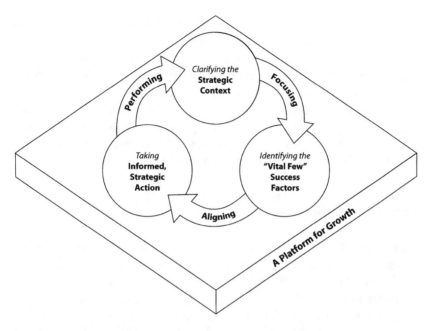

FIGURE 1.1 Strategic Learning Model: A Leadership Framework for Leveraging Diversity.

to enhance performance and facilitate organizational renewal. Organizational renewal is the ability to continuously adapt to the external environment and respond to emerging problems, challenges, and opportunities. While not the only factor, winning companies are beginning to understand that leveraging diversity can contribute greatly to creating and sustaining an adaptive enterprise.

The model's basic components include (1) three strategic learning capabilities, (2) three related outcomes associated with each learning capability, and (3) three different learning foci needed to generate the desired learning outcomes.

First, the model positions leveraging diversity as a form of human performance. Drawing on concepts from Jackson (1991) and Sanchez and Heen (2000), the model asserts that understanding this form of human performance is a function of examining the three dimensions of *context*, *content*, and *conduct*. The three strategic learning capabilities for leveraging diversity respond to the "where/when/ why," the "what" and the "how" of leveraging diversity. They are: (1) achieving and sustaining contextual awareness (know "why" or theoretical knowledge); (2) creating conceptual clarity (know "what" or strategic knowledge); and (3) taking informed action (know "how" or practical knowledge). Each strategic learning capability responds to important diversity and performance related questions. There are different outcomes associated with each, and each requires a different learning focus (Pietersen, 2002).

Contextual Awareness

Contextual awareness involves scanning the external and internal business environments. This capability is necessary in order to articulate the basic rationale for leveraging diversity in a given organization, identify the indicators for assessing progress toward diversity objectives and determine the overall success of diversity initiatives. The learning emphasis of contextual awareness is learning for expanded perspective and results in deep insight and focus.

Chapter 2 provides an extended discussion of the strategic learning capability of contextual awareness as a basis for establishing a unique organizational and personal rationale for leveraging diversity. The story on the following page illustrates the role of contextual awareness as a critical starting point for leveraging diversity in organizations.

Insight is often described as the "Aha" moment that occurs during the discovery process inherent in learning for contextual awareness. Diversity of team membership produces a divergence of opinions, thoughts and new learning. Making the leap from immersion in the challenge at hand to insight requires recognition of the universal tendency toward ethnocentrism.

Ethnocentrism is the tendency to view members of one's own group (in-group) as the center of the universe, for interpreting other social groups (out-groups) from the perspective of one's own group, and for evaluating beliefs, behaviors, and values of one's own group somewhat more positively than those of other groups. Left unchecked, ethnocentrisms diminishes the creative group synergy that leads to insight. However, superior strategic choices are a result of fresh insights arising from a diversity of perspectives.

UNDERSTAND THE ORGANIZATION'S STARTING POINT
(ADVICE FROM AN INTERNAL DIVERSITY LEADER)

The first thing I do as part of launching a diversity process is understand the organization, and in so doing, I'm going to take an organization where it's at, not where I think it should be. As a diversity practitioner, you always have to start where the clients are.

I'm looking for incremental change that will lead to an astronomical leap once the foundation has been built. I always expect on the front end of the process to make incremental changes that will position me for a monumental leap.

I look for those incremental changes that will have a politically strong impact on the organization, places that will give high levels of visibility to our diversity strategy and approach. I'm always looking for opportunities where can I partner with a business unit to integrate diversity for competitive advantage and if this business unit wins then diversity wins big time, and a strategic approach to diversity will successful.

Part of understanding the strategic context for diversity is to learn the competitive landscape for the business, what keeps leaders up at night, and figuring out ways to link diversity to the existing leadership agenda and business plan. You have to understand the contextual, cultural nature of this change and have the ability to act on this insight to devise strategies to change the systems that drive behavior in organizations.

— Corporate Director, Human Resources & Diversity
Major Producer, Marketer & Distributor of Energy Products & Services

Conceptual Clarity

Conceptual clarity concentrates on the knowledge areas necessary to leverage diversity for enhanced performance and competitive advantage. Conceptual clarity leads to making important strategic choices. These choices are more effective when based on the insight gained through contextual awareness. The emphasis of conceptual clarity is learning for knowledge. At this point strategic choices are made and the "vital few" critical success factors identified. These factors relate directly to "what we must know" and "what must go well" to win the competitive race and realize our intentions related to leveraging diversity for business success.

The idea of diversity-general work and diversity-specific work is addressed in detail in Chapter 2. In Chapter 3, the core components associated with the meaning of diversity are presented as a basis for gaining a deeper understanding of the strategic learning capability of conceptual clarity. The outcome associated with creating conceptual clarity is alignment between people and core processes across the organization. Enhanced focus allows for making important decisions related to how to deploy scarce resources. Alignment ensures that every element of the organization (i.e., measurement and reward systems, organizational structures and processes, culture and employees' skill and motivation) supports the strategic priorities.

Research shows that it is not enough for leaders to say they are committed to diversity; the organizational systems must reinforce values and behaviors consistent with the diversity strategy (American Society for Training and Development, 1996). The story below provides one perspective on the importance of the strategic learning capability of conceptual clarity.

THE CONTENT RANGES FROM DIVERSITY-GENERAL TO DIVERSITY-SPECIFIC WORK
(ADVICE FROM AN EXTERNAL DIVERSITY EXPERT)

The standard work around racism and sexism will continue in this [U.S.] country. Newer, emerging topics including sexual orientation, religion, cross-functional work and globalization will increase in their importance and integration into the diversity change process.

The foundation work is the same worldwide, it answers the question ... *What is diversity or pluralism? Why is that important? What are the fundamentals of how we do it?* However, the issue-specific work, that is specific to a given context, is where it's different (e.g., the dynamic interplay between specific identity groups and their proportions in a given region of the world influences the leverage points and related diversity priorities).

However it is important to acknowledge that racism, sexism, and the other "isms" are such sensitive, threatening, and potentially volatile topics, that people often perceive that they dominate diversity work, even when there is direct observable data (e.g., number of slides, program content, timelines, number of initiatives and so on) that prove that a broad spectrum of foundational and issue-specific topics were explored and included in the diversity strategy. This highlights the importance of continuing to emphasize the importance of understanding where individuals may be on the journey of learning and working with diversity.

— Author, Researcher and Former HR Executive
Independent Organizational Effectiveness and Diversity Consultant

Informed Action

We conclude Part I of the book with Chapter 4 by providing an overview of the diversity learning and change process reflective of the third and final strategic learning capability, taking informed action. Next, the four chapters in Part II of the book operationalize the capability of taking informed action by presenting six change drivers: (1) leadership, (2) diagnostic/discovery work, (3) broad-based involvement and communication, (4) education and training, (5) measurement and evaluation, and (6) total systems alignment.

The emphasis of taking informed action is on learning from experience and results in planned experimentation that provides a platform for performance excellence. Taking informed action allows organizations to quickly implement diversity related strategic choices and related plans, to take advantage of the next shift in the external business environment and changing workforce demographics. The reflective potential of learning during and from experience provides a capacity to repeat this cycle of learning for perspective, knowledge, and informed action, over and over again, and can result in personal and organizational renewal and transformation.

Strategic Learning Model: Theoretical Basis

Table 1.1 displays the theoretical and philosophical basis for our strategic learning model, including the guiding questions related to each strategic learning capability. First, contextual awareness is

TABLE 1.1 Strategic Learning: Theoretical Basis

Learning Capability	Philosophical Foundation	Guiding Questions
Achieving and sustaining contextual awareness	*Structuralism and Constructivism* An emphasis on the "where & when" in time, place and history; ultimately understanding the "why" of diversity.	What are the historical origins of one's cultural programming and its influence on thinking about diversity? What are the historical diversity profiles of senior executives (e.g., race, gender, ethnicity, nationality, etc.)? Impact on this history on current cultural and behavioral assumptions related to diversity? What is the organizational and personal rationale for leading to leverage diversity? What is the basic premise for diversity work? In what ways have current and historical systems and structures influenced the organization's diversity profile at all levels (e.g., strategy planning, selection and promotional practices, compensation policies and practices, succession planning processes, etc.)? Given this context, how will successes in leveraging diversity be evaluated today and in the future? What are the metrics and indicators?
Creating conceptual clarity	*Phenomenology* An emphasis on the "what" of leveraging diversity.	What is the organization's definition of diversity? What's included? What's excluded? Why? What are the organization's diversity priorities? The "vital few" areas of leadership and organizational focus? What is the organization's future vision for diversity? What are the strategic priorities and diversity strategies to realize its promise?
Taking informed action	*Behavioralism* An emphasis on the "how" of leveraging diversity.	What resources and interventions will be used to leverage diversity? What actions are used to leverage diversity daily?

Source: Authors' adaptation of concepts found in Terrence E. Maltbia's, *The Journey of Becoming a Diversity Practitioner* (2001, p. 32) and Terrance Jackson's, *Measuring Management Performance* (1991).

achieved by exploring the interplay between the social systems, the physical environment, the setting in which individuals function, and the evolution over time of all three (Katz and Kahn, 1966, 1978). Theorist from the fields of adult education and organizational behavior proclaim that in contrast to the structuralist view, reality is not always a given, but often a construction or an interpretation. Meaning is context-specific; to be comprehensive, the exploration of context should consider both perspectives (Argyris, 1993; Boud, et al., 1993; Brookfield, 1995; Freire, 1972).

Second, according to Jackson, the term "phenomenology" is drawn from *social philosophy* (Schutz, [1962]1971), and has been developed as a *sociological theory* (Berger and Luckmann, 1966; Cicourel, 1964). The emerging theory and practice of workplace diversity draw on a number of disciplines for guideposts including *psychology, sociology, anthropology,* and *organizational behavior* (Burke, 1994; Cox, 1993; Gardenswartz and Rowe, 1999); *business administration* and *organizational theory* (Thomas, 1996, 1991); *organizational, group,* and *individual development.* Knowledge, concepts, and models from each of these fields provide a basis for understanding the challenges and complexity associated with situations involving diversity.

Diversity is understood as both a set of characteristics and process resulting in patterns of behavior that account for how similarities and differences interact in the workplace. Diversity is a learning and change process. A review of diversity work in pioneering companies reveals three common phases associated with the learning and change process focused on creating an environment that attracts, understands, values, and leverages diversity, they are:

- Phase 1: Creating awareness and generating knowledge;
- Phase 2: Building skills and capacity; and
- Phase 3: Applying the learning in real work situations.

Enacting the diversity learning and change process often involves the transformation of self, others, organizational systems, and structures. In short, comprehensive diversity strategies involve work in three areas: *opening doors, opening minds,* and *opening systems.* The practical application of our strategic learning model rests in 12 leadership practices, which are described beginning in Chapter 2. Collectively, the three strategic learning capabilities presented in this book, when combined with the leadership practices listed in Table 1.2, provide a blueprint for devising strategies and tactics to leverage diversity for breakthrough performance. These leadership practices are introduced in the following chapters.

TABLE 1.2 Leadership Practices for Leveraging Diverity

Chapter	Learning Capabilities and Leadership Practices
Part I: Setting the Stage To Leverage Diversity	
Chapter 1 — Strategic Learning: A Leadership Framework for Leveraging Diversity	■ Achieving contextual awareness ■ Creating conceptual clarity ■ Taking informed action
Chapter 2 — Organizational and Personal Rationale for Leveraging Diversity	■ Balance diversity-general work with diversity-specific work ■ Establish a compelling organizational and personal rationale
Chapter 3 — The Meaning of Diversity	■ Get crystal clear about your organization's definition of diversity
Chapter 4 — The Diversity Learning and Change Process	■ Accept leveraging diversity as an emergent, ongoing & adaptive process
Part II: Building Your Strategic Story for Leveraging Diversity with Six Change Drivers	
Chapter 5 — Essential Change Drivers for Leveraging Diversity	■ Make your strategic story for leveraging diversity real
Chapter 6 — Evidence-based Leadership	■ Ground diversity interventions in a comprehensive discovery process
Chapter 7 — Teaching the Organization How to Leverage Diversity	■ Continue to gain buy-in. Model the way, lead as you learn
Chapter 8 — Diversity Measurement and Metrics	■ Lead from the future to leverage diversity today
Part III: Facilitators for Leveraging Diversity	
Chapter 9 — Leveraging Diversity: The Art of Human Interaction at Its Core	■ Leverage diversity with authentic leadership
Chapter 10 — Leverage Diversity Requires Addressing Conflict Head On.	■ Be prepared to address misunderstanding, resistance and conflict head on
Chapter 11 — Finding Help in All the Right Places	■ Consult prudent, capable and trusted advisor
Part IV: Final Thoughts	
Chapter 12 — Leveraging Diversity: A Leadership Mindset	■ Lead from the outside-in and the inside-out

References

American Society for Training and Development. *Elements of Competence: Creating Competence for Inclusive Work Environments.* Alexandria, VA: ASTD Publication Department, 1996.

Argyris, C. *Knowledge for Action: A Guide to Overcoming Barriers to Organizational Change.* San Francisco: Jossey-Bass, 1993.

Bennett, M. J. "Intercultural Communication: A Current Perspective." In M. J. Bennett (ed.). *Basic Concepts of Intercultural Communication.* Yarmouth, MA: Intercultural Press, 1998.

Berger, P. L., and Luckmann, T. *The Social Construction of Reality: A Treatise its the Sociology of Knowledge.* Garden City, NY: Anchor Books, 1966.

Boud, D., Cohen, R., and Walker, D. "Introduction: Understanding Learning from Experience." In D. Boud, R. Cohen and D. Walker (eds.). *Using Experience for Learning.* Bristol, PA: Society for Research into Higher Education & Open University Press, 1993, pp. 1–17.

Brookfield, S. *Becoming a Critically Reflective Teacher.* San Francisco: Jossey-Bass, 1995.

Burke, W. W. *Organization Development: A Process of Learning and Change.* New York: Addison-Wesley, 1994.

Cicourel, A. V. *Method and Measurement in Sociology.* New York: The Free Press, 1964.

Cox, T. H. *Cultural Diversity in Organizations: Theory, Research, and Practice.* San Francisco, CA: Berret-Koehler Publishers, 1993.

Freire, P. *Pedagogy of the Oppressed.* Harmonsworth: Penguin, 1972.

Gardenswartz, L., and Rowe, A. *Workplace Diversity: A Product of the SHRM Diversity Initiative.* Alexander, VA: Society of Human Resource Management, 1999.

Hamel, G. *Leading the Revolution.* Boston, MA: Harvard Business School Press, 2000.

Jackson, T. *Measuring Management Performance.* New York: Nichols/GP Publishing, 1991.

Katz, D., and Kahn, R. L. "Organization and the System Concept." In J. M. Shafritz and J. Steven Ott (eds.). *Classics of organization theory,* 4th ed., Orlando, FL: Harcourt Brace & Company, 1966, pp. 274–286.

Katz, D., and Kahn, R. L. *The Social Psychology of Organizations,* 2nd ed. New York: Wiley, 1978.

Maltbia, T. E. "The Journey of Becoming A Diversity Practitioner: The connection between experience, learning and competence." Unpublished Dissertation, UMI Dissertation Services, Ann Arbor, MI, 2001.

Marsick, V., and Watkins, K. *Informal and Incidental Learning in the Workplace.* New York: Routledge, 1990.

Pietersen, W. *Reinventing Strategy: Using Strategic Learning to Create and Sustain Breakthrough Performance.* New York: Wiley, 2002.

Sanchez, R., and Heen, A. "A Competence Perspective on Strategic Learning and Knowledge Management." In R. Cross and S. Israelit (eds.). *Strategic Learning in a Knowledge Economy: Individual, Collective and Organizational Learning Process.* Boston, MA: Butterworth-Heinemann, 2000.

Schutz, A. *Collected Papers I: The Problem of Social Reality,* 3rd ed. (unchanged). The Hague: Martinus Nijhoff, [1962]1971.

Thomas, R. R. *Redefining Diversity.* New York: AMACOM, American Management Association, 1996.

Thomas, R. R. *Beyond Race and Gender.* New York: AMACOM, 1991.

2

Organizational and Personal Rationale for Leveraging Diversity

Diversity is essential for life. Only where diversity is present can the ability to thrive be assured. Diversity makes chaos visible, as it pushes systems to forever adapt to changes in their environment.

— *Tim Porter-O'Grady and Kathy Malloch (2003), Quantum Leadership*

To successfully lead a diversity change initiative, leadership engagement is essential, as is the personal engagement of large numbers of people working throughout the organization. Engagement is the extent to which individuals commit to an initiative and demonstrate their commitment through their efforts and their intentions to see the project through to completion. Groundbreaking work by the Gallup Organization focused on "what the world's greatest managers do differently" and clearly documents the impact of employee engagement on basic, yet important outcomes such as employee and customer satisfaction, employee retention, and customer loyalty, as well as, higher level outcomes such as productivity, profitability, and overall organizational effectiveness (Buckingham and Coffman, 1999).

There is emerging evidence to support that engaged employees outperform others. For example, a report published by the consulting firm Towers Perrin, "Understanding What Drives Employee Engagement," reveals that highly engaged employees expend more discretionary effort, bring more energy and enthusiasm to their work, display a drive for efficiency, a flair for innovation, and demonstrate a talent for building supportive relationships with others, and as a result, out-perform their less-engaged peers (Stock, 2003). In his recent book *Social Intelligence* Daniel Goleman (2006) writes, "Socially intelligent leadership starts with being fully present and getting in synch [with employees]. Once a leader is engaged, then the full panoply of social intelligence can come into play, from sensing how people feel and why, to interacting smoothly enough to move people into a positive state" (p. 280). Your engagement counts! However, there is a cost for disenga-gement. According to research conducted by the Gallup Organization, disengaged employees cost the U.S. economy between $254 and $363 billion annually. As a leader your ability to leverage diversity is directly influenced by your ability to be engaged and to engage a diverse mix of employees in your efforts (Jesuthasan, 2000; Towers Perrin, 2003).

High levels of employee engagement involve both rational and emotional factors. The first step to attaining far-reaching employee engagement is establishing a compelling rationale for leveraging diversity. To accomplish this you must first come to thoroughly understand your organization's context. In Chapter 1 we described contextual awareness as the process of scrutinizing both your external and internal business environments. You do this to understand the impact of diversity on your organization: historically, currently, and in the future. Knowing your context from these three lenses helps you articulate your reasons for leveraging diversity. It also makes it easier to identify the ways in which you can assess where you are and where you want to go, so that you can later determine the overall success of your diversity initiatives. As you become more aware of your external and internal context, your perspective expands and insight results, especially when there is a diverse group engaged in the process. Finally, if you invest the time to generate clear responses to the following two questions you will have a foundation for devising a focused and aligned diversity strategy grounded in your organization's contextual reality:

- Why is leveraging diversity important to the success of our organization and its long-term survival?
- In what way is leading to leverage diversity in my best interests?

You will find that once you embark on a diversity change effort your employees will begin asking why the change associated with leveraging diversity is important to the organization, their work and, more importantly, how they will benefit personally. The work of diversity brings with it many uncertain paths. In order to commit to following a leader on this journey; they will want to know the leader's personal motivation. Good answers to these questions foster engagement through understanding and buy-in. In Chapter 5 you will be given an opportunity to write your strategic story for generating buy-in. It is this story that will prepare you for communicating your message clearly and concisely, over and over again.

The remainder of this chapter will help you answer the myriad of questions you need to address in order to successfully leverage diversity in your organization. First, we present a brief history of the diversity movement in the United States so that you can situate yourself and your organization historically. We follow this with a discussion of a twofold process of leveraging diversity in organizations: diversity-general and diversity-specific work. The chapter ends with a discussion of a variety of organizational and personal rationales for leveraging diversity. This chapter focuses on the two foundational leadership practices below:

Leadership Practice 1

Balance diversity-general work with diversity-specific work.

Leadership Practice 2

Establish a compelling organizational and personal rationale for leveraging diversity.

A Brief History of the Diversity Movement in the United States

Frederick R. Lynch (1997) describes the diversity machine as a "series of social movements designed to transform American ethnic relations" that have deep historical roots (p. 21). Understanding these roots and the "series of social movements" is a first and fundamental step to take when you begin the process of leveraging

diversity in your organization. Specifically, we believe that understanding diversity's historical context provides the foundation
needed to gain insight into the various ways society and organizations alike respond to difference. This sea-change has four historical
waves beginning in the middle of the last century and continuing
today (Maltbia, 2001). Each of these waves represents a shift in the
diversity paradigm operating in that era. To situate yourself
historically, we ask that you reflect on the following questions as
you review the four waves of change presented in Table 2.1:

- Where was I at this time?
- How did my experience of this time influence who I am today?
  - *My beliefs about the meaning of diversity?*
  - *My typical tendencies when faced with situations involving
    diversity?*
- Where were others I interact with today during this time and
  how might it influence them today?

Table 2.1 demonstrates the shifting diversity paradigm. The
diversity movement focused on moral and social action in the 50s.
The emphasis changed to a set of legal remedies in the 1960s and
1970s. During the 1980s the focus shifted again to an emphasis on
interpersonal relationships, specifically, understanding differences.
The 1990s focused on utilization of the workforce across systems.
With each paradigm shift important changes occurred. Unfortunately, as each new paradigm evolved the strengths of the previous
paradigm were not fully integrated, resulting in competing views and
a fragmented field of workplace diversity. The capability to leverage
diversity for performance breakthroughs requires integrating the
strengths from each of the prior diversity paradigms. We focus on
leveraging diversity — the paradigm of our current reality in the
emerging wave.

Contextual awareness situates the diversity movement in its
historical context and examines how various socioeconomic trends
have placed diversity on the social, political, and organizational
agenda in the United States. In this way, contextual awareness works
to answer the "where, when, and why" of diversity.

Table 2.1 is an example for the U.S., what are diversity's historical
roots in other countries for which you live and work?

TABLE 2.1 The Diversity Paradigm Shift: Four Waves of Change

What	When	Why	How
1st Wave The Civil Rights Era	1950s and 1960s	Social action Civil rights movement A moral imperative	Trigger: Women and minority groups expressed their mistrust and anger toward perceived injustice and equities embedded in many U.S. institutions. Response: Passage of the Civil Rights Act of 1964 and the related EEO guidelines. Impact: Organizations became more aware of fairness and equity issues and began to hire more minorities and women.
2nd Wave Affirmative Action (AA) & Equal Opportunity Employment (EEO) Era	1970s	Legal remedies Opening doors/representation focused	Trigger: Issues of race and sexual discrimination were taken into the court system as women and minorities entered the workforce in record numbers and faced barriers in systems that were not created for them. Response: To avoid more discontent many organizations demanded "equal" treatment of employees by their managers, which meant treating everyone the same, just like "me." Impact: A paradigm shift occurred as organizations moved beyond the social and legal imperative and sought more proactive strategies to address the potential financial loss associated with past and current inequities in the workplace.
3rd Wave Valuing Diversity Era	1980s	Understanding differences Opening minds/relationship focused	Trigger: Workforce 2000: Work and Workers for the 21st Century study highlighted a number of changes in America's workforce both in terms of demographic trends and a perceived "skills gap" between what a well-educated labor force needs to compete in a global economy and what skills they possess (Johnston & Packer, 1987). Response: Concept of diversity was now beginning to gain traction and emphasized the need to gain group-based, cross-cultural understanding and competence grounded in a growing economic business case to drive productivity gains in the workforce.

TABLE 2.1 (*Continued*)

What	When	Why	How
			Impact: Inclusiveness as a strategy for unleashing the power of diversity to generate business value began to emerge. Yet many women and minorities in organizations began to voice the need to "assimilate" to try to fit into the culture, which meant restricting their actions within a narrow band of "acceptable" behavior.
4th Wave Managing Diversity Era	1990s	Utilization focused Opening systems	*Trigger:* Challenges associated with equity in the workplace continued as evidence by increasing bias-based class action settlements (e.g., Texaco $176 million for racial discrimination & Mitsubishi $88 million for sexual harassment). *Response:* Federal Glass Ceiling Commission study examining the major barriers and enablers to driving equity in the executive suite. *Impact:* A realization that workforce utilization required an alignment of the systems that drove behavior in organizations with the aims of diversity initiatives, including: performance management, succession planning and compensation.
Emerging Wave Leveraging Diversity	2000+	Collective impact	This emerging diversity paradigm seeks to recognize the strengths and limitations of the previous approaches by focusing on the individual, group and organizational level outcomes that can be realized by leveraging diversity (see Table 1 introductory chapter).

Diversity-General Work & Diversity-Specific Work

In order for your organization to use diversity as a source of competitive advantage you must balance diversity-general work (or foundational work) with diversity-specific work (or issue-specific work). Diversity-general work provides a foundation for a comprehensive diversity strategy and change process and is a requirement for any diversity initiative or intervention. As a well known diversity expert explained, "the foundation work is the bricks of the process."

Diversity-general work includes a range of interventions that target individuals, workgroups, and organizational. Diversity-specific or issue-specific work concentrates on human interactions characterized by various mixtures of similarities and differences. Table 2.2 presents a comprehensive list of each and demonstrates both the expansive and complex nature of diversity.

TABLE 2.2 Two Primary Forms of Diversity Work in Organizations

Diversity-General Work (Foundational)	Diversity-Specific Work (Advanced)
Self-work and Self-awareness (developmental process with a focus on understanding the nature of one's cultural programming and its impact on thinking, acting and performance) *Organizational Rationale* (the "business case" and connection to organizational effectiveness) *Personal Rationale* (individual motivation) *Conceptual Clarity* (shared meaning of diversity and its promise for individuals and the organization) *Internal Cultural Assessment* (perspectives on the "current state" of diversity, a culture of respect and a commitment to equity for all) *Best Practice Research* (cataloguing effective practices and processes for leveraging diversity internally and externally) *Strategic Priorities* (select the "vital few" focus areas to guide results oriented diversity initiatives)	*Intercultural Competence* (enhanced communication and relationships between two or more cultures and/or identity groups) *Market Diversity* (multicultural marketing and culturally competent customer relations) *Functional Diversity* (breaking down silos and working productively across boundaries) *Generational Diversity* (fostering collaboration between veterans, boomers, Xers and Nexters) *Gender Diversity* (enhanced communication between men and women, pay equity) *Ethnicity/Racism* (addressing both explicit discrimination and "micro inequalities") *Physical/Mental Ability* (accommodating employees with physical disabilities and the often hidden dimensions of stress, depression and substance abuse) *Sexual Orientation* (inclusionary practices for gays, lesbian and transgender employees)

The importance of balancing diversity-general work with diversity-specific work highlights the developmental nature of the process (Hayles and Mendez-Russell, 1997). The three-phased workplace diversity process outlined in Chapter 1 is developmental in that it moves progressively from creating awareness and generating knowledge related to various aspects of diversity to actually applying the learning in a real-world context. However, there are multiple approaches and paths for realizing your specific intentions. Your challenge is to insist that there is an ongoing interplay between diversity-general work and diversity-specific work as displayed in Table 2.2. The table summarizes the major components needed for strategic diversity and change work in organizations. As one diversity leader suggested, "The foundation work will only get you awareness; it is just something to build on. From there, you should move to whatever are the significant diversity-specific problems and opportunities in your organization as a strategy for leveraging diversity."

At its core, foundation work has two critical components: (1) a clear rationale for addressing diversity and (2) understanding the fundamentals of cultural pluralism. The insights gained from foundational diversity work are often integrated into diversity awareness trainings and various communications media to disseminate clear, concise, and consistent diversity messages across the organization. However, advanced diversity work is where diversity is leveraged (e.g., race relations, gender communication, and market-driven cultural competence).

Table 2.3 lists a number of companies that had to various degrees engaged in foundational diversity, yet still found themselves in widely publicized lawsuits. In the 10-year period between 1995 and 2005, the 18 companies listed in the table settled discrimination and harassment claims exceeding 1.4 billions dollars. These figures listed do not include the cost of outside legal counsel and public relations consultants, top management's time, and potential damage to a company's reputation. For example, during Texaco's highly publicized racial-discrimination lawsuit in 1996, the company lost $1 billion in stock value in 2 days.

According to U.S. Equal Employment Opportunity Commission (EEOC), racial-discrimination complaints numbered 27,696 in 2004, while gender-based complaints were approximately 25,000. The companies in Table 2.3 (Hubbard, 2004) vary in size and industry, yet

TABLE 2.3 Sample of Legal Settlements: 1990s and Beyond

Organization	Category	Settlement
Abercrombie & Fitch	Racial discrimination	$40 million dollar settlement involving only 17 plaintiffs.
Amtrak	Racial discrimination	800 plaintiffs resulting in a $16 million dollar settlement.
Coca-Cola	Racial discrimination	$192.5 million dollar settlement based on 2,200 plaintiffs.
Cracker Barrel	Racial discrimination	$8.7 million dollar settlement based on 42 plaintiffs.
Denny's (Advantica)	Racial discrimination	$54 million dollars to nearly 300,000 patrons.
Ford Motor Co.	Racial discrimination	$11 million dollar settlement involving 3,400 plaintiffs.
MetLife	Racial discrimination	$160 million dollar settlement where the plaintiffs were 1.8 million policyholders.
Shoneys	Racial discrimination	$132 million dollar settlement.
Sodexho	Racial discrimination	$80 million dollar settlement distributed between 2,000 plaintiffs.
Sunoco	Racial discrimination	$5.5 million dollar settlement involving 200 plaintiffs.
Texaco	Racial discrimination	$176 million dollar financial penalty in 1996; a multi-year, government enforced decent decree and countless dollars in lost market share and ill will in consumer markets.
Home Depot	Gender discrimination	$88 million dollar settlement. Not including the costs associated with the required corrective action and investment in repairing market image.
Lucky Stores	Gender discrimination	$107 million dollar settlement.
Publix	Gender discrimination	$82 million dollar settlement.
State Farm	Gender discrimination	$250 million dollar settlement.
UBS	Gender discrimination	Paid $29 million to punitive & compensatory damages to former saleswomen sex-based bias and retaliation.
Mitsubishi	Sexual harassment	Settlement cost exceeded $34 million dollars.
Wal-Mart	Multiple categories	15 lawsuits filed against Wal-Mart for disability discrimination under ADA since 1994 (10 pending, 5 resolved including 3 jury verdicts in favor of the plaintiffs) — including $750,000 in fines for failure to comply with a Decent Decree; $11 million dollar settlement for hiring illegal immigrants; to stand trail for company-wide sex discrimination including more the 1.2 million employees, the Largest Civil Rights Class Action ever.

Source: Authors' adaptation from concepts found in Edward E. Hubbard's, *The Diversity Score Card* (2004, p. 20); Terrence E. Maltbia's, *The Journey of Becoming a Diversity Practitioner* (2001, p. 32); WageProject.org; and WorkplaceFairness.org.

collectively they demonstrate there is still much work to be done to eradicate various forms of discrimination and bias in the workplace. Massive lawsuits triggered major transformations in many of these companies' people practices, and a number became "diversity leaders."

The best way for you to reduce the possibility of discrimination complaints, lawsuits, and settlements is to transform your organization's diversity practices. Your over-riding challenge is to decide where to take strategic action to leverage diversity. There is often a desire to try to address the multiple dimensions of diversity all at one time (e.g., race, ethnicity, gender, sexual orientation, physical and mental ability, generational diversity, organizational role differences, etc.). However, when organizations have attempted to address the infinite number of differences reflective of the dynamic nature of diversity at once; the result is that very little, if any sustainable change occurred due to diversity's complexity.

To strategically build capability for leveraging diversity you must focus on the continuous interplay between diversity-general work (or foundational) and diversity-specific work (or advanced). Diversity-general work will provide you with the necessary context for the more difficult, developmentally advanced, diversity-specific work. The ultimate aim of cycling back and forth between diversity-general and diversity-specific activities is for your organization to develop the capacity to construct culturally competent responses to the challenges, complexity, and opportunities associated with any and all situations involving diversity.

Organizational Rationale for Leveraging Diversity

The brief history of the evolution of diversity in the workplace provides a backdrop for sharing the predominant factors we have found to motivate leaders and their organization to take on the work of leveraging diversity. There is evidence that some organizations promoted equity in the workplace long before the legal imperatives enacted by the United States government starting in the 1960s. For example, IBM is an organization with a heritage and demonstrated legacy of inclusion. IBM as we know it today is the result of a merger between the Tabulating Machine Company, the International Time Recording Company, and the Computing Scale Company to form the

Computing-Tabulating-Recording Company (C-T-R) in 1911, which eventually became IBM in 1924 (IBM company publication, 2000).

In 1935 then CEO Thomas J. Watson Sr. went public with his personal commitment to gender equity in the workplace in a quote that appeared in the *New York Sun*: "Men and women will do the same kind of work for equal pay. They will have the same treatment, the same responsibilities and the same opportunities for advancement" (IBM, 2000, p. 20). The company supported his words with action by hiring its first professional women — 25 college seniors — that same year. Progress continued with Ruth Leach, at the age of 29, becoming IBM's first female vice president in 1943, while one-third of IBM's manufacturing hires between 1940 and 1943 were women. In 1944 the company extended its commitment to inclusion when it became the first corporation to support the United Negro College Fund. Two years later, the company hired its first Black salesman, who in 1948 became a member of IBM's elite One Hundred Percent Club, an organization that recognized its most productive sales professionals.

In 1947, IBM added disability coverage to the company's benefits plan and joined the President's Committee on the Handicapped in 1948. Continuing this legacy of inclusion, in 1953, then President Thomas J. Watson, Jr. issued a policy statement proclaiming that "IBM will hire people based on their ability, regardless of race, color or creed." These are just a few examples of IBM's pioneering commitment to diversity. What's notable is that many of the company's early leaders preceded by a decade or more, the so-called legislative fairness of employment laws such as Title VII of the 1964 Civil Rights Act (which prohibits employment discrimination based on race, color, religion, sex, or national origin); the Equal Pay Action of 1963 and more recently the Americans with Disabilities Act of 1990.

When Lou Gerstner, former IBM's CEO, took the helm in 1993, he viewed one of his major responsibilities as building on the company's tradition firmly grounded in a philosophy that positioned "diversity as the bridge between the workplace and the marketplace." Gerstner believed doing so was critical in IBM's ability to win the war for global talent and success in a global marketplace. In 1998 they received the first annual Ron Brown Award for Corporate Leadership, Employee Initiatives; the company was honored with Japan's Equal Opportunity Ministries of Labor Award in 1999 and Universum magazine (Germany) named IBM the Number One Employer of Choice. The company has been recognized for its diversity leadership by numerous groups in the categories ranging from Asians, Blacks, Gays/Lesbians, Hispanic/Latino, Mature Adults, Minorities, Native Americans, People with Disabilities, Women to Worklife. Clearly, IBM's commitment to diversity is comprehensive and has a global footprint.

Today, IBM is a recognized leader in diversity, yet its commitment is a century-long. IBM's new CEO Sam Palmisano, who took the helm in 2002, is committed to continuing this legacy of leading to leverage diversity with his plans to transform the company to become an "on-demand" business and his focus is on innovation through collaboration. He states that "Diversity policies lie as close to IBM's core as they have throughout our heritage. Today, we're building a workforce in keeping with the global, diverse marketplace, to better serve our customers and capture a greater share of the on-demand opportunity. The lesson to draw from 50 years of leadership in diversity issues: we must stay true to our shared values. The marketplace demands it, and it's what we believe — and have always believed — is the right thing to do."

Diversity as "social responsibility," frames the organizational rationale for diversity as simply "the right thing to do" or the so-called moral imperative. For some, framing the organizational rationale this way might be considered too "soft" and risks diversity initiatives being criticized as merely responding to a "politically correct" social environment. In reality, evidence suggests that despite the guiding motive, organizations with a record of implementing effective diversity strategies realize a number of tangible benefits. For example, A Fact-Finding Report of the Federal Glass Ceiling Commission (1995) cites a Covenant Investment Management study that rated the performance of the Standard and Poor's 500 companies on a variety of equitable employment practices and found that companies in the bottom 100 on glass ceiling related measures earned an average of 7.9 percent return on investment, compared to 18.3 percent for the top 100.

In addition to perceiving diversity as simply the "right thing to do," six key themes emerged when reviewing a number of organizations' rationale for engaging in efforts to leverage diversity. Three factors are external drivers: new labor force demographics, related market demographics, and legal requirements. These factors, and how each is managed, collectively have an impact on three internal factors: teamwork, innovation, and productivity. Table 2.4 (Corporate Leadership Council, 2002a, 2002b, 2005; Gardenswartz

TABLE 2.4 Organizational Rationale for Leveraging Diversity

External Factors	Description and Implications
Labor Force Demographics	*Description:* Women, minorities, and foreign-born personnel are projected to produce 85 percent of the net new growth in the U.S workforce, while White male workforce representation is projected to decline from 85 percent in 1992 to 68 percent by the year 2020; male and female participation rates are converging with women projected to represent nearly 48 percent of workers by 2012; and the workforce continues to age as baby boomers move toward retirement resulting in a context where the foreign born population in the U.S. is twice as likely to be working age than the native born population (e.g., in 2002 almost half of the foreign-born population was between age 25 and 44 years old compared to 27.4 percent of the native-born population). *Implications:* Winning organizations will craft human capital strategies that effectively address the increased child and elder care demands of dual career couples; the challenges and opportunities associated with an intergenerational workforce (from Veterans to Generation Y). A study conducted by the consulting firm McKinsey & Co in 1998 concluded that "the most important corporate resource over the next 20 years will be talent." The work force today, and into the future, will demand to be treated as individuals, with respect & dignity. Talented people with the right capabilities, working in inclusive cultures, will generate more and better ideas, execute those ideas better, will help others to grow, and in the end be a major source of competitive advantage.
Market Demographics	*Description:* Dramatic shifts in the world's population have occurred in an increasingly diverse and global marketplace. Minority purchasing power is expected to increase from $1.3 to $6.1 trillion dollars between 2000 and 2045. According to the Selig Center for Economic Growth by 2010 purchasing power for Blacks is expected to reach $1 trillion, $69.2 billion for Native Americans, $579 billion for Asian Americans and $1,087 billion for Hispanics; compared to a projected overall U.S. purchasing power of 11.8 trillion in 2010. And by 2045, minority purchasing power may reach $4.3 trillion. In addition the gay and lesbian market in the U.S. reached an estimated $540 billion in 2000, while people with disabilities exceeded 796 billion dollars. *Implications:* A workforce that is sensitive to the needs of a variety of cultures and lifestyles can become a major a source of competitive advantage during the 21st century. Cultural competence in not only relevant to markets focused on consumer markets, such market driven capabilities are critical in business-to-business transactions as women and minorities increasingly attain positions with decision making clout and increases in women/minority owned business.
Legal Requirements	*Description:* Diversity's "legal imperative" is driven by a suite of statutes including Title VII of the Civil Rights Act of 1964 (prohibiting on-the-job discrimination on the basis of race, color, religion, sex or national origin); The Age Discrimination Act of 1967; The Vietnam Era Veterans Readjustment Assistance Action of 1972; the Rehabilitation Act of 1973; and a variety of other employment laws.

TABLE 2.4 (*Continued*)

External Factors	Description and Implications
	Implications: AA & EEO establishes a legal mandate for organizations to proactively eliminate discrimination in the workplace and recruit, hire, train and promote qualified employees of previously excluded groups. Failure to do so may result in financial settlements, lost of government contracts or funding and indirect costs associated with negative press and strained community relations.

Internal Factors	Description and Implications
Teamwork	*Description*: Groups are increasingly becoming the unit of work in today's organizations. Research suggests, with the right skills, diversity can have a positive impact on group performance, where multiple perspectives intensify problem solving processes, which can lead to a wider range of options and enhanced decision making. Specifically, the effects of diversity on group-level outcomes such as team productivity are mixed. *Implications*: Complexity and the potential for conflict increases with diversity. Effectiveness within and across diverse groups requires deliberate attention to creating conditions where pluralistic teamwork can flourish. Recognizing that team performance is a function of the collective capabilities of members and process loss. Selection of diverse team members is critical to success and ensuring that members have the capacity to productively manage conflict. Skilled facilitators can play a vital role in accelerating the start-up process of diverse teams to help clarify *goals* (i.e., shared purpose, alignment & commitment), *roles* and *operating procedures* (e.g., planning, structured problem solving, decision making, communication, meeting management and addressing disagreement) across differences.
Innovation	*Description*: Requisite variety, an adequate level diversity needed to maximize collective intelligence, is a platform used to ensure multiple perspectives are considered to foster creativity, innovation and adaptation in organizations. A critical mass of individuals must develop a capability to identify and productively work through differences of opinion; framing, reframing and discovering ways to integrate divergent ideas are critical skills in need of ongoing development. *Implications*: Leaders across the organization must recognize and strive to create the conditions that foster diversity including: (1) alignment, (2) empowered self-initiation, (3) time for reflection, (4) processing to capture incidental learning, (5) diverse stimuli resulting creative and dynamic tension to prompt insight, and (6) processes to promote sharing of ideas and knowledge. To promote innovation, leaders must recognize it as a learning and change process.
Productivity	*Description*: When productively leveraged, diversity has been shown to improve productivity at the *individual level* (e.g., attendance, turnover and work quality), *group level* (e.g., group cohesiveness and enhanced communication) and *organizational level* (e.g., achievement of goals such as market share and profitability).

TABLE 2.4 (*Continued*)

Internal Factors	Description and Implications
	Implications: Productivity gains result from the collective impact of leveraging diversity. Striving to create a positive work climate that respects diversity will contribute to individual affective outcomes (e.g., job satisfaction, organizational identity and job engagement) and achievement outcomes (e.g., performance ratings, compensation, development and mobility rates). Managers must be held accountable for creating such a climate and organizational systems must support managers in contributing to a strong performance culture that values diversity.

Source: Authors' adaptation from Corporate Leadership Council's, *Creating a Diversity Strategy* (2002a, pp. 1–4); Corporate Leadership Council's, *The Business Case for Diversity* (2002b, pp. 1–9); Taylor Cox's, *Cultural Diversity in Organizations* (1993, pp. 6–10); Lee Gardenawartz & Anita Rowe's, *Diverse Teams at Work* (1994, pp. 18–30); [13]Lee Garenswartz et al.'s, *The Global Diversity Desk Reference* (2003, pp. 19–23); and Jeffrey M. Humphreys', *The Multicultural Economy 2005: America's Minority Buying Power* (2005, pp. 1–27).

and Rowe, 1994; Gardenswartz et al., 2003; Humphreys, 2005) provides a brief summary of each trend and a description with implications to consider.

Fortune's 1999 "50 Best Companies for Minorities" outperformed the Standard & Poor's 500 companies not listed over three-and-five-year periods. Corporate social responsibility (CSR), a business concept that strives to bring a degree of balance to the complexity of public, corporate, and social policy with profitability goals, is emerging as a priority on the leadership agenda in boardrooms across the United States. CSR recognizes an expanding "bottom line," one that integrates concerns for environmental protection; labor rights, relations, and standards; stakeholder diversity; human and civil rights; investment in developing countries and disadvantage communities; and philanthropy with traditional profitability aims. In response to this trend there are a growing number of resources that monitor, track and report CSR organizations such as the Calvert Social Index, the Citizens Index and Dow Jones Sustainability Indexes.

Useful resources to gain additional perspective and supporting evidence include: (1) U.S. Department of Labor homepage (http://www.dol.gov/)/EEOC homepage (http://www.eeoc.gov/), (2) Workforce 2020: Work and Workers in the 21st Century (Hudson Institute 1997), (3) SocialFund.com, (4) U.S. Census Bureau (http://www.census.gov/), and (5) Diversity Inc. (e.g., magazine, website, and reports). Increasingly, these factors are being adapted on a global basis to reflect the growing reality of global markets and enterprise, for example the *Selig Center for Economic Growth* and *Futurist Magazine* are good sources for relevant global trend data.

Personal Rationale for Leveraging Diversity

Creating a shared understanding of your organization's rationale for leveraging diversity requires outside-in leadership; that is, being clear about how external environmental factors influence the inner working of your company. This form of leadership is necessary but not sufficient to sustain the energy needed to unleash the potential of diversity while productively addressing its embedded challenges and complexity. Leaders are effective when they model the way through authentic self-expression and cultural competence. Doing so starts with the self-reflective work required to clearly articulate your personal rationale for taking on, and leading, the diversity challenge in your organization. A part of the leadership journey moves inside out by examining one's core belief systems related to difference and then engaging in a series of conversations with other organizational leaders to gain insight into leadership behaviors that directly, and in some cases, unintentionally, shape the diversity climate of the entire organization.

Leaders who effectively leverage diversity continuously explore the shared cultural assumptions that guide the day-to-day experiences of various organizational members. These include perceptions, feelings, thoughts, behaviors, and ultimately perfor- mance. It is equally important to determine how these viewpoints and assumptions help or hinder your organization's capacity to leverage diversity. We have developed a process, "Understanding Your Starting Point," to guide self-reflection and group dialogue sessions between senior executives, as well as executives in the next two to three levels of the organization. Employing this process provides an opportunity for you to explore individual responses to diversity.

These conversations examine your role and stake in the existing organizational culture, while providing a platform for co-creating a vision of a more inclusive organizational culture. Structured dialogues provide an opportunity for you to examine assumptions about your role in leveraging diversity, as well as provide an opportunity to discuss positive diversity-related experiences. This process will help you explore individual and collective experiences related to diversity. You will find powerful new knowledge emerges as you explore the difference between your organization's "ideal self" and its "real self" with regard to diversity, inclusiveness, and equity. Table 2.5 (Bennett, 1998; Boyatzis et al., 2005; Cooperrider et al., 1999, 2005; Goleman, 1998, 2006; Goleman et al., 2002) on the following page suggests a three step process, each with a set of questions to guide these reflective conversations.

Using this process to facilitate a combination of one-on-one conversation and group dialogue sessions will help you appreciate how the experience of diversity in organizations occurs at multiple levels. For example, you will find that there are situational levels of experience regarding difference. These are contextually grounded in specific events and interactions (e.g., a minority employee promotion being attributed to Affirmative Action vs. Competence). Additionally, you will encounter the intrapersonal level of one's experience of difference where people assess the positive and negative aspects of a given situation (e.g., the expression of emotion in the workplace interpreted as being assertive for male employees and pushy by female employees). Finally, you will see that a social system level of the experience of diversity operates where people assess a given situation's positive and/or negative impact on others in general and across various dimensions of diversity (e.g., race, gender, age, sexual orientation, and so on).

Knowing that multiple levels of experience exist provides you with a new lens for understanding how diversity is experienced in your organization. The experience of diversity is defined not by one person's experience, but rather by the wide range of experiences happening to each member of the organization. Recognizing this allows for further understanding and insights about how we individually and collectively view the world. For you to navigate the journey of leading diversity with Authentic Leadership — that is, "walking the talk" — this understanding is essential.

TABLE 2.5 Understanding Your Starting Point!

Self-Reflective Questions	
Revealing the Best of the Past as a Platform for Envisioning a Better Future	What positive/productive experiences have I had related to diversity? What was the situation? Who were the players? What were the behaviors (my own, others)? How did it make me feel? What were the outcomes of this experience? What diversity related opportunities are I, or the organization, letting slip by? What diversity related opportunities should I, or the organization, work to leverage? Why? What difference will it make, to me, to others in the organization? What excites me about the possibilities that can result from this work?
Surfacing Diversity Blind Spots	Are there ways that I (and other senior leaders in the organization) take a different approach to diversity compared to other critical organizational initiatives? If so in what ways? Why (what might account from these differences)? What are my personal concerns about leading a cultural change intended to leverage diversity? What's troubling me? What is *really* going on at all levels of this organization related to diversity? Am I overlooking something important? What am I not seeing? Is there something I refuse to see?
Understanding Self as Cultural Being	What was the first time you noticed cultural differences? What was the affect (i.e., how did you feel about this observation)? When did you become culturally self-aware? How has your experience with other cultures influenced the way you think about diversity today? Think of a time when you "felt" like you were on the "outside" looking in... a time when you felt excluded for what ever reason. What was the situation? (Probes: Triggers? When? Who else was involved? How do you feel? Hopes? Thoughts? What did you do?/Handle the situation? What was the outcome of the situation? What was your learning as a result of the experience?)

Source: The process is grounded in concepts drawn from the practice of "Appreciative Inquiry," popularized by the work of David L. Cooperrider (2005, 1999), Associate Professor, Organizational Behavior at Case Western Reserve University; Emotional Intelligence as articulated by Daniel Goleman, Ph.D. (2006, 1998) and former senior editor for The New York Times & Psychology Today; Richard Boyatzis (2005, 2002), Professor in the Departments of Organizational Behavior and Psychology at Case Western Reserve University; and Intercultural Communications based on Milton J. Bennett's (1998) thinking, Founder and Co-Director, Intercultural Development Institute.

Get Personal, Get Real, Grow

Leading to leverage diversity is not a spectator sport; once you decide to lead you will need to engage in an inner discovery process, where you become keenly aware of your diversity lens. It is especially important that you come to know your personal tendencies toward bias and inclusion, as well as the origins, assumptions, and actions that are the result of these tendencies. The deep internal process of looking at yourself in relation to others will present many moments of truth for you. These may leave you feeling frightened, vulnerable, or embarrassed and at times outside of your comfort zone. Do not retreat, work with it. Face your hot buttons and uncover your blind spots. Be bone honest about what beliefs and behaviors you need to change, and then make the decision to change.

You also will find leveraging diversity demands you have the courage to take a stand against all forms of intentional and unintentional bias existing in your workplace, often by "good people." Your personal commitment is needed to stay the course, to address the hopes and fears associated with engaging in advanced diversity work, the kind that keeps companies out of the headlines while generating excellent organizational results.

References

Bennett, M. J. "Intercultural Communication: A Current Perspective." In M. J. Bennett (ed.). *Basic Concepts of Intercultural Communication*. Yarmouth, MA: Intercultural Press, Inc, 1998.

Buckingham, M., and Coffman, C. *First, Break All The Rules: What the World's Greatest Managers do Differently*. New York, NY: Simon & Schuster, 1999.

Boyatzis, R. E., and McKee, A. *Resonant Leadership: Renewing Yourself and Connecting Through Mindfulness, Hope and Compassion*. Boston, MA: Harvard Business School Press, 2005.

Corporate Leadership Council. *Creating a Diversity Strategy: Literature Review Findings*. Washington, DC: The Corporate Executive Board, 2002a.

Corporate Leadership Council. *The Business Case for Diversity: Literature Review Findings*. Washington, DC: The Corporate Executive Board, 2002b.

Corporate Leadership Council. *State of the Workforce 2005 — United States: Literature Review.* Washington, DC: The Corporate Executive Board, 2005.

Cooperrider, D. L., and Whitney, D. *Appreciative Inquiry: Collaborating for Change.* San Francisco, CA: Berrett-Koehler, 1999.

Cooperrider, D. L., and Sorenson, P. *Appreciative Inquiry: Foundations in Positive Organizational Development.* Chicago, IL: Stipes Publishing, 2005.

Cox, T. *Cultural Diversity in Organizations: Theory, Research and Practice.* San Franscisco, CA: Berrett-Koehler Publishers, 1993.

DiversityInc. *The Business Case for Diversity*, 4th ed. New Brunswick, NJ: Allegiant Media, 2003.

Federal Glass Ceiling Commission. *Good for Business: Making Full Use of the Nation's Human Capital.* Washington, DC: The U.S. Department of Labor, 1995a.

Gardenswartz, L., and Rowe, A. *Diverse Teams at Work: Capitalizing on the Power of Diversity.* Chicago, IL: Irwin Professional Publishing, 1994.

Gardenswartz, L., Rowe, A., Digh, P., and Bennett, M. F. *The Global Diversity Desk Reference: Managing an International Workforce.* San Francisco, CA: John Wiley & Sons, Inc, 2003.

Goleman, D. *Social Intelligence: The New Science of Human Relationships.* New York, NY: Bantam Books, 2006.

Goleman, D., Boyatzis, R., and McKee, A. *Primal Leadership: Learning to Lead with Emotional Intelligence.* Boston, MA: Harvard Business School Press, 2002.

Hayles, R., and Mendez-Russell. *The Diversity Directive: Why Some Initiatives Fail & What to Do about it.* Chicago, IL: Irwin, 1997.

Hubbard, E. E. *The Diversity Scorecard: Evaluating the Impact of Diversity on Organizational Performance.* Burlington, MA: Elsevier Butterworth-Heinemann, 2004.

Humphreys, J. M. *The Multicultural Economy 2005: America's Minority Buying Power.* Athens, GA: The Selig Center for Economic Growth, 2005.

IBM. *Valuing Diversity: An Ongoing Commitment, a Heritage of Leadership, a Legacy of Inclusion.* Armonk, NY: International Business Machines Corporation, 2000.

Jesuthasan, R. "The Total Performance Equation." *Financial Executive* (July 1), 2000. Retrieved from Factiva, December 20, 2005.

Lynch, F. R. *The Diversity Machine: The Drive to Change the White Male Workplace.* New York, NY: The Free Press, 1997.

Maltbia, T. E. "The Journey of Becoming a Diversity Practitioner: The connection between experience, learning and competence." *Unpublished Dissertation*, Teachers College, Columbia University, New York, NY, 2001.

Porter-O'Grady, T., and Malloch, K. *Quantum Leadership: A Textbook of New Leadership*. Sudbury, MA: Jones and Barlett Publishers, 2003.

Stock, H. "Intangibles Remain a Hidden Asset." *Investor Relations Business* (March 10), 2003. Retrieved from Factiva on December 20, 2005.

Towers Perrin. "Workforce Today: Understanding What Drives Employee Engagement." *The Towers Perrin 2003 Talent Report*, Towers Perrin, Valhalla, NY, 2003.

3

The Meaning of Diversity

You have to start with a belief and understanding that diversity is an institutional business imperative and that any institution that relies on any homogeneous population will sub-optimize in its performance ... You have to treat diversity like any other business imperative, and you must not be embarrassed about doing it that way.

— Henry Schacht
Director and Senior Advisor — E.M. Warburg, Pincus & Co. LLC,
Former Chairman & CEO, Lucent Technologies & Cummins

As you begin the process of leveraging diversity, you will likely face the challenge of defining the term "diversity." The way diversity is defined influences what is paid attention to, and what goes unnoticed in organizations. What you notice as a senior leadership team in turn impacts which set of diversity options are considered "valid," ultimately affecting your course of action. The more clearly you link the meaning of diversity to your organization's strategic priorities, the more easily diversity initiatives are understood, consistent with the DNA of the organization, and as a result translated into productive action and measurable results. This is the work of the strategic learning capability, *creating conceptual clarity*. As we noted in Chapter 1, this capability focuses on two core questions: (1) *What must we know to productively leverage diversity?* And (2) *What are the "vital few things" that must go well to assess our progress?*

The dictionary's definition of diversity is the "condition of being different; the state of being diverse; dissimilitude; variety; and a diversity of interests" (Webster, 1988, p. 369, 1997, p. 145). As generally used today, the word "diversity" has many layers and

39

a multitude of interpretations. Contemporary definitions of diversity range from "narrow" to all "inclusive." Narrow definitions of diversity focus on representation and compliance issues reflected in Equal Employment Opportunity (EEO) and Affirmative Action (AA) laws (Wheeler, 1994). Organizations focused on the narrow definition of diversity place an emphasis on integration through representation at all levels. In the United States, the focus tends to emphasize race and gender, then age and other physical and relatively observable dimensions of diversity. Any legal requirement that defines employee "rights" would also be included in this aspect of diversity.

Comprehensive definitions include a spectrum of dimensions that are characteristic of diversity. However this broad, "all inclusive" approach to diversity often lacks the strategic focus needed to drive measurable results. Using a two-prong approach to define diversity is valuable: diversity as a "subject" (the "what," or our human characteristics and experiences that make us each unique), and diversity as a "verb" (the "how," or the processes and actions individuals and organizations ascribe to diversity). This approach captures both the static and the dynamic nature of diversity. This chapter focuses on the third leadership practice:

Leadership Practice 3

Get Crystal Clear about Your Organization's Definition of Diversity.

The strategic learning capability of *achieving contextual awareness* described in Chapter 2 explores a number of important questions related to the *"where and when"* in time, place, and history of diversity, with the ultimate aim of gaining insight into the *"why"* of one's diversity processes, leadership practices, and related strategies. Here our attention turns to important *"what"* questions. These questions focus on obtaining the knowledge needed to take informed action aimed at productively leveraging diversity to realize performance breakthroughs in organizations. These "what" questions are the emphasis of the strategic learning capability creating conceptual clarity. In the next chapter we turn our attention to important "how" questions that focus on the approaches taken to achieve measurable results.

The "What" of Diversity

The descriptive nature of diversity entails a limitless number of similarities and differences that make each of us unique (Thomas, 1999). Table 3.1 lists the major components of diversity and related factors (Loden and Rosener, 1991; Loden 1996; Gardenswartz et al., 2003).

The inborn diversity characteristics form the core of one's identity. When meeting and interacting with others these are generally used unintentionally to determine in-group and out-group status. This sorting by in-group and out-group causes much of the diversity-related tension in organizations and leads to group-based stereotypes, prejudice, and discrimination.

The other dimensions of diversity, while important, are less salient to one's core identity. They represent mutable differences that are acquired, discarded, and modified throughout life. These diversity factors affect behavior in organizations and serve to ground both personal and organizational learning and change.

The "How" of Diversity

Diversity is also defined as a process or set of actions that typify how an organization responds to diversity. These include *acknowledging*

TABLE 3.1 Components of Diversity

Component	Factors
Inborn human characteristics	Race, ethnicity, gender, country of origin, age, physical and mental abilities, and sexual orientation.
Personal experiences	Educational background, family and personal income, geographic location, marital and parental status, religious beliefs, occupation, recreational habits, and military experience.
Organizational dimensions	Organizational level, line of business, work content, corporate or field location seniority, union affiliation, management status, and functional classification.
Personal style or tendencies	Learning style, approach to conflict, decision–making, and problem solving.
External factors	Suppliers, customers and external clients, the community and governments.

Source: Authors' adaptation of concepts from in Marilyn Loden and Judy B. Rosener's, *Workforce America* (1991, pp. 17–35); Marilyn Loden's, *Implementing Diversity* (1996, pp. 13–19); Lee Gardenswartz et al.'s, *The Global Diversity Desk Reference* (2003, pp. 25–25); Terrence E. Maltbia's, *The Journey of Becoming a Diversity Practitioner* (2001, pp. 8–9).

and *creating diversity* (i.e., legal and representation focused); *understanding differences* (i.e., enhancing interpersonal relationships across various dimensions of diversity); *valuing diversity* (i.e., seeing diverse cultural backgrounds as a resource); and *managing diversity* (i.e., utilization focused). In each of these examples, meaning is ascribed to the concept of diversity by placing a verb before the word. The verb ascribes an action, which determines the meaning of diversity in your organization, as well as how your organization responds to situations involving diversity.

Senior leaders' response to diversity greatly influences the collective organizational response. Milton Bennett (1998), an expert in the field of intercultural communication, suggests that a leader's denial, or defensive response to diversity spreads this response across the organization and impacts the entire workplace culture and climate. For some leaders its easier to simply minimize the influence diversity has on the workplace vs. dealing directly with its complexity. The unfortunate consequence of these responses is the promotion of organizational cultural patterns that exclude and even isolate those who are different from those with power. The net impact is an organizational climate where differences are suppressed and "outsiders" must assimilate to "fit in."

Leaders who accept differences adapt their behavior in interactions with others different from themselves. This type of response fosters more inclusive organizational work climates. The integration of differences in one's thinking and actions establishes a more conducive environment for creativity and innovation, as well as growth and renewal.

How Diversity is Defined in Organizations

Table 3.2 lists organizations that have received recognition for various aspects of their diversity strategies. The list includes the DiversityInc Top 50 Companies for Diversity number one ranked organization, the number one ranked company for minorities based on Fortune's 2004 listing, a U.S. Department of Labor Secretary's Opportunity Award winner and several Exemplary Voluntary Efforts

TABLE 3.2 Definitions of Diversity in Award Winning Organizations

Organization	Description
Altria Group	To build and maintain a collaborative work environment and culture by including diverse ideas and perspectives that will drive greater innovation and the best business solutions. In support of the Diversity Inclusion Mission, annual objectives will be developed and implemented our family of companies (i.e., focused on building a workforce that resembles our society at all levels; shared responsibility for fostering a participatory work environment; use open and honest communication; recognize manager and employees who get business results while leveraging diversity; and respect each employee as a whole person with different identities, abilities, life styles and family lives extending beyond the workplace).
Bank of America	Above all, we are about people. A philosophy of inclusion drives our organization every day and helps us win in a diverse, global marketplace.
Cornell University	Open Doors, Open Hearts, and Open Minds. Cornell University's enduring commitment to inclusion and opportunity, which is rooted in the shared democratic values envisioned by its founders. We honor this legacy of diversity and inclusion and welcome all individuals, including those from groups that have been historically marginalized and previously excluded from equal access to opportunity.
IBM	Valuing diversity: an ongoing commitment. Diversity ... the bridge between the workplace and the marketplace, and as such, the victory with customer begins with a winning workplace.
McDonald's	McDonald's is the world's community restaurant. We are proud of our long-standing commitment to a workforce that is diverse. We believe in developing and maintaining a diverse workforce that will strengthen the McDonald's system. Diversity at McDonald's means understanding, recognizing, and valuing the differences that make each person unique.
Procter & Gamble	Everyone at P&G is united by the commonality of the Company's values and goals. We see diversity as the uniqueness each of us brings to fulfilling these values and achieving these goals. Our diversity covers a broad range of personal attributes and characteristics such as race, sex, age, cultural heritage, personal background, and sexual orientation. By building on our common values and goals, we are able to create an advantage from our differences.
Sempra Energy	When we talk about diversity at Sempra Energy, we mean more than race, age, sexual orientation and gender ... includes *human diversity* characterized by our employees' physical differences, personal preferences or life experiences; *cultural diversity* characterized by different beliefs, values, and personal characteristics; and *systems diversity* characterized by the organizational structure and management systems in our workplace.
U.S. Department of Energy	The mission of the Department of Energy (DOE) is to contribute to the welfare of the United States, in partnership with customers, by providing technical and scientific information to achieve efficient energy use, diverse sources of energy, and a productive and competitive economy; to improve the quality of the environment through waste management and pollution prevention; and to secure national defense.

TABLE 3.2 (*Continued*)

Organization	Description
	Diversity means inclusion-hiring, developing, promoting, and retaining employees of all races, ethnic groups, religions, and ages; the able bodied and the disabled; and men and women. Through diversity we hear different points of view and approaches to problem-solving. Diversity and inclusion are the prerequisites to excellence.
Yale-New Haven Hospital	We value the diversity of our team as well as the diversity of the patients we serve and strive to create an environment that rewards personal contribution and enables each individual to achieve his or her full potential. Diversity at Yale-New Haven Hospital forms the cornerstone of its workforce, with women and minorities holding many of the key senior management positions. Valuing our employees is a natural outgrowth of caring for patients. Employees whose needs and concerns are taken into account are better able to provide compassionate, high quality care to patients and their families.

Award winners. Some have decades of experience with leveraging diversity in the workplace. What they share is an unwavering commitment to leveraging diversity as both a core organizational value and a platform for excellence in performance outcomes.

The descriptions listed in Table 3.2 reveal a number of important themes in diversity. Some emphasize defining the concept in a broad and inclusive manner. Most highlight connections between a culture of inclusiveness and organizational effectiveness. Many stress a comprehensive definition that reflects the need for understanding cultural and other human differences, as well aligning organizational systems across the spectrum of employment practices (see Appendix C for additional definitions from our study's participants).

The two stories that follow illustrate the challenges of clarifying the meaning of diversity. The first was told by a diversity leader who was involved in a turnover situation. The chief of global diversity for an award winning company shared the second story. These stories reflect a tension that exists between defining diversity in broad and inclusive terms and devising diversity strategies that result in significant change and measurable progress. This tension occurs in companies that find themselves involved in bias-based discrimination legal battles. A clear challenge for organizational leaders and internal diversity practitioners alike is figuring out how to achieve the balance between diversity-general and diversity-specific work outlined in the previous chapter.

BEYOND THE "POLITICALLY CORRECTNESS,"
MEANING OF DIVERSITY
(REFLECTIONS FROM INTERNAL DIVERSITY LEADERS

I know the politically correct answer is to define diversity all inclusively. But if we can get half the population to operate in productive collaborative relationships with the other half (that is the gender piece) and the other two-thirds of the population talking with the other one-third (that is the race piece); then I think everything else about diversity could be transferable to the other differences captured in the broader definition of diversity. And I believe this is the work, because I see all my years of being in this (i.e., diversity) business, it boils down to race and gender.

— Chief Diversity Officer,
Major Restaurant Group, Ranked Top 50 Companies for Minorities

There is a lively controversy about what is diversity. I use a definition of diversity that is generally accepted in my circles, that is, "all the ways in which we are different." Yet there continues to be the dichotomy, and I feel that I have the bridge to that dichotomy, that the dichotomy between those who say, "Diversity is all the ways in which we differ," including such things as thinking styles, learning styles, class and the like; and those folks who say, "This [defining diversity so broadly] is just a subterfuge for race and gender issues." I'm painfully aware of the dialog around this divisive issue in the field.

I believe that you cannot say, "Diversity is about all of us," without integrating and tagging in a statement that says, "Yes, it is about all of us, and we must understand that the race and gender issues are or can be at the core of many of these differences." So that if you say one, "It's about all of us," you must put in the other. Because, sometimes saying it's about all of our differences is a code word for, "Oh, thank God, we don't have to worry about the blacks and the women." And that's what bothers many people, women and people of color, but particularly women of color. It is a code word for, "Oh, thank God it's not about those blacks. So any trainer who says, "It's about all of us," really needs to be mindful that this is not a washed away program that masks some of the critical issues of racism, sexism, and homophobia.

— Corporate VP, Global Diversity & Foundations
Major Electronics Company,
Catalyst & Opportunity 2000 Award Winner

Table 3.3 (Herbst, 1997; Gardenswartz et al., 2003) provides a number of important diversity-related concepts. These will help as you define diversity for your organization in a way that captures its uniqueness. This is foundational to the strategic learning capability of creating conceptual clarity.

A Research Perspective

You do not need to be a researcher to know that people are diverse on many levels and in many ways. However, the following supporting research on the primary and secondary ways in which people differ is provided to help you learn about the different levels and types of diversity. The more you understand these, the more capable you will be in launching effective diversity initiatives.

Primary Dimensions

Organizational researchers often refer to inborn human characteristics as dimensions of diversity, or social category diversity (Jehn, 1999; Loden and Rosener, 1991). The theoretical foundations for primary dimensions of diversity include the *self-categorization theory* (e.g., Turner, 1982), the *social identity theory* (e.g., Tajfel, 1978), the *similarity-attraction paradigm* as articulated by Byrne (in Thatcher, 1999), and the *racial identity theory* (Jehn, 1999). Primary dimensions of diversity shape people's perceptions and behavior without regard to work-task relevance. Self-categorization theory, social identity theory, the similarity-attraction paradigm, and racial identity theory describe how people react to observable demographic characteristics. For example, self-categorization theory posits that people classify themselves and others into familiar categories in order to predict the nature of subsequent interactions. Further, these groupings are used to define the social identity of self and others (e.g., white, young, and female).

The similarity-attraction paradigm predicts that people are attracted to others similar to themselves. This paradigm also suggests that people apply negative assumptions to those different from them. Stereotypes and prejudice, based on race, gender, or other demographic characteristics, often reflect the categorization process

TABLE 3.3 Diversity-Related Concepts

Concept	Description
Equality and fairness	As a core value of a democratic society, equality refers to the ideal of the equal treatment of people in public matters and the distribution of scarce resources such as jobs, housing, and education. In practice, the idea of equality is often shaped according to individual and group interests. The concept of fairness gets translated into an attempt to treat everyone the same. Many proponents of diversity emphasize that in the context of very real power dynamics that exists in organizations and society, equal treatment results in unfair treatment of those not in the "in-group," that is those who have the power or influence to define the standards and requirements.
Stereotypes, prejudice, and the "isms"	Stereotypes are generalizations about what people are like, often an exaggerated image of characteristics based on identity group membership without regard to individual attributes and differences within a given group. Prejudice is often based on collective stereotypes and reflect one's general attitude toward a category or group of people, often an unfavorable or disparaging attitude including bigotry and/or hatred; negative experience with "difference," the "other" can result in prejudice; ethnocentrism, which judges others on the basis of one's own group standards is a major contributor group-based prejudice. At the group level, prejudice translates into the way people behave in concert with others including the so-called isms, racism, sexism, ageism, classism, and heterosexism; collective prejudice is often expressed in some from of discrimination.
Discrimination, power, and oppression	Discrimination occurs when an individual, group or institution has the power to deny equal treatment to people because of identity group membership (i.e., inborn characteristics such as ethnicity or experiences such as one's religion). Oppression is lacking freedom in some way as a result of the application of unjust social, political or economic forces. The social justice dimension of diversity is focused on eliminating or at least ameliorating oppression and discrimination in organizations.
Affirmative action and equal employment opportunity	A set of legal laws and related requirements intended to assure equal access to the employment processes of the organization including hiring, advancement and compensation; an attempt to open organizational "systems" to promote equality in the workplace; representation focused based on inborn human characteristics; often results in a focus on inclusion (see Appendix E).
Inclusion	To simply invite the "other" in or consider multiple perspectives whether or not they reflect the status quo; inclusion in the context of a dominant group means assimilation of "others;" integration goes beyond inclusion to by seeing all people as equals, which often requires changing or expanding systems so that all people have equal access to power.

TABLE 3.3 (*Continued*)

Concept	Description
Tension, conflict, and complexity	Conflict (i.e., opposition and disagreement), tension (i.e., anxiety, mental, or nervous strain, strained relations), and complexity (i.e., increased physical, mental, or emotional demand) all increase as diversity mixtures increase.
Human diversity	Focuses on holistic learning and requires engaging the whole person, i.e.: (1) the *cognitive domain* (i.e., knowledge or head work), (2) the *psychomotor domain* (i.e., behaviors and skills, or hand work), and (3) the *conative, affective domain* (i.e., affect and emotions including identity, or the heart work to expand one's values, attitudes and beliefs about the "other").
Cultural diversity	The integration of intelligence quotient and emotional quotient in adapting to different cultures; capacity to change or expand one's habits in response to culturally diverse factors.
Global diversity	Extending diversity processes and initiatives worldwide in multinational organizations.

Source: Authors' adaptation of concepts found in Philip H. Herbst's, *The Color of Words: An Encyclopedic Dictionary of Ethnic Bias in the United States* (1997); Lee Gardenswartz et al.'s, *The Global Diversity Reference* (2003); Terrence E. Maltbia's, *The Journey of Becoming a Diversity Practitioner* (2001).

of distinguishing between similarity and difference, and often lead to miscommunication. Thus, primary dimensions of diversity provide a source of both understanding and conflict in organizations.

Secondary Dimensions of Diversity

Experience-based diversity is referred to by organizational researchers as secondary dimensions of diversity, or informational diversity (Jehn, 1999). This form of diversity includes a wide range of differences that are acquired, discarded, and/or modified throughout one's lifetime and, as a result, are less pertinent to one's core identity. Informational diversity provides valuable insights into family structure, religion, and educational background. Organizational life provides context for one's work role, influenced by such factors as organizational level, classification (i.e., exempt, hourly, etc.), line of business, work content, location (e.g., corporate vs. field office), seniority, organizational type, mergers/acquisitions, and union affiliation.

In the workplace, numerous organizational dimensions of diversity can also result in goal diversity; that is, differences related to underlying work values and goals (Jehn, 1999). Goal diversity exists when members of a work group differ in what they believe is the task, performance outcome or mission. Although not always immediately detectable, many experience-based dimensions of diversity are important in the effective execution of work tasks and objectives, as well as the hiring, selection, advancement, and succession planning processes. The basis for secondary and organizational dimensions of diversity is information processing and decision-making theory. This perspective suggestions that diversity, when managed, will have positive implications on work group outcomes since such groups will have a wider array of views, skills, and information (Gruenfeld et al., 1996).

Educational background, functional and industry experience are part of competencies that one employs when undertaking a task (Bantel and Jackson, 1989; Zenger and Lawrence, 1989). Furthermore, the ability to productively discuss and examine task-related content issues grounded in a diverse set of perspectives can enhance performance quality (Tjosvold, 1991). Conversely, the lack of discussion, critical questioning, and thinking from multiple perspectives creates conditions of "group think." This condition hinders the ability to create interesting, creative, and "well-thought-out" solutions to the problems, challenges, and opportunities faced daily in the workplace.

Personal Dimensions of Diversity

The field of organizational behavior frames the theoretical basis for various personal dimensions of diversity (Organ and Bateman, 1991; Staw, 2004). Organizational behavior theory provides a foundation for understanding human differences, even within identity groups (e.g., race, gender, or sexual orientation), in terms of both personality and ability. For example, the Big Five Model of Personality identifies five general personality traits at the top of the trait hierarchy, they include: (1) *extraversion* (positive affectivity that predisposes individuals to experience positive emotional states and feel good about themselves and about the world around them), (2) *neuroticism* (negative affectivity which reflects people's tendency to experience negative emotional states, feel distressed, and generally view themselves and the world around them negatively), (3) *agreeableness* (distinction between individuals who get along well with other people and those who do not; general likeability; the ability to care for others and to be affectionate), (4) *conscientiousness* (the extent to which an individual is careful, scrupulous, and persevering; highly self-disciplined), and (5) *openness to experience* (the extent to which an individual is original, open to a side variety of stimuli, has broad interests, and is willing to take risks as opposed to being narrow-minded and cautious).

Many organizational behavior researchers use The Big Five framework to describe the personalities of people regardless of their inborn, primary, and secondary dimensions of diversity. Other important frameworks used to understand dimensions of personality include (1) the *locus of control*, (2) *self-monitoring*, (3) *self-esteem*, (3) *Type A* and *Type B personalities*, and (4) *needs for achievement*, *affiliation*, and *power* (Staw, 2004, pp. 10–13). An individual's personality represents the sum of a number of their traits, or particular tendencies related to how they think, feel, and behave.

Abilities, aptitudes, and skills represent another important component in understanding the role of individual differences in the workplace. What an individual is capable of doing, combined with personality factors, determines the level of performance that can be achieved. To assess and develop talent, leaders should consider and strive to understand cognitive ability, physical ability, and emotional intelligence need to be understood and when relevant considered (Staw, 2004, pp. 14–19). The most general aspect of cognitive ability is general intelligence. Specific types of cognition include verbal, numerical, reasoning, deductive, spatial, and perceptual abilities. There are also two types of physical abilities: *motor skills* (or the ability to manipulate objects in the environment) and *physical skills* (or personal fitness and strengths).

Daniel Goleman's New York Times bestselling books, *Emotional Intelligence* (1996) *and Social Intelligence* (2006), are largely credited for the emphasis on emotional intelligence, and social emotional learning in the workplace. A number of researchers believe it is plausible that emotional intelligence may facilitate job performance in a number of ways, and likewise, low levels of emotional intelligence may actually impair performance. There are several emotional intelligence assessment tools. The Hay Group markets the *Emotional Competence Inventory* (ECI) (2002), a multi-rater assessment that measures 18 competencies organized into four clusters (self-awareness, self-management, social awareness, and relationship management), the newly developed *Emotional and Social Competency Inventory* (ESCI), and the *Emotional Competency Inventory — University Edition* (ECI-U), which is available in both self-report and multi-rater formats. Other popular assessment tools include the *BarOn Emotional Quotient Inventory* and *Q-Metrics EQ Map* and the *Mayer, Salovey, Caruso Emotional Intelligence Test* (MSCEIT).

Collectively, primary, secondary, and other personal dimensions of diversity provide a foundation for understanding and effectively managing individual differences in the workplace. That is, they provide a basis for understanding the why and how we work, and by extension, contribute important knowledge to leveraging talent. The research supporting these three broad categories of diversity bring together the "nature" (or biological heritage) and "nurture" (or education, practice, and exercise) aspects of human performance.

Clearly, to effectively leverage diversity your definition of diversity must align with your core organizational values and operational strategy. Creating a shared meaning of diversity is important in establishing a shared future vision of diversity for the organization. In turn, shared vision helps to determine strategic diversity priorities for the organization. Leaders must recognize that diversity is a complex concept. It is important to decide and focus on a vital few diversity elements that align with core organizational values and are important to your business success to guide the diversity strategy. This is your true leadership challenge.

References

Bantel, K. A., and Jackson, S. E. "Top Management and Innovations in Banking: Does the Composition of the Top Team Make a Difference?" *Strategic Management Journal* 10 (1989): 107–124.

Bennett, M. J. "Intercultural Communication: A Current Perspective." In M. J. Bennett (ed.). *Basic Concepts of Intercultural Communication.* Yarmouth, MA: Intercultural Press, 1998.

Gardenswartz, L., Rowe, A., Digh, P., and Bennett, M. F. *The Global Diversity Desk Reference: Managing an International Workforce.* San Francisco, CA: Wiley, 2003.

Goleman, D. *Social Intelligence: The New Science of Human Relationships.* New York, NY: Bantam Books, 2006.

Goleman, D. *Emotional Intelligence: Why it Can Matter More Than IQ.* New York, NY: Bantam Books, 1996.

Gruenfeld, D., Mannix, E., Williams, K., and Neale, M. "Group Composition and Decision Making: How Member Familiarity and Information Distribution Affect Process and Performance." *Organization Behavior and Human Decision Processes* 67 (1996): 1–15.

Herbst, P. H. *The Color of Words: An Encyclopedic Dictionary of Ethnic Bias in the United States.* Yarmouth: Intercultural Press, 1997.

Jehn, K. A. "Diversity, Conflict, and Team Performance: Summary of Program of Research." *Performance Improvement Quarterly* 12(1) (1999): 6–19.

Loden, M., and Rosener, J. B. *Workforce America: Managing Employee Diversity as a Vital Resource.* Homewood, IL: Irwin, 1991.

Loden, M. *Implementing Diversity.* Chicago: Irwin, 1996.

Maltbia, T. E. "The Journey of Becoming a Diversity Practitioner: The Connection between Experience, Learning and Competence." *Unpublished Dissertation*, Teachers College, Columbia University, New York, NY, 2001.

Organ, D. W., and Bateman, T. S. *Organization Behavior.* Homework, IL: Irwin, 1991.

Staw, B. M. *Psychological Dimensions of Organizational Behavior*, 3rd ed. Upper Saddle River, NJ: Pearson, Prentice Hall, 2004.

Tajfel, H. "The Achievement of Group Differentiation." In H. Tajfel (ed.). *Differentiations Between Social Groups.* London, England: Academic Press, 1978, pp. 483–507.

Thatcher, S. "The Contextual Importance of Diversity: The Impact of Relational Demography and Team Diversity on Individual Performance and Satisfaction." *Performance Improvement Quarterly* 12(1) (1999): 97–112.

The Hay Group. *Emotional Competence Inventory*, Vol. 2, Philadelphia, PA, 2002.

Thomas, R. R. *Building a House for Diversity.* New York, NY: American Management Association, AMACOM, 1999.

Tjosvold, D. *The Conflict Positive Organization: Stimulate Diversity and Create Unity.* Reading, MA: Addison-Wesley, 1991.

Turner, J. C. "Towards a Cognitive Redefinition of the Social Group." In H. Tajfel (ed.). *Social Identity and Intergroup Relations.* Cambridge, England: Cambridge University Press, 1982, pp. 15–40.

Webster's Ninth New Collegiate Dictionary. Springfield, MA: Merriam-Webster Inc., Publishers, 1988.

Webster's Pocket Dictionary of the English Language: The International Edition. Naples, FL: Trident Press International, 1997.

Wheeler, M. *Diversity Training: A Research Report-1083-94-RR.* New York: The Conference Board, 1994.

Zenger, T., and Lawrence, B. "Organization Demography: The Differential Effects of Age and Tenure Distribution on Technical Communications." *Academy of Management Journal* 32 (1989): 353–376.

4

The Diversity Learning and Change Process

An awareness of diversity quickly leads to feelings of superiority or inferiority ... the work [of diversity] is about moving beyond these reactions.

— Margaret Mead, Anthropologist

The bottom line for leaders is that if they do not become conscious of the cultures in which they are embedded, those cultures will manage them. Cultural understanding is desirable for all of us, but it is essential to leaders if they are to lead.

— Edger H. Schein, Organizational Culture and Leadership

To succeed at your goal of leveraging diversity, you must create an adaptive organization. To do so you eventually need to shift your focus from the foundational work of the "why" and the "what" of leveraging diversity, to the "how" of making leveraging diversity a daily reality for you organization and its key stakeholders. How do we *take informed action* to sustain the gains that emerge from the foundational work enacted to leverage diversity in our organization? What must we do to adapt to our ever-changing global environment? We have discovered that taking informed action is a function of articulating a clear and compelling vision, igniting passion in individuals, and gaining their commitment to act.

Leveraging diversity involves an ongoing self-renewing cycle — there is no start to finish formula. Rather, it is a continuous process that begins with a period of discovery focused on achieving a deep awareness of the strategic context in which your organization operates. This discovery process is ongoing given the continuously changing nature of the strategic context. Yet at some point during this early stage of the strategic learning cycle, it will become clear to you that you know enough about your past and current context, and have some expectations for the future to take informed action about what is needed today to realize your diversity vision. This chapter explores the diversity learning and change process with an emphasis on the leadership practice below. There is no end to the journey of leveraging diversity. It is a process that requires ongoing learning and adaptation to respond productively to often unexpected changes in the internal and external business environments.

Leadership Practice 4

Accept Leveraging Diversity as an Emergent, Ongoing and Adaptive Process.

Distinguishing Between Operational Diversity Work and Adaptive Diversity Work

In their book, *Leadership on the Line*, Ronald Heifetz and Marty Linsky (2002) distinguish between operational and adaptive leadership work. Part of taking informed action is being clear about the nature of the presenting problems, challenges, and opportunities associated with various situations involving diversity. Table 4.1 applies Heifetz and Linsky's ideas to the diversity learning and change process by asking two questions: "What's the work?" and "Who does the work?"

The learning and process begins by being clear about the nature of the diversity leadership challenge: What aspects of diversity are operational in nature where current "know-how" can be applied or assistance from diversity "experts" is needed? What *aspects of diversity call for more adaptive forms of change — learning new ways of doing things — by the people closest to the work*? The point to remember is that each diversity challenge requires a leadership response appropriate to the situation.

TABLE 4.1 Distingushing Operational from Adaptive Diversity Work

	What is the Work?	**Who does the Work?**
Operational	*Apply existing know-how:* • Market intelligence • Workforce analysis and cultural assessment	*Authorities/experts:* • Market research professionals • Diversity/HR practitioners, external consultants
Adaptive	*Learn new ways:* • Understand cultural factors that support diversity and current diversity barriers • Commit to building a pluralistic work climate	*The people with the challenge:* • Senior executives with technical support • Managers and employees at all levels

Source: Authors' adaptation from in Ronald A. Heifetz and Marty Linsky's, *Leadership on The Line* (2002, pp. 13–20) and Terrence E. Maltbia's, *The Journey of Becoming a Diversity Practitioner* (2001).

Distinguishing between operational and adaptive diversity challenges provides a useful way to think about the various aspects of the learning and change process. Some aspects require, what organizational change expert W. Warner Burke (2002) calls *evolutionary change* — the more traditional forms of change (i.e., operational related diversity challenges that respond well to gradual and continuous process adjustments). And, other aspects of the change process call for more *revolutionary* forms of change (i.e., adaptive related diversity challenges that result from a sudden shift, a major break from the past, or intensified environmental conditions, and as a result require the co-creation of new processes.

When leaders take informed action they intentionally distinguish among operational and adaptive diversity-related challenges and opportunities and take action to leverage diversity. Diversity often takes a "wrong turn" when leaders try to apply a "one size fits all" approach to situations.

Operational Diversity Work

Operational forms of diversity work are often continuous and transactional in nature. Here specific organizational members apply their current "know-how" to determine how to design, deliver and/or upgrade diversity-related processes. Table 4.1 suggests that many facets of the work related to the diversity learning and change process are or can be performed by existing staff. Examples include:

- *Tracking* major trends in the external environment related to the economy, competitive moves, changes in societal attitudes, government regulation, technological innovation, and globalization;
- *Surveying* the workforce to determine how internal groups identify with and react to current organizational values, behaviors, management practices, and policies; and
- *Monitoring* the labor market and comparing these data with an internal workforce analysis to determine current and future workforce needs and core requirements to drive strategic implementation.

Operational diversity work focuses on the "what, where, and when" of various trends and applying current "know-how" to respond to changes in the external environment or internal requirements. You may find that much of the operational work needed to inform the diversity change process is already underway in your organization. However, if these efforts are spread across the organization and not integrated in a way that fosters broad strategic insight, you will need to establish a collaborative cross-functional group responsible for pulling this work together. We discuss various ways to create a group to lead the diversity learning and change process in Part II of the book.

Adaptive Diversity Work

Adaptive diversity work seeks to address broad questions that take the form of the "why" behind the "what, where, when, and how" of various diversity dynamics. As a result, adaptive forms of diversity work call for more revolutionary, transformational change in individuals and their organizations. Such situations call into question many "taken-for-granted" assumptions embedded in our thinking. Through examining these we gain a deeper understanding of how our individual and collective pictures of the world shape our daily actions and decisions, some with positive intended outcomes, along with many, unproductive, often unpredictable, and unintended consequences. When it comes to leveraging diversity, taking informed action is as much about reflecting on, and making meaning from our experiences, as it is about our behaviors.

Most likely, during the process of discovery, a number of external trends and changing conditions will emerge that could impact your organization's effectiveness and often its very survival. It is important to remember that in addition to operational work, the diversity change process requires new learning, experimenting, and adaptation across the organization. Organizations who fail to acknowledge this important insight are often surprised by unexpected tension and conflict at best, or find themselves in the headlines or worse. "Without learning new ways — changing attitudes, value, and behaviors — people cannot make the leap necessary to thrive in out new knowledge-based economy that is increasingly diverse and global (Heifetz and Linsky, 2002, p. 13).

Adaptive challenges require that people across the organization internalize and co-create productive responses to diversity's challenges and opportunities. Examples of adaptive diversity work during the discovery process include:

- *Reaching* agreement as to how your organization's culture facilitates your capacity to leverage diversity, while recognizing cultural factors that seem to get in the way;
- *Establishing* a clear business case and personal rationale across the organization based on these cultural insights; and
- *Deploying* a process to create a teaching culture that fosters learning across differences in pursuit of individual and organizational goals.

Engaging in the discovery processes associated with adaptive diversity work is as important, if not more, than the content and insights generated from this work. You may be temped to delegate this work or import a diversity vision and related initiatives from other, so-called best practice organizations, our advice, do not do it. Organizational leaders must be directly involved in joining others engaged in adaptive work. We have learned that it is the direct engagement in adaptive work by leaders and others at all levels of the organization that builds deep understanding and commitment to the diversity learning and change process.

Adaptive Diversity Work as Cultural Transformation

In the context of human interaction, we define diversity, and by extension the diversity learning and change process, in cultural terms. Here, we are defining culture in basic terms as a "set of beliefs and values about what is desirable and undesirable in a social system (or community) of people and a set of formal or informal practices to support the values" (Kreitner and Kinicki, 2007, p. 109). We are all cultural beings. We belong to groups, communities, organizations, professions, and nations, all of which have distinct cultural patterns, acceptable ways of thinking and behaving. Edgar Schein (2004), Professor at the MIT Sloan School of Management and considered one of the "founders" of organizational psychology, has pointed out that leadership and culture are two sides of the same coin, and understanding both is essential in leveraging diversity. He notes that cultural norms determine how organizations define effective leadership (i.e., who is heard, promoted, and rewarded). The essential role of leadership is to understand, create, manage, and work with culture (i.e., reinforcing existing culture when it supports goal attainment and to destroy it when it is viewed as dysfunctional). Given its importance, a critical question then is: *How does culture form?*

Origins of One's Cultural Programming: You as a Culturally Diverse Entity

The origins of cultural programming start early in life and are instilled in each of us by people most influential during our developmental years including family members, teachers, community and religious leaders, our friends, and other mentors. Those spontaneous and repeated interactions occurring during our direct and intimate contact with others gradually lead to the formation of lasting values and beliefs resulting in a set of rather stable patterns and norms of "acceptable" behavior. Most of our cultural knowledge is learned unintentionally as a result of daily interactions with others.

If you are a leader committed to leveraging diversity, one of your first steps is to make an in-depth examination of your cultural programming. We developed the tool that is presented in Table 4.2 (Walton, 1994; Gardenswartz et al., 2003) to help you gain important

TABLE 4.2 Tool: Exploring the Origins of Your Cultural Programming

Directions: Think about the cultural group you identify with (e.g., African American, Male, Corporate, Father, and Coach). Then go back as far as you can remember and list in the first column the people, groups and organizations that most influenced the person you are today. Next, reflect on the important values, beliefs, and assumptions that emerged from these relationships and list them in column two. Follow this with the biases, stereotypes, blind spots, or auto responses that result from your collective worldview in the third column. Lastly, note insights, surprises, and other observations from completing this activity. Ask yourself: Are any in conflict with one another? What impact might these insights have on your interactions with culturally diverse others? [Note: example from one of the co-authors]

Identity Groups (significant people, organizations, etc.)	*Worldview* (values, beliefs & assumptions)	*Potential Biases* (stereotypes and blind spots)
African American Family	Responsibility to "give back;" love and concern for family/friends	Internalized guilt when family does not live up to society's expectations (reversal)
Raised in Urban/Inner City Area	Belonging and self-interests	Conservatives seem very up tight, rigid, biased
Religion: Southern Baptist	The golden rule: do unto others as you would have them do unto you	Can see those with contrasting religious beliefs as radical — i.e., can ignore the platinum rule of treating others the way they want to be treated
Sports: Track	Competitive, persistence	Hard to see that sometimes not personally winning could be good for the team
Music: Band/Drum Corps	Collaboration and difference	Cannot always see internal faults
Friends	Loyalty and reliability (few/close)	Not open to "outsiders"
Corporate America	Conformity to succeed	Do not always see system level bias
University Faculty	Learning and discovery	Can lose sight of instrumental goals

Insights

Reviewing the sources of my cultural programming has helped me see the tension between the values I acquired early in life (age 12 when joining Drum Corps within my racial cultural heritage) and those that emerged once exposed to mainstream American values (spent 20 years in Corporate America being mentored by White Males over 40s since I was 22). Now that I am over 40 I am reclaiming my self-agency, not easy.

Source: Authors' adaptation from concepts in Sally J. Walton's, *Cultural Diversity in the Workplace* (1994, pp. 7–9); and Lee Gardenswartz et al.'s, *The Global Diversity Desk Reference* (2003, pp. 46–49).

insight into the cultural lenses influencing your thinking, feelings, and actions in organizational and other social settings.

Author Mark Williams (2001) in his book, *The 10 Lenses: Your Guide to Living and Working in a Multicultural World, Capital Ideas for Business and Personal Development*, frames the idea of cultural lenses as being composed of layers and legacies. "Diversity layers" represent the various groups and daily experiences that contribute to the foundation of one's cultural identity (includes unchangeable and elective). Legacies represent historical event(s) that have a powerful influence on the way we act and experience the world. We can experience such events directly (e.g., World Trade Center Attack on September 11, 2001) or indirectly through our ancestors, other family members, or the communities where we live and work (e.g., being a descendent of a "captured people"). Importantly, when we acquire a given group's identity we take on the legacies associated with that group, often unconsciously and uncritically.

The "Exploring The Origins of Your Cultural Programming" tool is designed to help you discover the elements that form your view of the world, in short, the origins of your cultural programming — the core of your cultural identity. You might consider the following list as you think about the various identity groups that have had a significant impact on you in the past, present, and in your imagined future (Table 4.2, Column #1):

- *Country of Origin* (American, French, Japanese, etc.)
- *Language* (English, Spanish, French, etc. and related accents)
- *Location* (Region within that country, urban or rural)
- *Family* (Parents, grandparents, uncles, aunts, and others)
- *Socio-economic Status* (Class and financial, growing up lower, middle, upper middle, upper class, and so on)
- *Race* (American Indian, Eskimo, or Aleut; Asian, Native Hawaiian, or Other Pacific Islander; Black; Hispanic or Latino; White; or some other race i.e., Mulatto, Creole, or Mestizo)
- *Ethnicity* (Irish, Italian, etc.)
- *Age/Cohort* (Baby Boomer, Gen X, Gen Y, etc.)
- *Ability* (i.e., Physical, Mental)
- *Gender* (Male/Female)
- *Sexual Orientation* (Heterosexual, Gay, Lesbian, Bisexual, or Transgender)
- *Marital Status* (Married, Single, Divorced, etc.)

- *Religion* (Christian, Jewish, Muslim, etc.)
- *Occupation* (e.g., Educator, Business Executive, Doctor, Musician, etc.)
- *Other Critical Identity Groups* (Hobbies, community groups, etc.)

The following definitions are provided to help you complete the second column of Table 4.2 (Argyris, 1993, pp. 87–88; Kreitner and Kinicki, 2007, pp. 78–79; Schein, 2004, pp. 25):

- *Values* — beliefs about what is important including your preferred ways of behaving and the outcomes you desire; your core values transcend situations, and as a result guide one's selection or evaluation of behaviors and/or events.

    Our *espoused values* are explicit statements about "what we stand for," while our *enacted values* are the values that are actually exhibited by our behavior; where there is a gap between our "audios" (or espoused values) and our "visuals" (or enacted values), people believe the visuals.

- *Assumptions* — are the master programs, deeply embedded, unconscious, and often taken-for-granted frameworks that guide what we pay attention to, the meaning we make of experience, the decisions we make, the action we take, and ultimately the outcomes and results we achieve in life, all of which happens in a nanosecond. This cycle is repeated many times in a given day.

    Our assumptions are so engrained, they are highly resistant to change; when others do not share our core assumptions we tend to view them as "out of synch" or experience their perspective as "foreign," and as a result we generally dismiss the opposing point-of-view.

- *Biases* — strong preferences for a particular point-of-view or ideological perspective that are not based on objective evidence and result in prejudging. In the context of human diversity we all hold biases toward specific social identity groups.

    Understanding the impact of biases is essential work in leveraging diversity. It is our biases, based on various social stereotypes that may cause us to, often unconsciously, accept or deny the truth of a given claim based on one's group membership. In most extreme cases, when we are in a position of power, our personal biases can result in certain groups being denied benefits and rights unjustly or, conversely, unfairly showing unwarranted favoritism toward others.

As you reflect on the influence your cultural programming has on the person you are today, use the following list of questions to stimulate deep insight about how your cultural programming has influenced your relationships with diverse others:

- What meaning do you make of the order in which you listed the significant cultural influencers? Which aspects came to mind first? Last? Why?
- Which aspects of your cultural programming are you most proud of and contribute greatly to your effectiveness? Less proud of? How are these values expressed in your life (e.g., when faced with difficult decisions)?
- In what ways do specific aspects of your cultural programming foster (or hinder): (1) equality and fairness, (2) stereotypes, prejudice, and the "isms," (3) discrimination or oppression, and (4) affirmative action goals?
- What impact do specific aspects of your cultural programming have on the inclusion of diverse others?
- What impact do specific aspects of your cultural programming have on your capacity to stay engaged and resolve conflict with diverse others?

Our colleague Michael Morris, a professor at Columbia University's graduate school of business, has conducted important research on cultural lenses. These cultural shades operate like transition lenses, that is, they are activated automatically whenever we encounter various triggers such as the pressure one experiences when faced with an important deadline, or any other experience that creates points of tension within or between people. We cannot eliminate our cultural lenses; we can only learn to manage them by considering a wider range of possibilities when interacting with culturally diverse others. The comprehensive nature of culture can be explained as operating at three levels: (1) artifacts, (2) espoused beliefs and values, and (3) underlying assumptions (Edgar H. Schein, 1992, 2004). Figure 4.1 illustrates the dynamic nature of culture ranging from the most visible to deeply embedded fundamental, taken-for-granted self-truths that are often not recognized even when pointed out.

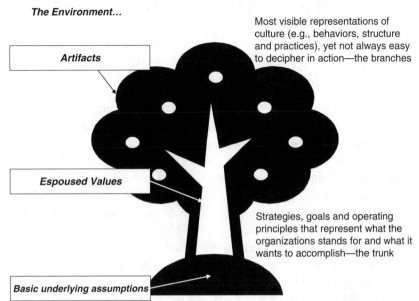

The Environment...

Most visible representations of culture (e.g., behaviors, structure and practices), yet not always easy to decipher in action—the branches

Artifacts

Espoused Values

Strategies, goals and operating principles that represent what the organizations stands for and what it wants to accomplish—the trunk

Basic underlying assumptions

Often unconscious, taken-for-granted beliefs, perceptions, thoughts and feelings that guide values & action in organizational life—cultural roots (collective worldview)

FIGURE 4.1 Levels of Culture: The Tree Metaphor.

The most visible cultural factors for individuals include behaviors, art, food and drink, manners, greetings, music, and dress (i.e., the artifacts of culture — branches and leaves). In organizations cultural factors are apparent in both structure and management practices. More surface factors include our words, conversation, patterns, norms, and values for individuals and groups — and strategies, goals, and operating principles in organizations (i.e., the trunk), which represent more mid range aspects of culture, often reflected in what we say we "stand for" as individuals and as collectives. Finally, the basic underlying assumptions are below the surface and include unspoken rules, and often unconscious, implicit standards that guide collective behavior in a social system (i.e., the collective, cultural roots). These are the most difficult to understand. The inner most layer of culture — our habits of mind, attitudes, hopes, dreams, fears, and even superstitions — are hidden from us. Yet, gaining access to these master programs, our own and those of others, that are the essential elements for taking informed, appropriate action in intercultural situations.

Formation of Organizational and Group Culture

Like individuals, organizations have describable cultures that began developing at the onset of their formation. The individual founder(s) bring with them a personal vision of the kind of organizations they want to create. This vision is combined with a set of goals, beliefs, values, and assumptions about how things should be; the origins of these, at least in part, are embedded in the founder's cultural programming. In the early stages of an organization's life the leader selects members with values and beliefs congruent with their own often unconscious, and deeply embedded cultural perspectives. This is consistent with the similarity-attraction paradigm pioneered by social psychologist Don Byrne (1971), which simply states that people tend to be attracted to and influenced by others they perceive to be similar to them, in this case shared values, beliefs, and other cultural factors.

Acts of leadership become stable, deeply embedded, and widespread in the organization's functioning when they address two criteria: (1) actions imposed by the leader result in success, survival, and growth as a result of effective adaptation to the external environment (e.g., competitive moves, customer requirements, market opportunities) and (2) internal integration (e.g., organizational strategy, structure, rewards, and other systems) permit effective daily functioning and the ability to learn, adapt, and change (Schein, 2004, pp. 17–18). When these factors are in place, the founder's beliefs become widely shared by others who move beyond mere compliance to commitment. Organizational culture is formed over time as members accept the prevailing behavioral expectations, espoused values and beliefs, and eventually customs and traditions.

Culture is developed in individuals and organizations through the accumulation of shared learning and includes behavioral, emotional, and thinking components. These reflect the group members' total way of thinking, feeling, and acting in response to challenges associated with external adaptation and internal integration (Schein, 2004, p. 17). Use the tool presented in Table 4.3 to access the degree of alignment between your personal values with those reflected in

TABLE 4.3 Tool: Aligning Individual and Organizatonal Cultural Values

Directions: Think about the people you are responsible for leading within the organization, list the personal attributes you value the most in the first column. In column two list what your subordinates' would say they value most about your leadership. Use column three to capture the factors that lead to success and those that lead to derailment.		
List the traits or personal attributes you value most in your subordinates:	List the traits or personal attributes that you think your subordinates value in you:	What does it take to succeed in your organization? What factors cause individuals to fail in the organization, or not reach their full potential?
Insights: Review the lists that you have created. What patterns and themes stand out for you? Use this space to summarize your reflections of the organizational culture in your workplace …		

Source: Authors' adaptation from concepts found in Sally J. Walton's *Cultural Diversity in the Workplace* (1994, pp 7–8); and Terrence E. Maltbia's, *The Journey of Becoming a Diversity Practitioner* (2001).

your workplace. Specifically, the tool is useful as establishing a foundation for the leadership context highlighting what gets paid attention to in terms of values and personal attributes, and by extension what types of personal factors often go unnoticed.

Diversity pioneer R. Roosevelt Thomas, Jr., (1996, 1999) notes the importance of distinguishing between customs, traditions, preferences, standards, and requirements (Table 4.4). Understanding the difference between these factors impacts numerous daily decisions, actions, and outcomes in organizations.

Table 4.5 makes the distinction between *culture* and *climate*. Culture is the work of leadership and climate is the work of management, both are essential to effectively leverage diversity in organizations. Additionally, Table 4.5 presents a number of definitions of organizational culture along with various perspectives on how "culture" shows up in action, as well as describes cultural intelligence.

TABLE 4.4 Standards and Requirements vs. Cultural Factors

Factors	Description
Customs	One's normal manner of doing or acting — habitual way of thinking or being, combine to establish one's customs.
Traditions	Over time customs become traditions, for both groups and organizations, as knowledge, opinions, practices, and ways of doing things are passed from member to member, and from generation to generation.
Conveniences	Making decisions based on customs, traditions, and conventions provide comfort and ease the complexity of contemporary life for many of us. Generally accepted social customs or modes of behavior are shaped by our worldviews and become rules and principles that guide behavior.
Preferences	Our master program or worldview is greatly influenced by customs, tradition, and convenience, which over time can result in perceived or real favoritism. Preferences result in choosing one thing, approach or person or another, or giving priority of one person over another.
Standards	Once established and accepted as a model, example, or test of excellence in performance and goal attainment — standards grounded in organizational requirements guide performance to promote equity.
Requirements	Organizational requirements represent success criteria informed by the external business environment; mission, vision, and strategy; the distribution of power; core people processes; and key stakeholders needs and concerns.

Source: Authors' adaptation of concepts in The New International Webster's Pocket Dictionary of the English Language, 1998 Edition; R. Roosevelt Thomas, Jr.'s, *Redefining Diversity* (1996, pp. 19–36); R. Roosevelt Thomas, Jr.'s, *Building a House for Diversity* (1999, pp. 53–63).

Cultural Continuum

Diversity work frequently involves striving to transform a mono-cultural work climate to one that is multicultural in orientation. In a mono-cultural organization individuals and groups hold ethno-centric points of view, where one's own set of standards and customs become the benchmark for evaluating all people regardless of background. Part of the work in our journey toward cultural competence is coming to grips with the inescapable reality that all human are ethnocentric, that is, we feel that what is "normal" in our culture is normal everywhere and to everyone (Triandis and Suh, 2002). This highlights the normality of bias. In mono-cultural organizations senior leaders serve as the "how to behave" benchmark by which all others are evaluated.

TABLE 4.5 Definitions of Culture and Related Concepts

Source	Description
Burke (2002)	*Culture* — "the way we do things around here and the manner in which these norms and values are communicated" (p. 205). Culture implies the rules that we follow to guide action (both explicit and implicit). *Climate* — "the way it feels to work around here ... the collective perceptions of members within the same work unit" (p. 207).
Schein (2004)	*Organizational Culture* — "a pattern of shared basic assumptions that was learned by a group as it solved its problems of *external adaptation* and *internal integration*, that has worked well enough to be considered valid and, therefore, to be taught to new members as the correct way to *perceive*, *think*, and *feel* in relation to those problems" (p. 17). *Levels of Culture* — the degree to which the cultural phenomenon is visible ranges from *artifacts* (i.e., the most concrete aspects of culture such as organizational structure and work processes), to *espoused beliefs* and *values* (e.g., strategies, goals, business philosophy, etc.) and *underlying assumptions* (i.e., deeply embedded, often unconscious, taken-for-granted dimensions of culture and include perceptions, thoughts and feelings) (pp. 25–27). *Dimensions of Culture* — deeply held, yet shared basic underlying assumptions about how the world works in terms of the nature of *reality* and *truth*, *time*, *space*, *human nature*, *human activity*, and *human relationships* (pp. 137–140). *Socialization* — the process of transmitting elements of culture on to new generations; how "new comers" learn to decipher operating norms and assumptions from "old timers;" an ongoing process that is often implicit and unsystematic (pp. 18–19).
Marshak (2006)	*Organizational Culture* — taken-for-granted assumptions about people, time, relationships, and the external and internal environment that create the dominant worldview of the social system (pp. 119–120). *Challenging Beliefs in the Prism* — a "prism" is composed of individual, group, organizational lenses shape the mental models, or the major frames through which we experience and make sense of, and act in the world around us (p. 22); significant organizational change require a critical mass of people to surface, expand or rethink core, often covert values, assumptions and beliefs that guide decisions and action (p. 121).
Walton (1994)	*Organizational Culture* — a pattern of values and beliefs formed over time by a group of people and is reflected in outer, accepted behaviors and eventually traditions ... the values supporting behaviors are a key to understanding cultural differences" (pp. 7–8). *Cultural Values Spectrum* — reflects 13 pairs of values commonly held by people around the world; the various mixtures result in a range of cultural profiles that help explain how culturally different individuals and groups show up in relationship and interact with others. These include: (1) *control* over environment vs. *fate*, (2) *individual* vs. *group* orientation, (3) preference for *change* vs. *stability*, (4) accomplishments attributed to *individual effort* vs. *birthright*, (5) *equality* vs. *hierarchy*, (6) focus on *time* vs. human *interaction*, (7) *competition* vs. *cooperation*, (8) *future* vs. *past*, (9) *doing* vs. *being*, (10) *informality* vs. *formality*; (11) *direct* vs. *indirect* approach, (12) *practicality* vs. *idealism*, and (13) *material* vs. *spiritual*.

TABLE 4.5 (*Continued*)

Source	Description
Hampden-Turner and Trompenaars (2000) Trompenaars and Hampeden-Turner (1998)	*Cultural Dilemmas* — when people from two or more different cultures interact and experience the contact as "foreign," this feeling is most often a result of the cultures being "mirror images of one another's values, reversals of the order and sequence of looking and learning, in short a reverse review of the world." The embedded dilemma is that neither culture is "normal" or "better" than the other, the cultures have simply made different initial choices about how to adapt to the external environment and internal interactions (pp. 1–2). *Dimensions of Cultural Diversity* — mirrored differences between cultures can be characterized by six dimensions: (1) *universalism* vs. *particularism*, (2) *individualism* vs. *communitarianism*, (3) *specificity* vs. *diffusion*, (4) *achieved status* vs. *ascribed status*, (5) *inner direction* vs. *outer direction*, and (6) *sequential time* vs. *synchronous time* (p. 11).
Coles (2005)	*Cultural Intelligence* — an analysis of social, political, economic, and other demographic information that provides understanding of a people or nation's history, institutions, psychology, beliefs, and behaviors.
Kreitner and Kinicki (2007)	*Cultural Intelligence* — "the ability to interpret ambiguous cross-cultural situations accurately" ... the ability to tease out of a person's or group's behavior those features that would be true of all people or all groups (i.e., universal factors), those peculiar to the person or group (i.e., idiosyncratic factors), and those that are neither universal nor idiosyncratic; culture lies between universal and idiosyncratic factors (pp. 114–115).
Earley and Ang (2003)	*Cultural Intelligence* — "a person's capability for successful adaptation to new cultural settings, that is, for unfamiliar settings attributable to cultural context; a person's capability to gather, interpret, and act on these radically different cues in order to function effectively across cultural settings" (pp. 9–12). *Three Aspects of Cultural Intelligence*: (1) *cognitive elements* (i.e., thinking and informational processing), (2) *motivational elements* (i.e., interests and drive), and (3) *behavioral elements* (i.e., action and interaction).
Thomas and Inkson (2003)	*Cultural Intelligence* — "being skilled and flexible about understanding a culture, learning more about it from your ongoing interactions with it, and gradually reshaping your thinking to be more sympathetic to the culture and your behavior to be more skilled and appropriate when interacting with others from the culture" (pp. 14–15). *Three Components of Cultural Intelligence* — (1) *knowledge* (i.e., understanding the fundamental principles of cross-cultural interactions, that is, knowing what culture is, how culture varies, how culture affects behavior), (2) *mindfulness* (i.e., the ability to pay attention, to be present in reflective and creative ways to different, often unfamiliar cues, during cross-cultural encounters), and (3) *behavioral skills* (i.e., the ability to choose appropriate behavior from a well developed repertoire to adapt and operate effectively in different intercultural situations).
Paige (1993)	*Intercultural Education* — a learning and change process with the aim of preparing persons to effectively live, work and operate in cultures other than their own; it is a highly personalized, self-reflective process that requires direct contact with the "other" — persons from the other culture (pp. 1–3).

In comparison, a multicultural organization has a critical mass of employees, including senior leaders, with the capacity to adapt both behavior and judgments in ways that are appropriate to a variety of interpersonal, intercultural situations (Bennett and Deane, 1994). These culturally competent organizations have the capability to unleash the vast talent and potential of a diverse workforce as a source of competitive advantage in our increasingly complex and global environment (Chesler, 1997; Cross, 1997; Jackson and Hardiman, 1994; Sue et al., 1998; Sue and Constantine, 2005; Wilson, 1996). Table 4.6 (Kockman and Mavrelis, 1999; Jackson and Hardiman, 1994; Miller, 1994; Sue and Constantine, 2005; Sue and Carter, 1998; Wilson, 1996) provides a comparison of characteristics relative of mono-cultural organizations and multi-cultural organizations.

TABLE 4.6 The Cultural Diversity Continuum

Characteristics of Mono-cultural Organizations	Characteristics of Multicultural Organizations
Organizational leaders take pride in being exclusive (e.g., focus recruiting at exclusive, top tier schools). Visible homogeneity in the senior ranks based on primary dimensions of diversity such as race, ethnicity, gender, age, and physical ability (i.e., "exclusiveness breeds sameness"). Prevailing values and beliefs grounded primarily in ethnocentric worldview structures and mental models. "Melting pot," those different from organizational "mainstream" expected to assimilate to existing culture, unilateral social accommodation. Culture-specific ways of doing things based largely on primary dimensions of diversity are neither recognized nor valued; "everyone should be treated the same "	Organizational leaders strive to embody inclusiveness to expand perspective. Commitment to visible, diverse representation throughout the organization, at all levels and across multiple dimensions of diversity. Prevailing organizational values and beliefs become progressively more ethnorelative as evidence in continuing attempts to accommodate various cultures. "Salad bowl," encourages the "Platinum Rule," of doing unto others as others would want done unto them, strive for reciprocal social accommodation. Actively engage in leadership and organizational practices that allow for equal access and opportunities, not treating everyone the "same" but in a culturally respectful manner.

Source: Authors' adaptation of concepts found in Thomas Kochman and Jean Mavrelis', *The Effective Management of Cultural Diversity*, Participant Manual (1999); Bailey Jackson and Rita Hardiman's, *Multicultural Organizational Development*, (1994, pp. 231–239); Frederick A. Miller's, *Forks in the Road: Critical Issues on the Path to Diversity* (1994, pp. 38–45); Derald Wing Sue and Madonna G. Constantine's, *Effective Multicultural Consultation and Organization Development* (2005, pp. 212–226); Trevor Wilson's, Diversity at Work: The Business Case for Equity (1996, pp. 41–46).

Further, Table 4.6 positions the two cultural responses to diversity at the organizational level in contrasting terms for the purpose of explaining the different dynamics at work, not to suggest that the conditions they describe are mutually exclusive. In reality, the two represent a continuum of the various ways diversity is experienced by different people in a given organization. To lead the transformation from a mono-cultural organization to a multicultural one, leaders must have the commitment and the capacity to communicate the reasons why such a major shift is necessary. This is nearly impossible when mono-cultural leadership reigns in an organization. In such cases, the learning and change process likely will require external experts serving as diversity coaches to those leaders charged with directing the process.

The continuum displayed in Figure 4.2 (Bennett and Bennett, 2004; Holvino, Ferdman, and Merrill-Sands, 2003; Jackson and Hardiman, 1994) builds on the descriptions provided previously in Table 4.6, and is a useful tool for clarifying individual and organizational learning needs in the context of diversity. For example, individuals and organizations on the mono-cultural end of the spectrum are less open to other perspectives than those on the multicultural end, and as such are less capable of understanding the reasons for engaging in diversity work. Making the transition from one point on the cultural continuum to the next requires creating awareness, acquiring the needed knowledge, learning new skills and applying new learning to real world situations. Each successive step on the continuum requires developmental growth. This growth is driven by the combination of an awareness, knowledge, and skills learning cycle, which continually repeats itself as the organization moves from the left end of the continuum toward the right. It is the leader's role during the diversity change process to guide this adaptive work.

We use Figure 4.2 to frame developmental stages along the path toward cultural competence, related learning associated with each stage, and the organizational impact of having a critical mass of individuals at any given stage. Organizational change experts emphasize the importance of understanding the concept of *critical mass* and the role it plays in the implementation of successful change strategies (Beckhard and Harris, 1987; Kotter, 1996). The concept of critical mass originated in the field of physics where it was used to define the amount of radioactive material necessary to produce a nuclear reaction. That is, an atomic pile "goes critical" when a chain

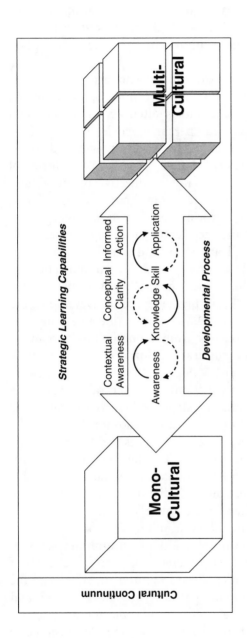

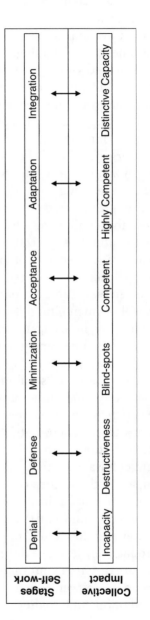

FIGURE 4.2 The Diversity Learning and Change Process.

reaction of nuclear fission becomes self-sustaining. When referring to social systems, Rogers (2003, p. 34) defines critical mass as the point at which there are enough individuals in the system to adopt an innovation so that the innovation's further rate of adoption becomes self-sustaining.

How individuals behave toward others who are not in their personal identity group depends on their perception of how others in their in-group are behaving. Individuals often act in rational and self-serving ways in pursuit of personal goals without fully considering how their actions might be disadvantaging others or the organization. The diversity change process is a form of organizational learning, where it is not a collective of individuals who are learning about diversity, instead, our focus is on stimulating learning to leverage diversity at various levels within the organization that builds on itself and accelerates learning capacity. In multicultural organizations, leadership and employee behavior reflect a degree of cultural sensitivity, that is, an indication of competence in understanding and integrating various diverse perspectives. Table 4.7 uses Milton Bennett's (2004) Developmental Model of Intercultural Sensitivity (DMIS) to describe a path for how leaders might navigate the journey from mono-cultural organizations toward becoming a multicultural organization.

Specifically, Bennett's (2004) DMIS describes three, ethnocentric stages, where one's culture is experienced as central to reality in some way, and three ethnorelative stages, where one's culture is experienced in the context of other cultures. Additionally, Table 4.7 aligns three "ethnocentric" organizational stages and three "ethnorelative" organizational stages linked to the related stages of intercultural sensitivity. And finally, the table suggests the collective impact of the various combinations of individual and organizational stages of cultural inclusion has on the entire system.

At the ethnocentric end of the continuum, the combination of denial and the "Club" organization results in cultural incapacity to productively leverage diversity. This mode of operating is a result of the organization's prevailing bias toward cultural superiority of the group in power, often unintentional discriminatory hiring and promotion, and holding lower expectations of non-dominant group members. The combination of defense and the "exclusionary" organization results in cultural destructiveness due to forced oppression and informal, yet forced segregation. The combination

TABLE 4.7 The Cultural Diversity Continuum: Monocultural Stages

Personal Intercultural Development Stages — Ethnocentric		
Denial — an inability or tendency to not notice cultural differences; a state where one's own culture (expressed as a pattern of beliefs, behaviors and values) is experienced as the only "real" one; tendency to dehumanize outsiders (e.g., "foreigner" or "immigrant"; common forms include disinterest and avoidance. *Developmental Task* — attend to the existence of others cultures by gathering information about other cultures to expand one's own worldview; strive to move beyond the comfort of familiar cultural patterns.	*Defense* — recognition, yet negative evaluation of variations from one's own culture; more openly threatened by cultural differences; dualistic in-group/out-group thinking and overt negative stereotyping; common forms include denigration of others, feeling of superiority, and reversal (i.e., see another culture as superior). *Developmental Task* — strive to maintain emotional control when encountering other cultures; mitigate polarization by emphasizing "common humanity" and recognize not doing so is a barrier to equality.	*Minimization* — recognition and acceptance of superficial cultural differences (e.g., eating customs), while holding that all people are basically the same with basic needs and motives, subtext "just like me"; common forms include human similarity and universalism (e.g., universal laws of nature). *Developmental Task* — moving beyond the "golden rule" of treating others the way you want to be treated toward the "platinum rule" (the way they want to be treated); learn to recognize the reality of institutional privilege.
Ethnocentric Organizational Stages		
The "Club" Organization — characterized by one dominate group in power, while not explicitly racist or sexist, holds on to traditional privileges, and only allows "others" in only when they accept and adhere to the norms of those in power ("fit").	*Exclusionary Organization* — here the dominate group in power actively excludes, or dominants, other groups based on race, gender, and other society identity characteristics; members of non dominant-groups experience the culture as hostile.	*Compliance/Affirmative Action Organization* — addresses discriminatory practices in limited ways, and in accordance with legal requirements; women, or people of color are included, yet core organizational practices remain unchanged.
Collective Impact		
Incapacity to Act Productively — when a critical mass of organizational members in power reside in denial characteristic of the "club," the organization lacks the capacity to effectively address the needs, interests and preferences of diverse employees, customers, markets and other stakeholders.	*Destructiveness* — the organization's norms, attitudes, policies, structures, and operational practices have a negative impact on non-dominant group members; institutional and systemic bias disproportionately benefit the dominant group, while discriminating against non-dominant groups.	*Blind-spots* — the organization's expressed philosophy of treating all people the same actually encourages assimilation for non-dominant group members if they are to have any attempt at succeeding in the organization; while alienating diverse others outside of the organization.

TABLE 4.7 (*Continued*)

Personal Intercultural Development Stages — Ethnorelative		
Acceptance — a state where one's own culture is experienced as just one of many alterative ways of being in our complex world (i.e., a recognition and appreciation of cultural differences); common forms include behavioral differences and value-based differences.	*Adaptation* — a state where one is able to reflect on the experiences of another culture and shift's one's perspective to understand and operate in multiple cultures; recognition of multiple realities.	*Integration* — a state in which one's experience of self reflects an internalization of multicultural view points; encapsulated marginality (i.e., "no where is home" and constructive marginality ("everywhere is home").
Developmental Task — emphasis on refining analysis of cultural contrast, a tolerance for cultural ambiguity and recognizing one's inaction can be a form of acceptance of unearned privilege.	*Developmental Task* — focus on improving empathic accuracy, culturally appropriate social adaptability skills, and learning to change one's perspective; work to address power dynamics.	*Developmental Task* — work to expand role and identity flexibility needed to address potential identity confusion and authenticity; embrace multicultural identity; use mediation approaches.
Ethnorelative Organizational Stages		
Utilization Focused Organization — strives to actively support the growth and development of all employees, with an eye toward previously excluded groups; the "isms" are discouraged; emphasis is placed on rewarding performance based on pre-defined requirements and standards; behavioral change.	*Redefining Organization* — questions how its cultural perspective (embedded in its vision, mission, strategy, structure and management practices) serve to engage its workforce, while enhancing relationships with key external stakeholders (e.g., customers); makes changes to take advantage of a diverse workforce.	*Multicultural Organization* — contributions of diverse cultural and social groups are embedded in the firm's vision, mission, strategy and way of operating; a diverse group of organizational members and other key stakeholders influence key decisions at all levels; committed to the ongoing eradication of social group-based oppression.
Collective Impact		
Competent — organization expressly values the creation and delivery of high quality products and services for culturally diverse groups; capacity to assess needs of diverse groups; yet organization lacks clear plan for achieving cultural competence.	*Highly Competent* — organizations where a majority of members have knowledge, skills and personal attributes that facilitate the construction and implementation of culturally appropriate responses to diverse identity groups.	*Distinctive Capacity* — organization that consistently includes and productively utilizes the wide range of skills and perspectives of its distinct identity groups; operates effectively across a wide range of intercultural business interactions.

Source: Authors' adaptation from concepts found in Milton. J. Bennett's, *Becoming Interculturally Competent* (2004, pp. 62–77); Evangelian Holvino et al.'s, *Creating and Sustaining Diversity and Inclusion in Organizations: Strategies and Approaches* (2003, pp. 245–276); Janet M. Bennett and Milton J. Bennett's, *Developing Intercultural Competence: A Reader* (2004).

of minimization and "compliance" organization results in cultural blindness. Here organizational leaders strive to "treat everyone the same" and are well intended. However, given the lack of emphasis on identifying cultural factors that serve to reinforce institutional bias, the leader is lured into the belief that "getting the numbers right" and "adhering to the law" will result in an inclusive organizational climate. Despite their efforts, organizations at this stage of cultural development find themselves surprised by the ongoing tension and conflict among identity groups, non-dominant group member's complaints about perceived discriminatory organizational practices, and unexpected bias based legal action.

Moving to the ethnorelative end of the continuum one finds that the combination of acceptance and a focus on utilization creates an organization where members have moved beyond simply recruiting, developing, and retaining a diverse workforce, to working to assess the needs of both diverse employees and external stakeholders. At this stage the presence of a diverse group of organizational decision makers, with sufficient resources to meet the unique needs of diverse employees, customers, and other organizational stakeholders, begins to emerge.

Selective intercultural competence is experienced when a majority of senior executives and other organizational members reside developmentally at the "adaptation" and "redefining organization" stage of the continuum. Here organizational members engage in continuous self-assessment regarding cultural competence. Diversity, based on *primary* (e.g., race and gender), *secondary* (e.g., educational background), and *personal dimensions* (e.g., learning style), is present at all levels of the organization. There is an explicit commitment by organizational members to continuously improve intercultural skills to provide culturally appropriate products and services.

From our experience the combination of placement along the continuum at "integration" and the notion of becoming a multicultural organization are ideals that leaders and high-performing organizations use as a target. The key distinction between this ideal stage and others is an explicit and unweaving commitment for social responsibility to fight social discrimination (i.e., doing "good"), while at the same time leveraging diversity to enhance organizational effectiveness and performance (i.e., doing "well"). Such organizations strive to attract and retain people with demonstrated cultural competence, and provide resources as needed to enhance cultural competency skills for all employees.

Use the questions below to apply the insights gained from reviewing Table 4.7 to your organization:

- Which stage is most similar to your organization and senior executives? In what ways?
- Given your starting point, which stage could your organization achieve within the next year? Within 3 years? 5 years?
- What would be the benefits for the organization, and for senior executives, for achieving the organization's next progressive stage of cultural competence? What would be potential drawbacks of doing so?
- What specific action strategies would be required to reach your first year objective? Within 3 years? 5 years?
- What dimensions of the current culture could serve to push the organization to the next level of cultural competence? What dimensions would get in the way?

We know from experience that it takes a majority of workers who accept differences and enjoy interacting with culturally different others for the creative and innovative potential of diversity to surface. Innovation and other positive outcomes associated with leveraging diversity are realized on a more consistent basis when a large group of people intentionally shift their perspective by adapting both their thinking and behavior to adjust to various cultural contexts. Conditions that facilitate multicultural, culturally competent organizations include:

- Committing to diverse representation throughout the organization, with measurable results to support stated commitment;
- Striving to maintain an open, supportive culture that is responsive to differences and can demonstrate improvement through periodic progress on employee climate surveys;
- Emphasizing diversity in the various operations of the organization, e.g., in strategic plans, marketing, community outreach, and supplier purchasing; and
- Having a comprehensive approach to diversity by aligning organizational employment and reward systems to support the effort to leverage diversity.

In this last chapter of Part I we focused on the "how" of diversity specifically emphasizing that you will need to commit to an ongoing, adaptive process to be successful in your efforts. In Part II we present six change drivers with the hope of providing you with a roadmap for leading the diversity learning and change process.

References

Argyris, C. *Knowledge for Action: A Guide to Overcoming Barriers to Organizational Change.* San Francisco, CA: Jossey-Bass, 1993.
Beckhard, R., and Harris, R. T. *Organizational Transitions: Managing Complex Change,* 2nd ed. Reading, MA: Addison-Wesley, 1987.
Bennett, M. J. "Becoming Interculturally Competent." In J. Wurzel (ed.). *Toward Multiculturalism: A Reader in Multicultural Education,* 2nd ed., Newton, MA: Intercultural Resource Corporation, 2004.
Bennett, J., and Bennett, M. "Developing Intercultural Sensitivity: An Integrative Approach to Global and Domestic Diversity." In D. Landis, J. M. Bennett and M. J. Bennett (eds.). *Handbook of Intercultural Training,* 3rd ed., Thousand Oak, CA: Sage, 2004, pp. 102–120.
Bennett, M. J., and Deane, B. R. "A Model for Personal Change: Developing Intercultural Sensitivity." In E. Y. Cross, J. H. Katz, F. A. Miller and E. W. Seashor (eds.). *The Promise of Diversity: Over 40 Voices Discuss Strategies for Eliminating Discrimination in Organizations.* New York, NY: Irwin Professional Publishing, 1994, pp. 286–293.
Burke, W. W. *Organization Change: Theory and Practice.* Thousand Oaks, CA: Sage, 2002.
Byrne, D. *The Attraction Paradigm.* New York, NY: Academic Press, 1971.
Chesler, M. A. "Strategies for Multicultural Organizational Development." In E. Y. Cross and M. B. White (eds.). *The Diversity Factor: Capturing the Competitive Advantage of a Changing Workforce.* Chicago, IL: Irwin Professional Publishing, 1997, pp. 34–46.
Coles, J. P. "Cultural Intelligence & Joint Intelligence Doctrine." *Joint Operations Review 2005.* Joint Forces Staff College, 2005.
Cross, E. Y. "Confronting Oppression and Discrimination." *The Diversity Factor* 5(2) (1997): 2–8.
Earley, P. C., and Ang, S. *Cultural Intelligence: Individual Interactions Across Cultures.* Stanford, CA: Stanford Business Books, 2003.
Gardenswartz, L., Rowe, A., Dign, P., and Bennett, M. F. *The Global Diversity Desk Reference: Managing an International Workforce.* San Francisco, CA: Pfeiffer, 2003.

Hampden-Turner, C., and Trompenaars, F. *Building Cross-Cultural Competence: How to Create Wealth from Conflicting Values*. New Haven, CT: Yale University Press, 2000.

Heifetz, R. A., and Linsky, M. *Leadership on the Line: Staying Alive through the Dangers of Leading*. Boston, MA: Harvard Business School Press, 2002, pp. 13–26

Holvino, E., Ferdman, B. M., and Merrill-Sands, "Creating and Sustaining Diversity and Inclusion in Organizations: Strategies and Approaches." In M. S. Stockdale and F. J. Crosby (eds.). *The Psychology and Management of Workplace Diversity*. Malden, MA: Blackwell Publishing, 2003.

Jackson, B., and Hardiman, R. "Multicultural Organizational Development." In E. Y. Cross, J. H. Katz, F. A. Miller and E. W. Seashore (eds.). *The Promise of Diversity: Over 40 Voices Discuss Strategies for Eliminating Discrimination in Organizations*. New York, NY: Irwin Professional Publishing, 1994, pp. 231–239.

Kochman, T., and Mavrelis, J. *The Effective Management of Cultural Diversity Program*. Chicago, IL: Kochman Communication Consultants, 1999, Attended workshop April 25–30, 1999.

Kotter, J. P. *Leading Change: An Action Plan from the World's Foremost Expert on Business Leadership*. Boston, MA: Harvard Business School Press, 1996.

Kreitner, R., and Kinicki, A. *Organizational Behavior*, 7th ed. Boston, MA: McGraw-Hill Irwin, 2007.

Maltbia, T. E. "The Journey of Becoming A Diversity Practitioner: The Connection between Experience, Learning and Competence." Unpublished Dissertation, UMI Dissertation Services, Ann Arbor, MI, 2001.

Marshak, R. *Covert Process at Work: Managing the Five Hidden Dimensions of Organizational Change*. San Francisco, CA: Berrett-Koehler Publishers, 2006.

Miller, F. A. "Forks in the Road: Critical Issues on the Path to Diversity." In E. Y. Cross, J. H. Katz, F. A. Miller and E. W. Seashore (eds.). *The Promise of Diversity*. New York, NY: Irwin, 1994, pp. 38–45.

Paige, M. R. "On the Nature of Intercultural Experiences and Intercultural Education." In R. Michael Paige (ed.). *Education for the Intercultural Experience*. Yarmouth, MA: Intercultural Press, 1993, pp. 1–19.

Rogers, E. M. *Diffusion of Innovations*, 5th ed. New York, NY: Free Press, 2003.

Schein, E. H. *Organizational Culture and Leadership*, 2nd ed. San Francisco, CA: Jossey-Bass, 1992.

Schein, E. H. *Organizational Culture and Leadership*, 3rd ed. San Francisco, CA: Jossey-Bass, 2004.

Sue, D. W., and Constantine, M. G. "Effective Multicultural Consultation and Organization Development." In M. G. Constantine and D. W. Sue (eds.). *Strategies for Building Multicultural Competence: In Mental Health and Educational Settings*. Hoboken, NJ: Wiley, 2005, pp. 212–226.

Sue, D. W., Carter, R. T., and Associates. *Multicultural Counseling Competencies: Individual, and Organization Development*. Thousand Oaks, CA: Sand Publications, 1998, pp. 3–15

Thomas, R. R. *Redefining Diversity*. New York, NY: American Management Association, AMACOM, 1996.

Thomas, R. R. *Building a House for Diversity*. New York, NY: American Management Association, AMACOM, 1999.

Thomas, D. C., and Inkson, K. *Cultural Intelligence: People Skills for Global Business*. San Francisco, CA: Berrett-Koehler Publishers, 2003.

Triandis, H. C., and Suh, E. M. "Cultural Influences on Personality." *Annual Review of Psychology* 53 (2002): 133–160.

Trompenaars, F., and Hampeden-Turner, *Riding the Waves of Culture: Understanding Diversity in Global Business*. New York, NY: McGraw-Hill, 1998.

Walton, S. J. *Cultural Diversity in the Workplace*. Burr Ridge, IL: Irwin, 1994.

Webster's Pocket Dictionary of The English Language. Naple, FL: Trident Press International, 1998.

Williams, M. A. *The 10 Lenses: Your Guide to Living and Working in a Multicultural World, Capital Ideas for Business and Personal Development*. Herndon, VA: Capital Books, 2001.

Wilson, T. *Diversity at Work: The Business Case for Equity*. New York, NY: Wiley, 1996, pp. 42–46

II

STRATEGIC STORIES: A LEVER FOR INDIVIDUAL AND ORGANIZATIONAL CULTURAL CHANGE

Part I discussed the strategic learning framework for leveraging diversity and introduced the three strategic learning capabilities: achieving contextual awareness, creating conceptual clarity, and taking informed action.

We begin Part II by suggesting you craft your strategic story for leveraging diversity. This story is your organization's roadmap for initiating and driving change. We follow this by introducing you to six change drivers. In Chapters 6 we address the first two change drivers: Leadership and Diagnostic Work and focus specifically on creating a leadership structure and conducting evidence-based situation assessment — both important change drivers for kicking off your strategic process.

In the next chapter we continue our efforts to demonstrate ways in which you can lead the leveraging diversity process by discussing the importance Broad Involvement and Commitment, and Education and Training (Change Drivers #3 and #4). Here we look at what needs to be communicated and to whom, as well as what are the educational needs to ensure that people have the capacity to leverage diversity.

Finally, we end Part II by emphasizing the value of Measurement and Evaluation and the significance of Systems Alignment to successfully implementing your strategic initiatives (Change Drivers #5 and #6).

5

Essential Change Drivers for Leveraging Diversity

You have to start with a belief and understanding that diversity is an institutional business imperative and that any institution that relies on any homogeneous population will sub-optimize in its performance ... You have to treat diversity like any other business imperative, and you must not be embarrassed about doing it that way.

— *Henry Schacht, Former CEO, Lucent Technologies &*
Cummins Engine

Strategic storytelling is a powerful tool used by 21st century leaders as they set the stage for change. These stories are used to build a stronger organization, improve business operations, and in this case, to leverage diversity for enhanced performance. Creating a strategic story for leveraging diversity provides a cohesive platform for linking your organization's history, to current reality, and to an envisioned, ideal future.

A strategic story can be made up of a series of short strategic stories, where each story serves a unique purpose, such as gaining buy-in or capacity building, yet when combined, the stories contribute to one powerful, inspiring, overriding story. This story provides your organization with a roadmap for initiating and driving change focused on building an organization that leverages diversity with intention and staying power. In this chapter we call attention to a fourth leadership practice by outlining a process of crafting strategic stories that can be used in combination with six change drivers for leveraging diversity in organizations:

Leadership Practice 5

Making your strategic story for leveraging diversity real.

Diversity Leadership through Storytelling

The diversity learning and change process begins with a visible, broad-based, and committed leadership team, who are charged with among other things, developing the organization's strategic story. When this process begins, as Jim Collins (2001), author of the best-seller *Good to Great* notes, leaders must "confront the brutal facts" about their cultural reality by grounding diversity strategies and related interventions in solid diagnostic work. Leveraging diversity in organizations requires perspective taking, which is achieved by ensuring broad involvement during all stages of the learning and change process, supported by focused and ongoing communication. Through this communication between diverse groups holding a wide variety of *personal* and organizational stories, the strategic story emerges grounded in multiple realities on multiple levels within your organization. Figure 5.1 displays the need to explore emerging stories from multiple perspectives, *personal* (i.e., your story), *interpersonal* (between individuals), *intra-group* (within identity groups, our story), and *inter-group* (between identity groups/their story).

Determining Your Buy-In Objective

Mark S. Walton (2004), former CNN anchor and award winning journalist, provides useful guidelines for framing vision statements as strategic stories that get attention and generate buy-in. He notes that gaining other people's buy-in has emerged as a paramount leadership skill for the 21st century. In short, gaining other people's buy-in requires their understanding, commitment, and action in support of organizational goals. From a perspective of leadership, it

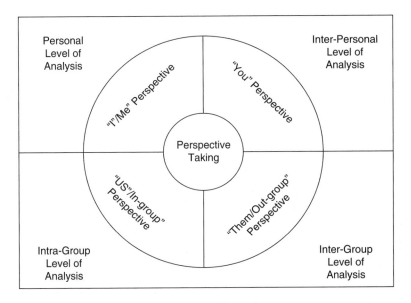

Personal Level of Analysis

Inter-Personal Level of Analysis

Intra-Group Level of Analysis

Inter-Group Level of Analysis

"I"/Me" Perspective

"You" Perspective

"US"/In-group" Perspective

"Them/Out-group" Perspective

Perspective Taking

FIGURE 5.1 Human Interactions and Levels of Perspective Taking.

is important to begin the process of crafting your story for leveraging diversity with a singular strategic objective — getting the attention, interest, and buy-in of everyone within its line-of-sight. In short, the process of strategic storytelling starts with determining your buy-in objective. Figure 5.2 displays a familiar, yet useful, tool for clarifying buy-in objectives (i.e., SMART goals). The strength of this simple tool is to start with the action you want your target audience to take, make explicit the accomplishment intended as a result of the action, communicate a concrete performance indicator, and conclude with a time frame for completion.

Strategic stories are designed to project a positive future, in this case a clear picture of the benefits to individuals and the organization to expend energy and effort to leverage diversity to drive performance breakthroughs, a leap from current levels and results. Walton believes the most effective way to influence the human mind is through its basic mental programming, a story. Walton's (2004, p. 23) approach for developing a strategic story displayed in Figure 5.3 builds on a clearly stated buy-in objective, that is, the actions you want people to take regarding the diversity vision and involves three steps: (1) establish a compelling strategic storyline; (2) develop the strategic storyline in three chapters; and (3) call people to action.

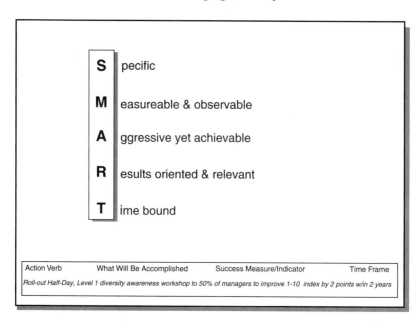

FIGURE 5.2 Writing SMART Buy-in Objectives.

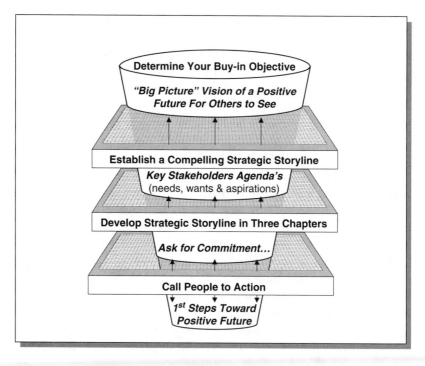

FIGURE 5.3 Strategic Storytelling Framework.

TABLE 5.1 Strategic Storytelling and Essential Questions

Component	Questions and Clear Points
Determine your buy-in objective(s)	Question — *What actions do you want your audience to take regarding your idea, proposal and related strategies for leveraging diversity?* Clear Point — Developing a story for buy-in requires an initial exercise in goal setting. Action is buy-in's bottom line!
Establish your strategic storyline	Questions — *What is the "big picture" or vision of a positive future you want your audience to see for leveraging diversity? In the desired future what will employees, customers, suppliers and other critical stakeholders do, think and feel differently from today?* Clear Point — *Tap into their imagination from the start!*
Develop your storyline in three chapters that target your audience's agenda	Questions — *What are the three most important ways in which your audience's agenda will be fulfilled? What is each stakeholder's incentive for leveraging diversity?* Clear Point — *Focus on the client's agenda and you will achieve your own*
Call your audience to action	Question — *What is the first step toward living from the future, today?* Clear Point — Ask for a commitment framed as a first step!

Following this process provides a way for leaders to bridge the gap between their desired future, with regard to leveraging diversity, and the preferred future of key stakeholders. The act of storytelling is consistent with the idea of using questions to spark your thinking. Each component of the framework is guided by one or more essential questions (Table 5.1).

Establish a Compelling Strategic Storyline

A compelling storyline is clear and concise. It begins with an attention-grabbing headline that places you and the story you are about to share in the spotlight. Select words and phrases that illuminate the future you imagine. Examples of powerful storylines from a variety of contexts include AT&T's "Reach Out and Touch Someone," former President J. F. Kennedy's "The New Frontier," The Nature Conservancy's "We Preserve These Places Forever," and the U.S Navy's "Its Not a Job, It's an Adventure" (Walton, 2004, p. 30). Effective leaders create a strategic story for leveraging diversity and continue to adapt it for various stakeholder groups, while maintaining the core message.

The following diversity-related example demonstrates how a central storyline can be modified for three different stakeholder groups.

CITIGROUP'S STRATEGIC STORY FOR DIVERSITY

For our people ... Employer of Choice — Citigroup values a work environment where diversity is embraced, where people are promoted on their merits, and where people treat each other with mutual respect and dignity. Around the world, we are committed to being a company where the best people want to work; where opportunities to develop are widely available; where innovation and an entrepreneurial spirit are valued; and where a healthy work/life balance is encouraged. Join Us, Stay with Us, Grow with Us!

For our Customers ... Provider of Choice — Citigroup strives to deliver products and services to our customers that reflect both our global reach and our deep local roots in every market where we operate. The diversity of our employees enables us to better understand our customers, while the breadth of our product offerings allows us to serve them better. Let Us Serve You!

For our Suppliers ... Business Partner of Choice — Citigroup works to create mutually beneficial business relationships with minority-, women-, and locally owned businesses. We recognize that working with a wide range of professionals, suppliers, and consultants strengthens the communities we serve and creates value for our shareholders. Collaborate with Us!

Develop Your Strategic Storyline in Three Chapters

Research shows that most people lock their mental gates between five and nine bits of information, with three being optimal for many of us. Examples of this truism are omnipresent in our lives in fields as diverse as *religion* (e.g., Father, Son, and Holy Ghost), to the *motion picture industry* (e.g., Lights, Camera, and Action). Building on this idea, once you have the attention of the audience, continue telling your story in three chapters (i.e., "big" ideas) providing support, evidence, and examples. Each key message should respond to your audience's agenda — speak to their needs, wants, and future goals — their hopes, dreams, and aspirations.

Construct each target chapter with a key message that makes explicit how developing a leveraging diversity capability will enable the fulfillment of personal, team and organizational needs, wants and goals. Each chapter must be laser-beam focused on providing a target message that asserts an agenda for the future combined with credible supporting evidence for each assertion.

Call People to Action

What differentiates strategic storytelling from other stories is their intentionality. While a well told story imparts an emotional source of value for listeners, as a leader the measure of your strategic storytelling success is the action and results that each triggers in others. You must bring the process home by: (1) asking your audience to take the actions you are proposing, and (2) calling on each person explicitly requesting that they come along with you and start making the story a reality today.

In Table 5.2 (Walton, 2004; Tyler, 2002) we suggest a tool for beginning to develop your strategic story applied to the Strategic

TABLE 5.2 Tool: Strategic Story Telling Framework — Generating Buy-In

Introduction: This planning tool applies a strategic learning framework to the art of storytelling and includes clarifying the context, defining the story's content, and encouraging your audience to take action.
Context — Determine Your Buy-In Objective Guiding Prompt (Link organization/business objective to diversity priority) ■ Action: ■ Performance Indicator: ■ Timeframe: *Example*: Complete demographic market research for core service areas in order to penetrate new segments to support annual 10 percent growth target during the next 3 years.
Content — Establish a compelling strategic storyline and develop your strategic storyline in three chapters Guiding Prompts ■ List the needs wants and future aspirations of the target audience ■ First target message with supporting evidence: ■ Second target message with supporting evidence: ■ Third target message with supporting evidence:
Conduct — Call People to Action Guiding Prompts ■ What is the best way to ask for commitment from your audience? What is the first step toward the desired future?

Source: Authors adaptation from concepts found in Mark S. Walton's *Generating Buy-in* (2004, pp. 23–77) and Jo Tyler's *Strategic Storytelling: The Alchemy of Putting Stories to Work* (2002, pp. 462–463).

Learning Framework introduced in Chapter 1. The six change drivers introduced in this chapter provide a focus for developing strategic stories aimed at leveraging diversity (see Figure 5.4). Once you have your overall strategic story — one that clearly establishes the case for building a leveraging diversity capability — as the change process unfolds, you can use the following framework and related tool to create versions of the story. Then, these versions can be used to breathe new life as you move into and through the various stages of the diversity learning and change process.

Early on you will find that you will need to share your personal leadership story for leveraging diversity time and time again. You should eventually reach a point when it is viewed as an essential component of your leadership platform. Your story should provide listeners with an engaging drama that reveals how leveraging diversity is a part of your autobiographical story and life history, not simply a new idea. The stories you tell about yourself should generate responses such as "I didn't know that about him" or "Now I see what she's driving at."

Personal leadership stories help you connect with others. They serve to make your commitment to leveraging diversity real, not some abstract ideal. These stories highlight your personal rationale for leveraging diversity as we discussed in Chapter 2. Combine your personal stories with diagnostic stories, ones that provide clear evidence for the need for the desired future embedded in your strategic story. Doing so helps you establish a powerful foundation for leveraging diversity. Once in place, build on this foundation to craft and widely communicate the story of what the organization stands for in regards to leveraging diversity, its branding story. When employees in the organization experience the organization's commitment to leveraging diversity everything begins to change. Your employees' enthusiasm spreads to your customers, suppliers, and other stakeholders, who in turn become your agents telling others about their positive experiences with your organization's products and services.

Leadership stories, a clear rationale for leveraging diversity, and the stories that emerged from various stakeholder groups' direct, and lived, experiences with your organization are important to record. They will provide a basis for the stories that frame diversity education and training initiatives. Measurement and evaluation stories are used to monitor progress, make adjustments as needed,

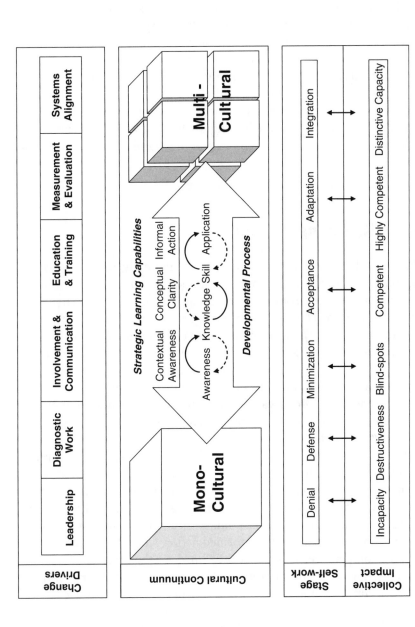

FIGURE 5.4 Diversity Learning and Change Process (Six Change Drivers).

and to share diversity-related successes internally and externally. Finally, systems alignment strategic stories ensure that people are clear that those core processes that drive organizational behavior (e.g., succession planning, performance management, selection, and compensation) are all consistent with the organization's commitment to leveraging diversity and related strategies. Or as Steve Kerr, former Chief Learning Officer at General Electric and Goldman Sachs, suggests you end up in a situation where you are "Rewarding A, while hoping for B," and as all of us involved in the work of leadership clearly understand, "hope is not a method."

Diversity Change Drivers

Although "best practice" companies differ greatly in their specific approach to diversity, they share a common commitment to framing diversity as a deeply rooted learning and change process. There are several important change drivers that provide a clear map of where leaders and other organizational change agents must focus to launch the process of leveraging diversity for performance breakthroughs and to sustain momentum throughout the journey. Table 5.3 provides a set of guiding questions related to each of the six change drivers. These questions can be used to guide the development of your strategic story in the chapters that follow.

Figure 5.4 links directly to the Strategic Learning Model. The bottom section of this figure addresses the strategic context (individual and collective impact). Knowing where you and your organization are situated on the continuum is contextual data that you must gather in order to determine what needs to be done to get where you want to go. The middle section of Figure 5.4 (cultural continuum) relates to taking informed action from the perspective of cultural competence. It links to the "how" of the Strategic Learning Model. *How will the organization move from a mono-cultural organization to a multicultural organization?* And the upper tier of the figure (change drivers) is the "what" of the Strategic Learning Model. That is, what are the vital few things that you need to focus on to drive change in your organization? These are the change drivers we introduce in this chapter and spell out in detail in Chapters 6, 7, and 8.

TABLE 5.3 Diversity Change Drivers and Guiding Questions

Change Driver	Guiding Questions
Leadership	Who needs to be involved in leading this process? Who has passion for the work? Are there members of my leadership team who will resist or sabotage this work? If so how should I deal with each? (Moments of Truth) What leadership structure needs to be in place to guide this change process? How can we leverage current leadership processes? (Structure and Roles)
Diagnostic Work	What information do we need to make critical leadership, structural and strategic choices regarding diversity that aligns with organizational priorities? (Content) Where and how will we gather and analyze data quickly to generate the critical insight needed to leverage diversity to spark performance breakthroughs? (Process)
Broad Involvement and Communication	Given what we have learned, what do we need to communicate? Why? How should we communicate? What results do we want to achieve? (Focus and Targeted Communication)
Education and Training	What do people need to learn to develop a capacity to leverage diversity? How? When? (Learning Strategies)
Measurement and Evaluation	How will we know progress is being made in each area of strategic focus? What are the early indicators of progress? Early warning signs of problems? (Performance Metrics)
Systems Alignment	What are the core people systems (e.g., benefits) and management practices (e.g., delegation) that drive behavior in our organization, which need to be aligned with our vision and aspirations to leverage diversity? (Reinforce Execution)

Each change driver is guided by several leadership questions. Tables 5.3 and 5.4 provide a description of each. The insights that emerge from working with the change drivers provide additional evidence to support your stories crafted to spread the diversity vision.

Change Driver #1: Leadership

An early step to insure your diversity initiative is real across your organization is to create a highly visible leadership structure, made up of the best minds available, to serve as your strong guiding coalition for leveraging diversity. Early on their mission critical work is to create a sense of urgency and build additional insight for taking informed action today, and in the future. Using the

TABLE 5.4 Change Drivers for Leveraging Diversity

Change Driver	Description
Leadership	Leadership commitment is a critical success factor for the effective execution of diversity strategies. Specifically, two factors are important: (1) constructing a *clear leadership structure* (i.e., Executive Level Diversity Sponsor, Enterprise Diversity Councils, Business Unit/Functional Councils and Affinity/Employee Resource Groups) for driving the diversity learning and change process and (2) demonstrating *leadership behaviors* (e.g., direct involvement in diversity initiatives, CEO surrounded by diverse senior management team, discussing progress toward diversity goals during strategy review meetings) consistent with fostering an environment that make working productively with diversity possible.
Diagnostic Work	External and internal research and assessment work provides a foundation for devising fact-based diversity strategies in addition to a baseline for the ongoing monitoring of progress and evaluation. Comprehensive diagnostic work includes three forms: (1) *self diagnostic work* by examining one's current knowledge and understanding of those who are different from oneself based on various primary, secondary, or organizational dimensions of diversity; (2) *external best practices* and *diversity research* and (3) *internal analysis* of representation and employee attitudes by organizational level and primary dimensions of diversity; assess equitability of employment practices from recruitment and exiting.
Broad Involvement and Communication	Engaging multiple perspectives in the work of crafting organization-specific responses to the three core diversity questions (i.e., the "why," the "what" and the "how" of diversity) ensures understanding, buy-in and creative approaches to productively addressing the problems, challenges, complexity and opportunities associated with situations involving diversity.
	Components of an effective diversity communication process include: (1) *clarifying key diversity messages* such are the organization's rationale, diversity vision and related values, definition of diversity, employee benefits, description of process, demonstrated commitment and progress updates and (2) *using a variety of channels* such as staff meetings, memos, posters, policy statements, articles in newsletters, orientation sessions, lunch sessions and various informal discussion opportunities.
Education and Training	Education and training are essential for helping leaders, and others in the organization, develop the *knowledge*, *skills* and *personal attributes* needed to construct competent responses to the problems, challenges and opportunities associated with situations involving diversity.
	Diversity educational activities *build awareness* and *understanding* as a foundation for driving behavioral changes consistent with the core diversity values of: (1) *respect for the individual*, (2) *treating all people with dignity*, and (3) *unleashing talent and potential*. The focus of education is to enhance one's intellectual capacity to process diversity's complexity with increasing levels of perspective and insight.

TABLE 5.4 (*Continued*)

Change Driver	Description
	Training aims to provide individuals with specific skills needed to excel in a diversity workplace and global context. Skill building focuses on enhancing a *culturally competent set of behaviors* needed to apply the insights gained from diversity education to real world situations ranging from establishing rapport with someone difference from another cultural context to productively resolving diversity-related conflicts.
Measurement and Evaluation	Measurement tools provide a powerful vehicle for reinforcing expectations and monitoring progress toward diversity objectives. A comprehensive measurement framework includes four diversity accountability areas: (1) *diversity mixtures* (workforce representation and executive parity focused, e.g., hiring and promotions), (2) *managing diversity* (utilization focused, e.g., performance rating and productivity), (3) *valuing differences* (climate focused, e.g., climate and employee engagement levels), and (4) *leveraging diversity* (collective impacted focused, e.g., achievement of work unit objectives). Measurement framework should include both *process measures* (i.e., leading indicators) and *result measures* (improvements in quantity, quality, time, resource allocation and/or impact). As such, diversity measurement systems help leaders determine: (1) *areas of success*, (2) *areas of venerability* that if not targeted and addressed could evolve into major issues, and (3) *areas of needed improvement*.
Systems Alignment	Systems alignment ensures that the core factors that drive behavior in a given organization are congruent with the overall enterprise strategy and supporting diversity strategies, including: (1) *measurement and rewards* (i.e., strategy and performance planning, compensation, succession planning and promotions), (2) *culture* (i.e., shared organizational core values and beliefs, leadership practices), (3) *structure and work processes* (i.e., organization and work design, decision processes and information systems), and (4) *people practices* (i.e., people first, competencies and motivation, development, selection, mentoring and coaching). High-performing organizations align systems to reinforce strategic focus; diversity must be treated in the same manner. This is a leadership challenge, yet without clear systems alignment and line-of-sight accountability, no strategy, no matter how brilliant will succeed.

organization's emerging definition of diversity to create a broad understanding of your current reality related to diversity, these leaders should represent and consider the multiple realities existing throughout the organization as they launch a comprehensive organizational diagnostic process.

Change Driver #2: Diagnostic Work

The diagnostic process begins by asking questions that engage others in deep conversation about diversity. The focus of these conversations is to gain an understanding of how to successfully navigate the territory between "What is" and "What can be." Examples include: In what areas of the organization are we effectively leveraging diverse talent today (i.e., identifying and appreciating the best of "what is")? What do we need to do differently to make this a reality across the organization (i.e., envisioning "what could be" and determining "what should be")? How will we know we are making progress (i.e., innovating "what will be")? These early conversations become the basis for co-creating the organization's emerging strategic story for leveraging diversity. At this point your strategic story gets real — real for all organizational leaders, all employees, customers, and other key stakeholders. Change drivers 1 and 2 will be explored in more detail in Chapter 6.

Change Driver #3: Broad Involvement and Communication

Persuasion is the process of engaging others in powerful conversations. The research on influence is very clear about the fact that people believe what they say themselves more strongly than they believe what other people say. Leaders who give people inside and outside of the organization the opportunity to become involved at each stage of the diversity learning and change process are more persuasive than those who simply state the diversity vision and communicate the diversity vision, goals, and related strategies. Involving a cross section of organizational employees and other stakeholder groups is an essential strategy for leveraging diversity.

Leaders who effectively leverage diversity know that getting information from key stakeholders about the organization's responses to difference and providing people a forum to have a voice is as important as giving information about accomplishments. Leadership for leveraging diversity also acknowledges that opposition is a process of intercultural interactions and is a sign of involvement. Leaders must strive to bring a "learner mindset" to such interactions and consider that responses of denial and defense are indicators of one's position along the intercultural development continuum toward cultural competence, and should not be viewed as negative.

The more involved individuals are in co-creating the vision of the future the more committed they are to making it a reality. As is discussed in Chapter 7, developing an effective diversity communication plan involves responding to four questions: (1) Why you want/ need to communicate (guided by an understanding of "context")? What do you want to communicate (or "content")? (3) What results do you want to achieve as a result of your communication (or "content" in terms of success indicators)? And (4) How do you want to communicate? (or taking "informed action")?

Change Driver #4: Education and Training

Education and training are important vehicles to ensure that everyone in the organization has an opportunity to learn the knowledge and skills needed to adapt to the changing leadership and performance requirements of the 21st century. Professional development in diversity and multicultural education is increasingly important as workplaces, markets, schools, and communities become more diverse and connected with the rapid advances in technology and transportation. The diversity learning and change process is both externally focused to promote understanding and internally focused to facilitate change. Also, in Chapter 7 we make important distinctions between diversity education and diversity training grounded in adult development theory and principles of effective adult learning.

Change Driver #5: Measurement and Evaluation

Early diagnostic work provides a clear picture of the organization's starting point with respect to leveraging diversity and a gauge of overall readiness for change, while ongoing measurement and evaluation are essential to monitor progress, make adjustments as needed, reward those taking on the diversity challenge and dealing with leaders who do not. Contextually, if the language of business is money, then the alphabet is numbers. While leaders may come under fire for instituting a diversity measurement process, if diversity is to be considered "real" by organizational members and other stakeholders, then it must be approached like any other strategic initiative. As is the case with many areas of organizational performance, when it comes to leveraging diversity a leader must acknowledge that at the end of the day, no metrics no movement. In Chapter 8 we provide general guidelines for building a diversity measurement system linked to organizational strategy.

Change Driver #6: Systems Alignment

Finally, it is important to acknowledge that many people in the organization have been rewarded for their current way of doing things, and so the new behaviors and skills needed to leverage diversity must be reinforced with reward and recognition strategies. Without *total systems alignment*, we often unintentionally implement various diversity strategies in the context of rewarding "A" (or old behaviors) while hoping for "B" (or cultural competence). In general, high performing organizations align critical systems that drive behavior including measurement and rewards, structure and processes, culture and people. Chapter 8 details how to align these systems to effectively leverage diversity.

Our research revealed that the people and organizational systems essential to leveraging diversity include *succession planning* (i.e., who will run the place in the future), *performance management* (i.e., creating line-of-sight accountability for diversity goals), *compensation and reward* (i.e., recognizing those who take on the diversity leadership challenge and excel). Many organizations focus on recruitment and training in the early phases of the diversity learning and change process and get stuck there. While these are important people systems in any organization, they are necessary but not sufficient for the leveraging diversity challenge, it takes courage on the part of leaders to demonstrate their commitment to this work by aligning diversity tightly with the systems that count.

You will find that implementing each of these six change drivers provides the power for moving your change process along. However, it is the combined momentum of all six that determines whether your efforts to leverage diversity are successful. The next three chapters provide a thorough discussion of each and set forth what we consider best practices for their execution.

References

Collins, J. *Good to Great: Why Some Companies Make the Leap ... and Others Don't*. New York, NY: Harper Collins, 2001.

Tyler, J. "Strategic Storytelling: The Alchemy of Putting Stories to Work." Unpublished Doctoral Dissertation, Teachers College Columbia University, New York, 2002.

Walton, M. S. *Generating Buy-In: Mastering the Language of Leadership*. New York, NY: American Management Association (AMACOM), 2004.

Evidence-based Leadership

Effective leaders pose strategic questions and challenge their people to pursue the answers.

— Michael Marquardt, Leading with Questions

How do you bring people into the change process? Start with reality! When everybody gets the same facts, they'll generally come to the same conclusion.

— Jack Welch, Former CEO, General Electric

Leading to leverage diversity requires personal and organizational transformation, where diversity in terms of "us" versus "them" is reframed to a mindset guided by collaboration across and among differences. The establishment of a leadership structure combined with thorough evidence-based, diagnostic work is essential for creating a strong foundation from which to build strategic diversity learning and change processes. In the previous chapter we introduced a strategic storytelling framework. Here our focus shifts to the first two change drivers (i.e., leadership and diagnostic work) that align with enacting the leadership practice below to ensure your strategic story for leveraging diversity is perceived by others in "real" terms:

Leadership Practice 6

Ground diversity interventions in a comprehensive discovery process.

You start this leg of the journey by uncovering your organization's history from multiple viewpoints to achieve a level of requisite variety that cultivates (not just tolerates) diverse perspectives and stimulates breakthrough thinking — do not distort with a myopic lens. Comprehensive, evidence-based diagnostic work is a critical platform for launching an effective strategic diversity process, such interrogation examines both the past and present looking to create an equitable and productive future that taps into the hearts and minds of your entire workforce, while generating results key organizational stakeholders (e.g., customers, investors, and community) truly value. Include baseline data on past and current performance measures and their impact across differences. You must rest future diversity interventions on a firm foundation of "fact" integrative of multiple "realities" — and, you need to know the facts cold. One way you make your strategic story for leveraging diversity real is by supporting each key message with solid evidence.

If strategic stories appeal to the emotions of employees and other key stakeholders regarding your core diversity messages (or "heart" work); then the comprehensive diagnostic work involved in setting-up an evidence-based leadership structure for leveraging diversity intends to stimulate analytical thinking (or "head" work). A well-crafted and well-executed discovery process is a perfect vehicle for demonstrating leadership commitment. It provides a platform for cascading formation and authority to those closest to the work, creating diverse teams as a basic building block, implementing high-speed communication channels to share insights, and fostering collaboration across disciplines. Compared to earlier chapters, here we take a more directive approach for setting-up the overall diversity discovery process by:

- Describing guidelines for creating a structure to enact leadership behaviors needed to leverage diversity (i.e., Change Driver #1) and
- Outlining four tracks for conducting evidence-based diagnostic work (i.e., Change Driver #2).

Together, these two change drivers help to ground diversity learning and change processes in the organization's current reality while continuing the work of crafting a compelling picture of a desired future focused on the effective utilization of human capital and talent. Our goal in this chapter is to present you with a series of frameworks and tools to use as guideposts while preparing to implement the six change drivers introduced in Chapter 5.

Begin with an End in Mind: Organizational Discovery Process, a Systems Perspective

Stephen Covey (1989), author of the best-selling book, *The Seven Habits of Highly Effective People*, identifies the first habit as "Begin with An End in Mind." We draw your attention to the right of Figure 6.1 where we list a number of potential results leaders can expect from a well-executed discovery process. We encourage leaders to invest some time getting crystal clear about the results they want to achieve by leveraging diversity in general, and how the discovery process will contribute to the overall objective. For example, many of the leaders we work with want to benefit from existing knowledge, research, and diversity "best practices" so they often commission a team to identify and explore how various trends are impacting their organization today and the impact they might have in the future. Our clients also are interested in understanding how various identity groups within their organization experience the culture and work climates.

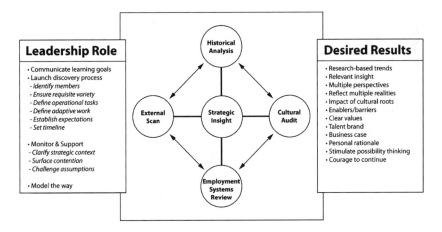

FIGURE 6.1 Organizational Discovery Process: A Systems Perspective.

Once you are clear about your intentions for launching the diversity discovery process it is time to express the "what" and "why" of leveraging diversity, as well as the important role leadership must play in guiding this process with simplicity, clarity, and sincerity. We list the essential factors of clarifying leadership's role in the discovery process in the left of Figure 6.1 and include:

- *Communicating* learning goals of the process, related outcomes, and connections to organizational strategy;
- *Launching* the process with personal involvement in determining the member of the various discovery teams, ensuring diverse membership, and ensuring the teams get off to a good start;
- *Demonstrating* your personal commitment to the process by continuously monitoring progress with clear milestones and scheduled reviews combined with providing support and resources as needed; and importantly
- *Modeling* the way by making decisions and applying the results from this work to key organizational systems and as an input to generating solutions.

In the next section of the chapter we provide detailed guidelines for establishing a leadership structure outlined here. Having given some time to thinking about the results you want to achieve from the discovery process and the importance of establishing a clear leadership structure, you are ready to implement the process with a focus on four tracks all with the purpose of contributing to strategic insight needed to take informed action in leveraging diversity (Table 6.1).

Various strategies for engaging in the important self diagnostic work of examining one's current knowledge and understanding of those who are different from oneself based on various primary, secondary, or organizational dimensions of diversity were presented in Part I, here our attention turns to the group and organizational level of analysis by taking a systems approach to inform our discovery process work. Evidence-based, diagnostic work is a form of organizational research that includes two major components: (1) a review of external diversity "best practices" and supported with relevant empirical data, and (2) an internal analysis of various employee attitudes to gain important insight into the organizational culture and climate as experienced by various identity groups.

TABLE 6.1 Organizational Discovery Process: Four Diversity Tracks

Track	Description
External scan	Research focused on examining a number of external economic, societal and demographic trends to speculate on their impact on the world of work, both opportunities and threats. Chances are this type of research is already underway in various parts of the organization in market research, competitive analysis, and forecasting functions. Often times existing data and procedures can be leveraged to support the aims of the diversity discovery process.
Historical analysis	A form of internal, organizational research that involves engaging in a series of individual and group conversations with senior executives to decipher deep-rooted cultural assumptions to gain historical knowledge of the organization's experience with in-group and out-group dynamics. The insights gained from this track can be combined with those that emerged during the self-diagnostic work described earlier: (1) Table 2.5 "Understanding Your Starting Point" and (2) Table 4.2 "Exploring the Origins of Your Cultural Programming."
Cultural audit	This form of internal, organizational research is broader in scope when compared to the historical analysis and involves gathering data from a cross-section of organizational members to identify factors that both enable, and serve as barriers to people developing to their potential and contributing fully to key organizational results. The traditional cultural audit uses "closed-response" and limited open-ended questions in the form of employee surveys generally combined with a series of identity group structured focus groups, communications, and action plans. Recently this approach as been combined with advances in "social networking" and "social network analysis" to reveal deeper patterns in an organization's informal systems.
Employment systems review	A third form of internal organizational research involves an in-depth review of the organization's employment and people systems that drive behavior. The scope of this work includes front-end processes such as recruitment, selection, staffing, and on-boarding of new hires; to ongoing processes such as training and employee development practices, performance management and recognition; to back-end processes such as layoffs, outplacement and retirement. In practice a number of themes that emerge during the cultural audit will relate to how various employee groups experience the way management implements the organization's employment systems with respect and in an equitable manner.

The basic open systems model includes inputs, throughputs, and outputs. In the case of the organizational diversity discovery process the inputs involve clear leadership roles and supporting structure, the throughput involves discovery teams focused on one of the four tracks all with the aim of generating strategic insight and related action plans, and outputs include factors such as those displayed in the right of Figure 6.1 or others of strategic importance to a given organization. In the final section of this chapter, starting with Table 6.5, we provide process maps you will find useful to focus the work of the four diagnostic tracks associated with the diversity discovery process.

Change Driver #1: Leadership

The first change driver involves creating a leadership structure to enact a set of leadership behaviors needed to leverage diversity, and ensuring that all organizational leaders are clear about their role. The leadership work for leveraging diversity as a strategic change process involves, as author Jim Collins (2001), author of the best-seller *Good to Great*, would say, first "getting the right people on the bus." Then the work shifts to co-creating a general approach for leveraging diversity, gaining broad-based buy-in and commitment, and going about the business of executing each specific strategy. As outlined in Table 5.2, a number of leadership questions must be addressed early on, for example: *Who is going to be involved in the work? Who will be responsible for moving the work ahead? What is the right mix of line and staff executives, officers, managers, and individual contributors to achieve and sustain momentum? Will the diversity change process be managed centrally, locally, or some combination of the two?*

Structure

Establishing a clear leadership structure to guide the work of leveraging diversity should be a leadership priority. Once a core leadership team that serves as a guiding coalition is established, their first task is developing the strategic story for gaining buy-in. This is done by devising clear messages with supporting evidence to frame the organization's rationale for leveraging diversity. The strategic learning capability of achieving contextual awareness described in Chapter 2 provides a number of useful resources for the leadership team to employ in service of this important work. The leadership team's first task is to examine the organization's external and internal reality with respect to diversity. This data is then used to articulate a clear and concise "call to action" that tells your strategic story and creates a sense of urgency. Be certain your guiding coalition has the power, expertise, resources, and creditability to lead the change as they collaborate to achieve specific diversity aims (Kotter, 1996).

Several award winning companies, recognized for their demonstrated leadership in a variety of diversity practices, differ greatly in how they managed and structured the diversity process in their organization. Some use a centralized model, others a decentralized one and the most common structure seems to be a hybrid model that combines the two. There clearly is no "best way" to manage and structure your process to leverage diversity, each option has strengths and limitations, yet it is critical that you are intentional about your choices.

The advantages of a centralized model include a strong focus on diversity initiatives, economies of scale, and integrating diversity components into organization-wide accountability systems to ensure sustainability and consistency of approach. The major disadvantage these organizations found is that it is unwise to customize enterprise initiatives and processes to meet local diversity-related demands, particularly in a global context. The advantage of a decentralized model is its flexibility. The diversity strategy can be customized to address the unique diversity challenges and opportunities of specific operating units. The primary disadvantage of this approach is duplication of effort in both the design and development of diversity processes and inconsistency across the enterprise.

Hybrid models were the most common approach we found in our research and in the findings reported in a number of Corporate Leadership Council studies (2000, 2001, 2003, 2004, 2005a, 2005b). Under this approach broad-based diversity objectives and priorities are established by a central body (focused on the "what" and "why" of diversity), while operating units are charged with devising location-specific diversity tactics (the "how" of diversity) and reporting progress. In the centralized, decentralized, and hybrid models centralized "centers of expertise" can be developed and deployed to provide advisory services to operating units as needed to leverage "best practices" and ensure that local approaches are consistent with overall organizational values.

The title and reporting relationship of the diversity function sends an important message across the organization. In other words, who the chief diversity officer reports to establishes top leadership commitment and sets the expectation as to how this function should be viewed by others. This message influences a range of factors including the amount of attention the diversity initiative will receive from managers, the degree of integration of diversity efforts into core organizational processes, as well as employees' perceptions of diversity's significance to leadership. When the Chief Diversity Officers reports directly to the CEO a clear message that "we mean business" reverberates across the organization.

Roles

Regardless of the specific structure, it is important to understand four critical roles related to any large-scale organizational change process: *sponsors, agents, advocates,* and *targets* (Conner, 1993, pp. 106–107). Table 6.2 provides a summary of major structural considerations, focus, and responsibilities associated with each role.

Sponsors

Sponsors (or diversity champions) include the individual or group with the power to sanction a large-scale change initiative. Champions have sufficient positional power and the personal influence to provide the people, financial and other resources needed to guide the diversity change process. Organizations that effectively leverage diversity have champions at multiple levels. Corporate (or Enterprise) Diversity Councils (or advisory boards) are generally made up of top executives, directors, and senior managers, representing cross-functional and cross-divisional perspectives to ensure diversity is aligned with other critical strategic priorities. Headquarter diversity councils play a critical role in defining the direction of core diversity strategies, deciding diversity priorities, ensuring priorities are communicated throughout the organization and monitoring progress. Diversity champions at the regional or local level are senior-level employees in their respective unit(s) charged with cascading the overall diversity strategies to their unit, monitoring progress and ensuring results.

Agents

Diversity change agents are the individuals or groups responsible for working closely with sponsors and others to make the diversity

TABLE 6.2 Typical Divesity Leadership Structure and Roles

Role	Focus	Responsibilities
Diversity champions	*Focus*	*Distributive leadership*
Enterprise-level diversity council ⇕	Devise strategies and priorities; provide direction and oversight	*Launch diversity discovery process (e.g., cultural audits, external research, and business alignment).*
Operating unit diversity councils ⇕	Define objectives and create action plans	*Integrate diversity priorities into strategic planning and implementation processes.*
Location diversity councils/ action teams ⇕	Customize operating unit plans, implement and report on-going progress	*Create diversity objectives and monitor progress (e.g., community outreach; inclusive work environment; multicultural marketing, etc.).*
		Ensure line-of-sight accountability and feedback (i.e., clear goals setting process and progress reporting).
		Establish diversity metrics (e.g., AAP goal attainment; employee survey data; executive parity and balanced workforce statistics; customer feedback; supplier diversity statistics, etc.).
Change Agents		Support champions in establishing and maintaining diversity councils (member of core and supporting diversity councils).
Diversity Executive/ practitioners ⇕	Co-create enterprise strategic direction and partner w/ change agents, advocates, and targets	Work with operating unit and functional heads to establish diversity objectives, strategies and action plans.
HR/OD professionals ⇕	Align people practices with diversity strategy and support implementation	Design communications relating to diversity objectives, expectations and progress.
Other staff partners ⇕	Provide functional advice and support (e.g., legal, Enabling Technology etc.)	Monitor external and internal demographics and other critical workforce trends; devise ways to disseminate strategic information to decision makers.
		Implement diversity training and education programs.
		Maintain relationships with communities, associations, educational institutions and vendors.
Advocates		*Provide input to diversity champions and change agents regarding initiatives that would benefit group of affiliation (e.g., Women, GLBT, etc. such as mentoring).*
Employee Resource Groups (ERGs) ⇕	"Bubble Up" issues; pilot initiatives; external linkages and self growth	*Identify and help develop external customer business opportunities & community connections.*
Change Targets		*Integrate diversity perspective into daily tasks from employee selection and staffing to coaching and performance evaluations.*
Managers/Supervisors ⇕	Implement management practices that promote employee engagement	*Strive to develop individual capacity to work productively with diverse others by expanding personal knowledge about various cultures and applying insight to daily work.*
Individual contributors	Personal responsibility for cultural competence	

initiative come to life. Organizations typically use two common models to guide the functional ownership of diversity: (1) diversity oversight within the Human Resources (HR) function or (2) diversity oversight outside of the HR function. To be successful, diversity change agents must effectively collaborate with colleagues within the HR and diversity function, other staff groups such as communication and technology, as well as, front line managers and employees. Strong diagnostic, influence, facilitation and project management skills are essential for success in this role.

Advocates

Advocates are individuals or groups who strongly support the diversity learning and change process, but lack the organizational power to sanction specific initiatives. The talents of advocates are often leveraged through their service on various organizationally sponsored Affinity Groups (or Employee Resource Groups, ERGs). Common categories include: (1) Gay, Lesbian, Bisexual, and Transgender (GLBT), (2) Hispanic/Latinos, (3) African Americans, (4) Asian, (5) people with disabilities, (6) older workers, (7) new employees, (8) women, and (9) working parents. ERGs perform a dual role. They serve the organization by providing valuable information ranging from giving feedback on a variety of HR processes (e.g., diversity training, performance coaching), product, and service ideas for target multicultural markets. Affinity Groups provide a link to diverse communities through mentoring programs, scholarships, and adopt-a-school initiatives. However, ERGs provide a context for employees to develop and exercise leadership skills, work through challenges with colleagues in a supportive environment, and gain access to senior-level executives.

Targets

While sponsors, change agents, and advocates each play vital roles, it is the entire workforce that is the target of the diversity learning and change process. It is only when a critical mass of leaders, managers, and individuals across the enterprise are committed that distinctive capacities associated with leveraging diversity through cultural competence is possible. The targets of the change must clearly understand the organization's expectations regarding diversity and must be involved appropriately in the implementation of each initiative. The role of the guiding coalition for the diversity learning and change process is to align individual and collective interests.

Leadership structures for leveraging diversity exist in various permutations in the organizations we studied. A number of major insights emerged from our work. The first is that distributive, broad-based leadership is a critical success factor across organizations. Learning to leverage diversity requires direct and intimate contact with individuals from different cultural backgrounds combined with willingness to listen and grow from interactions with each other. For this reason, diversity councils composed of primarily officers and other senior executives generally include lower-level and less-tenured employees such as high-potential managers and affinity group members to promote new learning about diverse perspectives as a result of engaging in the council's work.

The second insight is that diversity council members have demanding jobs independent of their council activities, and as a result diversity objectives can be viewed as a second-level responsibility, resulting in organizations unintentionally prolonging the realization of core diversity objectives and subverting the importance of diversity as a business objective. While diversity councils have emerged as a key structural framework since the late 1980s, some diversity experts are beginning to question this taken-for-granted practice.

Voices against the use of diversity councils during the early phases of change initiatives cite conflicting member priorities and poor group process outcomes as a result of large membership, with diverse backgrounds, tackling difficult, sensitive issues without the cultural competence to do so. As we pointed out in Chapter 4, there is growing evidence demonstrating that for such groups to be effective, a critical mass of group members must be positioned in the range of "minimization" and "acceptance" stage of intercultural sensitivity.

Our study results show a highly effective way of handling the diversity change process is to hire a diversity expert as a dedicated diversity professional and a full member of the senior executive team, who reports to the CEO to strategically approach diversity as a business objective. In one of our study cases where such a person was hired, she was able to make quick, precise alterations and changes that transformed the company from an organization with countless diversity challenges to an organization publicly recognized for top tier diversity practices.

The third insight related to creating leadership structures for leveraging diversity is that some organizations are beginning to explicitly add an external perspective to their process. For example the Eastman Kodak Company created a diversity panel comprised of external leaders from the private, public, and academic sectors as strategic advisers. The panel presents it recommendations to company's Board of Director's public policy committee. Merrill Lynch formed an external Diversity Advisory Board in addition to its Internal Employee Advisory Council. This external board is also compromised of leaders from industry and the academy and advises senior executives on maters related to attracting, developing, and retaining a diverse talent pool. The Corporate Leadership Council, Diversity Inc. and The Conference Board are excellent sources for additional research and company case examples of leadership structures for leveraging diversity.

Leadership Behaviors

In addition to creating a clear and explicit leadership structure to guide the diversity change process and clarifying various leadership roles; commitment for the work is reflected in leadership behavior. Commitment starts with one's core beliefs about others different from one's self, and is expressed in the actions that grow from these values. There are several ways in which commitment to diversity is experienced daily in organizations. Table 6.3 provides a sample list of behaviors related to each category and the related cultural competencies needed to reduce any organizational resistance to the diversity change process.

Firstly, the degree to which the composition of the executive officer rank reflects the available diversity in the talent pool demonstrates diversity at the top of the organization. Next, the ways in which senior executives hold themselves and others throughout the organization accountable for living the core values of inclusion and integration in critical decisions that are made regarding hiring, selection, promotion, termination, and downsizing.

Finally, the distribution of performance-based rewards and recognition, participation in development programs, succession planning and explicit sanctions for violation of ethical behavior including bias comments and harassment whenever it occurs

TABLE 6.3 Leadership Behaviors that Leverage Diversity

Visible Internal Diversity Champion	Integrate Strategic and Diversity Objectives	External Involvement
⇩	⇩	⇩
Continually articulates diversity vision. Puts diversity on meeting agendas and organizational reviews. Publicly recognizes people who leverage diversity to generate results. Takes explicit actions toward those not living the values. Mentors a diverse set of protégés.	Communicates personal, diversity performance objectives. Links diversity initiatives to strategic priorities. Sets a clear diversity change agenda for direct reports aligned with personal objectives. Emphasizes desired results, measures, and rationale. Requires direct reports to repeat the process with their employees until people at all levels of the organization understand how they make a contribution to the diversity vision (line-of-sight).	Participation in civic work that promotes social responsibility. Involvement in college relations activities at a wide range of schools. Supports philanthropic organizations that promote diversity objectives and develop future diverse talent. Collaborates with community and civic leaders. Membership on external broad that reflect diverse interests.

Enabling Leadership Behaviors
Recognize the emergent nature of developing a capacity to leverage diversity by holding people accountable for learning from their experience, experimenting, tracking results, and adjusting tactics as needed.
Align actions with the "Platinum Rule" of diversity by understanding how others want to be treated, and treating them that way versus treating others how you want to be treated.
Lead discussions about progress toward diversity initiatives with questions that surface insights about what's working, what's not working, the causes for both and what's needed to take informed future action.

regardless of who commits the infractions, all reflect leadership commitment. Supportive leadership behaviors fall into three board categories: (1) visible, internal diversity sponsors and champions, (2) cascade diversity objectives at all organizational levels, and (3) intentional external involvement.

Change Driver #2: Diagnostic Work

The second change driver involves conducting diagnostic work to ground the process in the organization's current reality while crafting a compelling picture of a desired future. Data drives change. It is clear and explicit evidence linked to each stakeholder's agenda that makes your strategic story real. Without doing a full-fledged diagnostic effort, you will not have the data needed to develop your business case for diversity, to gain buy-in, and to build commitment, nor will you be able to measure progress. Again, Table 5.3 provides a starter list of questions to provide a general guide for driving the diagnostic work to leverage diversity (i.e., content and process). A number of data-driven questions must be addressed to ensure that diversity strategies are established on the solid foundation of a good diagnosis.

Diagnostic work ranges from gathering data for baseline assessments to understanding your organization's current level of effectiveness at managing and capitalizing on diversity, to evaluating the effectiveness of implementing a diversity strategy, and so on. Further, the purpose of diagnostic work shifts throughout the diversity learning and change process. During the early stages the emphasis is on best practice research and an internal assessment of the organization's readiness for change. External best practice research helps to catalogue exemplars of outstanding diversity programs across organizations and provides a picture of what success might look like in terms of practices that attract, develop, deploy, and retain diverse talent.

Information from best practice research is generally combined with data gathered from cultural audits to examine current organizaztional realities related to diversity. Cultural audits (Hutcheson and Kruzan, 1996, p. 13) are a form of research designed to:

- *Identify* the core assumptions (i.e., values and beliefs) that reflect an organization's culture;
- *Access* how a given organization's cultural roots either hinder or facilitate its capacity to leverage diversity; and
- *Provide* a foundation for guiding the design, implementation, and evaluation of various diversity learning and change processes.

Organizations either hire an external diversity expert to assist in completing this upfront diagnostic work or charge an internal organizational development professional to guide this process. When external resources are acquired, the consultant works with a team of internal resources to complete the cultural audit and build capacity to continue the work beyond the consulting engagement. If the decision is made to complete this process internally there are several resources available (see Appendix D). Whether you decide to internally do the heavy lifting associated with completing the task of generating a comprehensive, evidence-based foundation to drive your diversity strategy, or you decide to hire an external consultant to do the work, we recommend this work be guided by the diagnostic four tracks we introduced in Table 6.1 (i.e., external scan, historical analysis, cultural audit, and employment systems review (ESR)).

Strategic Insight Process

We frame the diagnostic work involved in conducting a diversity-focused situational analysis as a transformational learning process. As you will see, the diversity discovery process is similar to various forms of effective competitive analysis. Further, this diagnostic process is characterized as transforming raw data into strategic insight. Figure 6.2 graphically displays the key elements of this transformational learning process by showing how the process moves progressively from "data" to strategic "insight."

While each diagnostic track plays a role in filling in a different part of the organization's diversity story, the aim of each track is the

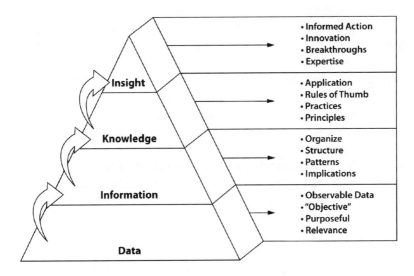

FIGURE 6.2 Achieving Strategic Insight.

same, to generate strategic insight. This process can be applied to each of the four diagnostic tracks used to guide the diversity discovery process. This analytical thinking process can be applied to external scanning and internal scanning activities.

Data

The foundation of the strategic insight process is "data," collecting lots of it, from multiple sources, over a specified period of time. The data you collect to better understand the comprehensive nature of diversity (and the multiple ways diversity is experience inside of the organizations by your employees and outside of the organization by customers, suppliers, and other key participant's in the value chain) must be inclusive of two forms: (1) *objective data* (i.e., fact, figures, statistics, demographic data, diverse market trends, and other sources of relatively direct observable data) and (2) *perceptual data* (i.e., the thoughts and feelings of various groups based on their experience with diversity — the emotional and cultural aspect of diversity). Objective and perceptual data must be collected and analyzed for each diagnostic track.

Information

Given the sheer volume of data associated with the diversity discovery process, it is important to have an explicit process for transforming the raw data into information. Thus, the second stage of the strategic insight process is to organize the objective data and perceptual data into a uniform structure to facilitate the identification of patterns and trends embedded in the various data sets. This will be particularly critical in managing perceptual, more qualitative forms of data. Teams should explore various "data displays" such as tables, matrices, charts, graphs, mind maps, and process flows to help facilitate the transformation of data to information. These tools will help to crystallize the major organizational, identity group, and individual diversity themes.

Knowledge

The work associated with data collection and transforming "raw" data to information is largely an organizational research process, which we have described as an operational form of diversity work in Chapter 4. The transition from information to knowledge is comparatively more adaptive work and requires broader involvement. The essential tasks related to the "data" and "information" stages of the strategic insights process relate to understanding important "what" and "how" questions. As the diagnostic process makes the shift from information to knowledge, these questions are combined with the all important "why" questions that are so central to our understanding of the cultural factors that support diversity and current diversity barriers.

Knowledge work focuses on applying the information that emerges from various diagnostic tracks to "live testing" with representatives from target identity groups that reflect a cross-section of the organization along various primary and secondary dimensions of diversity as outlined in Table 3.1. This is also where the strategic conversation guidelines described in Chapter 9 of Part 3 of the book can be of great benefit. It is at this stage of the strategic insight process that you begin to pull together convincing evidence from a variety of sources, targeted to agenda's of various stakeholder groups that the organization's strategic story for leveraging diversity becomes real and has the capacity to tap into not only the minds, but importantly the hearts of others.

Insight

Strategic insight is the result of structured, systematic process of broad-based data collection; transforming data to information for analysis and pattern identification; and applying data and information to a specific context while involving key stakeholders in the system to make explicit the on-the-ground principles and practices in action, and how each is experienced by various identity groups inside and outside of the organization. Strategic insight results in expertise, fosters innovation, and importantly drives performance breakthroughs, in this case by leveraging diversity through cultural competence.

Four Diagnostic Tracks

We believe the starting point for any situational analysis is to decide what you need to know and where to search for the data. Having a clear purpose for each area of exploration provides focus and allows people in the organization to seek relevant data that, when closely examined, will provide value-added insight to guide ongoing diversity strategy formulation and related interventions. The search for new insight continues by gathering data from a variety of sources and testing the reliability of each source. Whether you rather engage in data-gathering process directly or you decide to delegate it to researcher, be sure to set the expectation to focus on trends not a given point in time. As Willie Pietersen notes "trends tell a story, snapshots never do." So, it is important when you identify relevant data to map the trend and try to gain an understanding of its underlying drivers.

The four diagnostic tracks summarized in this section outline a set of procedures for collecting data from numerous sources, using a variety to data collection methods to ensure a comprehensive, evidenced-based diversity discovery process. Be certain to gather your data from a cross-section of executives and employees. You should use a mixture of interviews, focus groups, and surveys. This ensures the opportunity for broad levels of participation and the ability to analyze the data by the various dimensions of diversity (e.g., race, gender, age, and other central descriptors) and organization dimensions of diversity (e.g., level, function, locations, and other factors). There are numerous sources that provide a more detailed account and related tools for each of these discovery tracks, our purpose here is to provide general "action maps" for each track.

The following descriptions of the four tracks that guide the diversity discovery process will also aid in helping the leader set clear expectations for each team and engagements with external resources by highlighting the purpose, information needed, topics, and the desired outcomes of each track of discovery work. Although the amount of work may seem overwhelming, you will find that much of the data needed for these efforts is overlapping and that the combined results of the four tracks provide you with a holistic perspective.

External Scan

We start with this track because it is likely to be the most familiar to leaders across organizations. Many organizations use some version of environmental scanning as input to the strategy planning process. Specifically, the process employs various frameworks to generate useful information to assist leaders in grappling grapple with a number of external trends and issues that could create both threats and opportunities to the organization's ability to realize its core mission and effectively execute its strategy. In short, ongoing environmental scanning can provide windows into the organization's past and current realities, as well as, possible futures. Depending on the organization, this work is most likely already underway by market and product research, competitive analysis, and competitive intelligence professionals. Table 6.4 lists the purpose and topics related to this track of work.

The goal of the external environment scan phase of the situation analysis is to make sense out of these changes and to examine current and probable future directions. To do this, you will need to look at the historical picture, examine the current situation and finally, explore the impact of what the demographers and economists

TABLE 6.4 External Scan: Action Map

Purpose	Type of Information	Methods	Topics/Focus
Examine a number of external economic, societal and demographic trends to speculate on their impact on the world of work, both opportunities and threats.	Trend data	Mix method: qualitative and quantitative (secondary sources)- document analysis ■ Research Reports and Studies ■ Trade Publications/ Associations ■ Bureau of the Census Data ■ Bureau of Labor Statistics ■ U.S. Department of Education	Strategic context ■ Recent industry/ market developments (e.g., competitive moves and market demographics) ■ Forces shaping the American and Global economies (e.g., technology, globalization, population trends, workforce demographics and educational attainment)
	Perceptual and experiential	Qualitative analysis ■ Benchmarking ■ Discussions with industry/market experts	Implications ■ Competitive/market position ■ Opportunities ■ Threats ■ Workforce/attract and retain talent

Source: Authors' adaptation of concepts found in Terrence E. Maltbia's, *The Journey of Becoming a Diversity Practitioner* (2001).

suggest are the likely outcomes of the shifting demographics. You will want to map diversity-related trends specific to your labor force, as well as in your customer and supplier base.

As a starting point, many diversity practitioners in our study learned about existing organizational environmental scanning procedures and worked to leverage those wherever possible. Often the insight gained from ongoing organizational intelligence efforts related trends in technology, markets, economics, and various regulatory requirements. These are useful inputs for diversity-focused environmental scanning activities. In addition, demographic, educational, and societal trends are areas in which the diversity practitioner's in our study were well-versed. Diversity practitioners and leaders also worked to stay current on best practices.

There are a number of economic, societal, and demographic trends that are expected to continue to shape the world of work. Broadly speaking, the changing demographic reality of today's workforce is shaped by the six mega-social trends (see Appendix D for data from the Center for Strategic and International Insight, 2005; Cetron and Davies, 2003). As you review each megatrend think about "where," "when," and in "what" way the trends will impact your organization, your workforce, and the clients you serve. Which of these trends do you need to continue to monitor? How will you work to transform this information into useful insight to inform future action? The external scan is an excellent way to develop the strategic learning capability of achieving and sustaining contextual awareness.

Historical Analysis

We strongly endorse including an historical analysis of the organization that includes an exploration of the institution's executive profile over time as a central feature of the diversity discovery process. Table 6.5 outlines the purpose, type of information needed, and the topics that guide data collection, conversations, and analysis during this track of work.

We propose two major interventions in this track: (1) a series of conversations with a group of selected executives to examine organizational culture and (2) one-on-one conversations with senior executives in the top two to three levels of the organization to gain a deeper understanding about their leadership assumptions, the implications of the organization's historical executive profile and

TABLE 6.5 Historical Analysis: Action Map

Purpose	Type of Information	Methods	Topics/Focus
Engage in a series of individual and group conversations with senior executives to decipher deep-rooted cultural assumptions and understand the organization's historical experience with in-group and out-group dynamics.	Historical/ Current	Qualitative analysis ■ Large Group Dialogue Session(s) ■ 1-on-1 Executive Dialogue Sessions ■ Company historical documents	Cultural assumptions ■ How to think about culture ■ Cultural artifacts Incumbent executive profile ■ Historical and current ■ In-group/out-group dynamics at senior level ■ Key influencers
	Perceptual and experiential	Qualitative analysis ■ Large Group Dialogue Session(s) ■ 1-on-1 Executive Dialogue Sessions	Cultural assumptions ■ Identify values ■ Surfacing shared underlying cultural assumptions Personal beliefs about … ■ People and work ■ Leadership ■ One's own strengths and limits ■ What is important in life Critical incidents examples ■ Diversity "high-points"

Source: Authors' adaptation from Edgar H. Schein's, *Organizational Culture and Leadership*, 2nd ed. (1992, pp. 147–168) and 3rd ed. (2004); Chris Agryris', *On Organizational Learning*, 2nd ed. (1999); and Terrence E. Maltbia's, *The Journey of Becoming a Diversity Practitioner* (2001).

organizational culture. We introduced the tool, "Understanding Your Starting Points," to facilitate these reflective conversations in Table 2.5.

Given the nature of this work, the executive team might consider identifying a skilled external diversity consultant, with specific expertise in organizational culture, intercultural dialogue and analysis. This resource should work in collaboration with the lead internal diversity professional and key human resource leaders. The facilitator can help guide a group of selected executives through a series of conversations designed to situate the diversity challenge within the broader strategic context of the organization, while working to identify the degree of congruence between *what the organization says it stands for* (i.e., espoused values) and *wants to achieve* (i.e., business and diversity-related results) on the one hand, and the *shared underlying assumptions* (i.e., organizational culture or what Agryris calls theories-in-use/action) that influences what actually happens on a daily basis in the organization on the other hand.

We use a process designed by Edgar H. Schein (1992, 2004) to guide the design and execution of a series of two or four sessions (depending on each time block) to help insiders decipher their organizational culture:

- *Align* expectations with an executive sponsor (CEO, President or other senior leader) and obtain commitment needed to invest the time and energy needed to complete this upfront culture work;
- *Conduct* a series of two or three large group meetings with executive sponsor and other selected executives (focus on how to think about organizational culture, elicit descriptions of the organization's cultural artifacts — things like dress code, desired modes of behavior, use of time and space, etc.; identifying organizational espoused values — what the leaders say the organization stands for and the results they collectively hope to achieve; and make tacit, shared assumptions that make the culture explicit);
- *Identify* culturally based enablers and barriers to co-creating an inclusive, high-performance organizational culture that leverages diversity in subgroups (time is spent in subgroups refining each assumption, identifying additional assumptions, then categorizing them as enablers or barriers to diversity and inclusion); and
- *Report* subgroup generated assumptions and engage a conversation focused on a joint analysis of culture in the large group (critical to reach consensus on what the important shared assumptions are and what the implications of those assumptions are for co-creating a culture to leverage diversity).

At its core, the historical analysis track of the diversity discovery process is to gain a contextual understanding of the organization's pattern of in-group and out-group dynamics over an extended period of time. A realistic approach to understanding these patterns is to integrate the following set of questions into the inquiry process of the top 50 roles in the organization (based on level, pay grade, and control of resources) by asking each: (1) *What are the names of the individuals who have held your current position in the past* (or most similar), *starting with the most recent and going back as far as you can?* (2) *What do you know about the major contributions each made to the organization while in your role?* (3) *What do you know about the diversity profile of each of these job incumbents* (i.e., age when entered and exited the role, race, ethnicity, gender, country of origin, political affiliation, and so on)? and (4) As you reflect on these various individuals who have held your position in the past; *What patterns do you notice? What are the implications for how diversity is currently managed and leveraged in the organization?* We find the collective insight from these conversations to be some of the most revealing and are consistent with recent discoveries of the importance of informal relationships from the emerging field of social network analysis.

Cultural Audit

The cultural audit builds on insights gained during the historical analysis. In the context of the diversity discovery process, the cultural audit is based on the assumption that "understanding organizational culture is necessary to decipher what is going on and identify priority issues in organizations" (Schein, 1992, 2004). There are many good resources to help you direct your cultural audit process. Table 6.6 highlights the process with a focus on diversity. A thorough audit requires three types of information: (1) current and historical documents, (2) leadership and workforce demographic profiles, and (3) perceptions of a cross-section of employees from diverse groups.

Because a cultural audit is broad in scope and provides perspectives from a diverse group of employees it can take 2–4 months to complete (Thomas, 1991). Depending on the context, the audit focuses on a variety of diversity components in broad categories of inborn characteristics, personal experiences, organizational dimensions, personal styles or tendencies, and a number of relevant external factors (as presented in Table 6.6). It is important

TABLE 6.6 Cultural Audit: Planning Map

Purpose	Type of Information	Methods	Topics/Focus
Gather data from a cross-section of organizational members to identify factors that both enable, and serve as barriers, to people developing their potential and contributing fully to key organizational results.	Historical and documentary	▪ Document review	▪ Histories of organization ▪ Biographies of Founder(s) ▪ Public relations and recruitment materials; newsletters (over time that include policy and strategic statements from executives) ▪ Vision, mission and strategy statements; strategic plans, annual reports and goals progress reports ▪ Organizational structure/chart ▪ AA/EEO policies and practices; handbooks and training materials ▪ Training materials for managers and supervisors
	Leadership and workforce profile	▪ Human resource information system	▪ Board of Directors ▪ Top 50 Paid ▪ Officials and managers ▪ Hiring and retention rates ▪ Promotion rates ▪ Pay rates ▪ Legal employment claims and supplements
	Perceptual and experiential	▪ Surveys ▪ Quantitative analysis ▪ Focus groups ▪ Qualitative analysis	▪ Employee expectations ▪ Sources of fulfillment/frustration ▪ Perceptions of "What it takes to be successful?" ▪ Perceptions of diversity

Source: Authors' adaptation from Dr. R. Roosevelt Thomas', *Beyond Race and Gender* (1991, pp. 50–71) and Terrence E. Maltbia, *The Journey of Becoming a Diversity Practitioner* (2001).

for diversity sponsors to clarify the focus on specific, relevant diversity categories from the start, with an explicit strategy for expanding the scope over time. Vas Taras, Ph.D. of the University of Calgary has developed a catalogue of publically available instruments for measuring culture that is an excellent resource for devising organization-specific culture assessments (see http://www.ucalgary.ca/~taras/_private/Culture_Survey_Catalogue.pdf).

Cultural audit surveys and related focus groups need to explore employee perceptions along five broad categories (again refer to Appendix D for sample resources):

- *Employee Expectations of Organization* (i.e., factors that attracted employees to organization; extent to which expectations have been met; sources of fulfillment and frustration);
- *Success Factors* (i.e., beliefs about what it takes to be successful in the organization; characteristics of successful employees; the extent to which employees themselves feel successful; facilitators and barriers to success; what characteristics would employees seeks in hiring someone to do their job; perceptions about "unwritten rules" and related consequences and payoffs);
- *Management and Supervisions* (i.e., quality of management; positive and negative management attributes; what managers pay attention to/what gets rewarded; clarity of what's expected and feedback; empowerment; assimilation; people skills and technical competence);
- *People Practices and Systems* (i.e., staffing; training and developing including mentoring and succession planning; reward and recognition including pay, support, promotion; performance assessment and coaching and communication); and
- *Response to Diversity* (i.e., respect for the individual; full utilization of talent; degree of optimism or pessimism about the future of diversity in the organization; value of different views and perspectives; degree to which "isms", racism, sexism, and so on can be discussed with supervisor, others? Repercussions? What needs to be done to improve the situation).

The historical analysis and cultural audit combine to construct a comprehensive picture of cultural assumptions that negatively or positively impact your organization's capacity to leverage diversity.

Employment Systems Review (ESR)

Leveraging diversity requires changing, modifying or expanding systems that influence behavior in organizations. The ESR examines how the various employment and people systems drive your capacity to leverage diversity (Table 6.7).

TABLE 6.7 Employement Systems Review: Action Map

Purpose	Type of Information	Methods	Topics/Focus
In-depth review of the organization's employment and people systems that drive behavior.	Trend data	<ul><li>Distribution rates by primary dimensions of diversity</li><li>Run adverse impact analysis and other statistical procedures</li></ul>	Systems:<ul><li>Recruitment</li><li>Selection</li><li>Training and development</li><li>Promotion</li><li>Job evaluation</li><li>Compensation</li><li>Conditions of employment</li><li>Performance assessment</li></ul>
	Perceptual and experiential	<ul><li>Focus groups surveys</li></ul>	Equity factors:<ul><li>Adverse impact</li><li>Job relatedness</li><li>Business necessity</li><li>Objectivity/validity</li><li>Consistency</li><li>Legality</li></ul>

Source: Authors' adaptation from Trevor Wilson's, *Diversity at Work: The Business Case for Equity* (1996, pp. 143–159); and Terrence E. Maltbia's, *The Journey of Becoming a Diversity Practitioner* (2001).

Much of the data regarding these systems is collected and analyzed during the historical analysis and cultural audit. An effective way to re-examine this data from an employment systems perspective is to ask that line managers analyze the data from their assigned area across a set of six equity factors listed at the bottom right side of Table 6.7. Trevor Wilson's book, *Diversity at Work* (1996, pp. 143–159), is a good source for guiding questions of each employment system. The line managers (individually and in teams) should make recommendations, related action plans, and improvement metrics to an assigned executive sponsor for approval, refinement, and agreement to pilot the system changes.

The outcome of this upfront work should include a comprehensive review of core employment systems. The important systems to include in your analysis are: recruitment and staffing, training and development, promotions, job evaluation, compensation and benefits, performance management systems; conditions of employment. Additionally, you will want data that are used to analyze your past and current employment practices including layoffs, recall, disciplinary action, and termination.

For all diagnostic tracks, once analyzed each team share findings with a cross-section of employees to further analyze, verify and confirm the key insights from the external scan, historical analysis, cultural audit, and ESR. If you want a thorough interpretation of the results, do not skip feedback sessions. They surface gaps in the data, as well as misinterpretations. As a result there is a shared sense of the meaning of diversity, clarity around the various ways diversity is experienced by different organizational members, a focus on ways to better leverage diversity, and importantly, the identification of core organizational systems in need of alignment to diversity priorities.

Next, stakeholders across the organization engage in the creation of experiments and pilot projects to generate early successes. Full-scale implementation of diversity strategies is generally more successful in large, complex organizations when pilot programs can clearly demonstrate the value of diversity in a real-world context. The knowledge generated during this work serves as a critical input for co-creating a shared vision of diversity to guide emerging diversity strategies.

Making Learning Explicit: The After-Action Review Process

Conducting an After-Action Review (AAR) session is a useful way for team members and their executive sponsor to capture insights gained as a result of conducting various diversity discovery process activities by (1) sharing what each learned from implementing the system changes (2) recommending additional modifications to the system based on their assigned employment system, and (3) partnering with their executive sponsor to gain senior management approval to implement the practice across the organization.

The AAR is a tool adapted from the U.S. Army and can be used to capture the learning from diversity-related pilot projects (Baird et al., 2000). Specifically, AAR facilitates learning while doing. It involves those closest to implementing each diversity pilot project, regardless of level, to gain the various perspectives needed to understand what was learned from the pilot project and to determine what future action makes sense. Conducting each AAR immediately upon completion of your pilot projects, leads to clear insights and improved future actions (five-step AAR process is outlined in Table 6.8).

TABLE 6.8 Tool: After-Action-Review (AAR) Protocol

Step 1 Intentions	Step 2 What happened? Why? (Understanding reality/Outcomes)			Step 3 Lessons Learned	Step 4 Action	Step 5 Dissemination
Objectives (SMART criteria)	What happened? How? Results?	Why did it happen?	What are the implications?	What are the lessons learned from this experience?	What do we do now? (What, Who and When)	Who needs to know? How to communicate?
Situation:						

It is important to have clear performance objectives at the start of each project (Step 1), that is SMART objectives that are specific, measurable/observable, aggressive yet attainable, results-oriented and relevant and time bound (see Figure 5.2). The process begins with a brief, yet explicit review of intentions. Step 1 is followed with a review of outcomes — what happened and why? In Step 2 your focus on "getting the facts." At this point you make your best effort to capture specific action taken. It is important to first gather all of the data, that is, to focus on "what actually happened" before engaging in a conversation about "why things happened." Doing this reduces the tendency to look for someone to blame for things that did not go as planned. Reconstructing the events chronologically is a useful strategy. Asking individuals to recall key events during the implementation is another approach. Both strategies focus on asking people to reflect on "content" (what happened), as well as, the "process" (how it happened).

Once a foundation is in place, the group can begin to examine "why" the events occurred in the way they occurred. What went according to plan (successes)? What did not go as planned (performance gaps)? What are the related implications? This part of the AAR process requires reflective thinking on the part of the people involved in the discovery process. This type of critical thinking can lead to deep and powerful learning because it calls into question the assumptions that informed the way the objective and related actions were originally understood and framed.

The goal of Step 3 is to capture the learning embedded in the experience by exploring the gap, or degree of congruence, between intentions and outcomes. Guiding questions during this step include: based on what we tried to do and what actually happened, what did we learn? What do we understand now that we did not know when we started? Answering these questions naturally leads to the "informed future action" conversation, which is the focus of the next step.

The fourth step in the process answers the questions: Given our experience, what must we keep doing, stop doing, and start doing? Why? In addition, it is helpful to think about future action along the three time horizons of short-term actions (i.e., quick actions related to tweaking the process), mid-term actions (i.e., action that require modifications to systems or policies, such as changing compensation and hiring practices), and long-term actions (i.e., relate to strategies, goals, and values at the core of organizational culture such as redefining strategic intent).

The collective insight and public commitment that results and often motivates people to reengage in action are what makes the AAR process powerful. True lessons are not learned until there is action resulting in an actual change. The dissemination of lessons learned throughout the process contributes to individual, team, and organizational learning.

As you learned in this chapter, the leadership practice, "Ground Diversity Interventions in a Comprehensive Discovery Process," is vital to successfully leveraging diversity. The outcome of each of the strategic learning capabilities depends on your initial discovery process, as well as your ongoing data collection and analysis process. To achieve and sustain contextual awareness you must ground yourself in data. Without solid data you will not fully understand the internal and external factors influencing your workplace, you would not be able to build a rationale for the changes you propose, nor will you have a baseline for measuring the results of initiatives you implement. You need data to determine where you've been (historical perspective), where you are (current reality), and where you want to go (future vision).

The outcome of each of the three strategic learning capabilities depends on your initial and ongoing discovery process. Clearly, *achieving and sustaining contextual awareness* demands a thorough and ongoing data analysis effort. This analysis helps to create *conceptual clarity* — that is, now that we know what we know, what do we need to do? Finally, you can only take *informed action* if you have the data to guide your strategic initiatives, as well as measure their results. Do not find yourself in a legal battle because you fell short in the discovery process. It may not be as exciting as implementing changes that make a difference for the people in your organization, but we are certain it will make a difference in your final outcomes.

References

Agryris, C. *On Organizational Learning*, 2nd ed. Malden, MA: Blackwell, 1999.

Baird, L., Deacon, S., and Holland, P. "From Action Learning to Learning from Action: Implementing the After Action Review." In R. Cross and

S. Israelit (eds.). *Strategic Learning in a Knowledge Economy: Individual, Collective, and Organizational Learning Process*. Boston, MA: Butterworth Heinemann, 2000, pp. 185–202.

Center for Strategic and International Insight. Global Challenges. Retrieved from http://www.csis.org/ (August 1), 2005.

Cetron, M. J., and Davies, O. "Trends Shaping the Future: Technological Workplace, Management, and Institutional Trends." *The Futurist 37(2)* 2003: 30. March/April.

Collins, J. *Good to Great: Why Some Companies Make the Leap ... and Others Don't*. New York, NY: Harper Collins, 2001.

Conner, D. R. *Managing at the Speed of Change: How Resilient Managers Succeed and Prosper Where Others Fail*. New York, NY: Villard Books, 1993.

Corporate Leadership Council. *Fact Brief: Managing and Fostering Diversity — Structure, Roles, and Responsibilities of Diversity Owners*. Washington, DC: The Corporate Executive Board, 2000.

Corporate Leadership Council. *Fact Brief: Executive Involvement in Diversity Initiatives*. Washington, DC: The Corporate Executive Board, 2001.

Corporate Leadership Council. *Fact Brief: Developing, Communicating, and Measuring Diversity Initiatives*. Washington, DC: The Corporate Executive Board, 2003.

Corporate Leadership Council. *Fact Brief: Global Diversity Functions*. Washington, DC: The Corporate Executive Board, 2004.

Corporate Leadership Council. *Fact Brief: Executing and Measuring Diversity Goals*. Washington, DC: The Corporate Executive Board, 2005a.

Corporate Leadership Council. *Fact Brief: Executive-Level Diversity Councils*. Washington, DC: The Corporate Executive Board, 2005b.

Covey, S. *The Seven Habits of Highly Effective People*. New York, NY: Simon & Schuster, 1989.

Hutcheson, J. D., and Kruzan, T. W. *A Guide Culture Audits: Analyzing Organizational Culture for Managing Diversity*. Atlanta, GA: The American Institute For Managing Diversity, 1996.

Kotter, J. P. *Leading Change: An Action Plan from the World's Foremost Expert on Business Leadership*. Boston, MA: Harvard Business School Press, 1996.

Maltbia, T. E. "The Journey of Becoming A Diversity Practitioner: The Connection between Experience, Learning and Competence." Unpublished Dissertation, UMI Dissertation Services, Ann Arbor, MI, 2001.

Schein, E. H. *Organizational Culture and Leadership*, 2nd ed. San Francisco, CA: Jossey-Bass, 1992.

Schein, E. H. *Organizational Culture and Leadership*, 3rd ed. San Francisco, CA: Jossey-Bass, 2004.

Thomas, R. R. *Beyond Race and Gender*. New York: AMACOM, 1991.

Wilson, T., *Diversity at Work: The Business Care for Equity*. New York, NY: Wiley, 1996, pp. 42–46.

7

Teaching the Organization How to Leverage Diversity

Leadership requires a learning strategy. A leader has to engage people in facing the [diversity] challenge, adjusting their values, changing perspectives, and developing new habits of behavior.

— Ronald Heifetz, Co-Director of the Center for Public, Leadership, Harvard University

Beyond your guiding coalition, it is important that you insist on engaging multiple perspectives from across the organization in the work of leveraging diversity. This ensures understanding, buy-in, and creative approaches to productively addressing the challenges, complexity, problems, and opportunities associated with situations involving diversity. Additionally, education and training help leaders, and others in the organization, develop the knowledge, skills, and personal attributes needed to effectively leverage diversity. This chapter focuses on our seventh leadership practice for leveraging diversity:

Leadership Practice 7

*Continue to Gain Buy-In. Model the Way.
Lead as You Learn.*

The following two change drivers, which are described in this chapter, combine to enact the leadership practice of gaining buy-in, while modeling the way and leading as you learn to leverage diversity:

- Facilitate broad involvement and communication; and
- Devise developmentally sequenced diversity education and training interventions in support of the cultural diversity learning and change process.

As a leader you model the way by demonstrating your unwavering commitment to leveraging diversity beyond your words by your ongoing direct involvement and by putting diversity on the strategic agenda. As you continue the journey toward diversity leadership you will discover that being a learning organization is a continuous process that requires you to lead as you learn. In our fast paced, changing, and increasingly diverse business environment, you simply cannot afford to wait until you have figured it all out before leading this critical business process.

Change Driver #3: Broad Involvement and Communication

To gain buy-in and commitment, employees at all levels of the organization should play a role in identifying the organization's current and desired values related to workplace diversity. They should be called upon to provide input related to defining not only the diversity vision, but also the action plans developed to make the vision a reality. Broad involvement combined with ongoing communication keeps employees aware of all aspects of diversity strategies, thus generating buy-in at all levels of the organization.

Early diagnostic work provides a platform for communicating the multiple realities within your organization with regard to diversity. The diagnostic findings provide a basis for creating a shared future vision for diversity and related strategies. So, what do we mean by broad involvement? Specifically, you need to enlist a diverse group of individuals, who represent a diagonal slice across your organization. Doing this sets the stage for achieving a critical mass of people truly committed to the vision of diversity and related strategies. Shared vision creates energy and excitement about the prospects of a desirable future related to diversity (i.e., 5 years or longer), while focused strategies provide direction for the ongoing learning and change effort.

Learning organizations use the dynamic tension between a shared vision of a desirable future, and the organization's current reality in relation to that future, as a source of energy for personal and organizational renewal (Senge, 1990). A diversity vision without a clear and realistic view of how different organizational members experience the culture and climate lacks dynamic tension. Upfront diagnostic work is intended to create a snapshot of the organization's current reality. The idea is to use tension to move toward the diversity vision. This vision then drives buy-in.

Extensive research conducted by Richard Beckhard and Reuben T. Harris (1987), and confirmed by other key management thinkers (e.g., Nadler, 1998), reveals that "the greatest single threat to successful change results from inadequate early attention to defining the desired end states for the change, both the ultimate vision and the interim future state, or midpoint goal" (pp. 46–48). Addressing this gap for diversity initiatives involves building on the work of clarifying the organizational and personal rationale for leveraging diversity discussed in Chapter 2. The change driver of broad involvement and communication has two leadership tasks: (1) creating a shared vision and (2) devising and implementing a communication plan.

Creating A Shared Vision

Your diversity vision should be comprehensive, and sufficiently imaginative to be engaging, inspiring, value adding, desirable to stakeholders, challenging yet attainable, focused, flexible, easy to communicate, and energy releasing (Kotter, 1996; Nutt and Backoff, 1997). In addition, your vision must be explicitly linked to your organizational mission and value statements, as well as, strategic priorities. Effective diversity visions capture one's attention by tapping into the whole person. Be certain your vision expresses a clear rationale for the desired future state (i.e., the "head"), outlines what actions and behaviors must change to realize the vision (i.e., the "hand"), and speaks to each key stakeholder's motivation for engaging in the change process with a personal, emotional appeal (i.e., the "heart"). In time, the diversity vision will become your strategic story projecting a desired future (Walton, 2004).

Creating a shared vision of diversity for which organizational members can commit requires a collaborative and cascading process involving three levels (Nutt and Backoff, 1997). The process begins with a leader (i.e., a diversity champion) whose role is to develop a personal vision of diversity focused on linking organizational priorities to a broad range of possibilities where diversity can be leveraged (or Vision 1). Next, the diversity champion taps into a variety of possibilities by sharing their personal vision with, and integrating the ideas of, a small group of trusted advisors, other diversity champions, and change agents (or Vision 2).

Then the vision is further refined by drawing on the ideas, interests, and perspectives of an even broader group of internal stakeholders (i.e., Employee Resource Groups, Supervisors and Individual Contributors) and external stakeholders (i.e., Customers, Suppliers, Government Officials, and Community Leaders) to make the final diversity vision comprehensive (or Vision 3). The goal of this collaborative visioning process is to gather together a critical mass of people to collectively engage in possibility thinking that effectively paints a picture for some future point.

Given the long-range nature of the diversity learning and change process, you should develop a detailed description of the desired midpoint conditions needed to realize your vision of diversity. This information is added to your strategic story. As we have discussed, creating a focused leadership structure as a guiding coalition is an important early step in creating the conditions necessary to leverage diversity in organizations. A critical mass of leaders who consistently demonstrate behaviors that leverage diversity inside and outside of the organization takes longer and requires ongoing education, training, and systems reinforcement. Key organizational components such as performance management and reward systems, staffing and promotional practices, succession planning, strategy and other systems that drive behavior in the organization must align with diversity strategies and key initiatives.

Devise and Implement A Diversity Communication Plan

Ongoing, strategic communication is essential for any organizational change process and diversity is no exception. You begin by establishing formal communication channels for diversity. Crafting and

TABLE 7.1 Developing an Effective Diversity Communication Plan

Why Communicate?	What to Communicate?	How to Communication?
Rationale ■ Clarify performance and behavioral expectations internally with regard to diversity ■ Establish organization as "employer of choice" to wage the war for talent ■ Strengthen the organization's brand reputation with customers, suppliers and the community *Target audiences* (the "who") ■ Internal champions, change agents, advocates and targets ■ Customers/client ■ Investors/financial community ■ Local community ■ Government agencies ■ Professional/Trade Associations ■ Salesforce/Distribution Networks ■ Other Key Stakeholders	*Key messages* ■ Case for diversity ■ Diversity vision/mission ■ Meaning/definition of diversity ■ Relationship to EEO/AA ■ Diversity-related policies and procedures ■ Employee benefits (e.g., domestic partner, work-life balance such as child care, etc.) ■ Organization's diversity Story (i.e. history, key events) ■ Leadership structure and key contacts ■ Approach to diversity/core strategies ■ Short- and long-term diversity objectives ■ Key milestones, measures and metrics ■ Resources (for individual and organizational development) ■ External recognition (e.g., Fortune Top 50 for diversity) ■ Progress toward objectives	*Communication channels* ■ Executive Memos and Handouts ■ Policy Manuals ■ New Employee/Manager Orientation ■ Newsletters/Speeches ■ Education and Training ■ Annual Report/Recruiting Materials/Diversity Brochure ■ Websites (internet/intranet) ■ Videos by Senior Executives ■ Meetings (e.g., executive reviews, workgroup, town-hall forums, etc.) ■ Brown-bag lunches on focal topics (e.g., multicultural marketing, gender communications, etc.) ■ Informal Networks (linkage with informal opinion leaders) ■ Employee Resource Groups ■ Frequently Asked Questions (FAQs) ■ External Publications ■ Organizational Sponsorship
Impact of Communication		
■ Three possible results: (1) to inform, (2) to persuade, and (3) to motivate ■ Commitment to diversity vision and related strategies ■ Participation in diversity-based programs and initiatives (e.g., training, surveys, focus groups, Employee Resource Groups, multicultural marketing projects, etc.)		

Source: Authors' adaptation of concepts found in Terrence E. Maltbia's, *The Journey of Becoming a Diversity Practitioner* (2001, p. 32); Michael Wheeler's, *The Diversity Executive: Tasks, competencies, and strategies for effective leadership* (2001); Trevor Wilson's, *Diversity at Work: The business case for equity* (1996, pp. 107–134).

implementing an effective diversity communication strategy requires a collaborative partnership with key players across your organization. These include communication professionals, HR professionals, diversity champions, and legal counsel. Table 7.1 summarizes the major components of a diversity communication plan guided by four questions: (1) *What is the rationale for diversity-related communication?* (2) *What message(s) is to be communicated?* (3) *How will we communicate?* and, (4) *What is the desired result of the communication?* (Wilson, 1996; The Corporate Leadership Council, 2003). Much of the content needed to execute this component of Change Driver #3 emerges from the diversity discovery process described in Chapter 6, which is the emphasis of the strategic learning capability of contextual awareness.

An organization's unfolding strategic story provides a common platform to highlight strengths and accomplishments related to its support for diversity internally, in the community and in the marketplace. As we noted in Chapter 5, an essential component of crafting effective strategic stories is combining a compelling storyline of the organization's vision for leveraging diversity with three core messages focused on your target audience's agenda. The results of a comprehensive, evidence-based discovery process well positions leaders to align core diversity messages to various relevant identity groups. Doing so allows the organization to continue to gain buy-in to leverage diversity. In each category the following information should be catalogued for customizing diversity messages for key stakeholder groups:

- Specific initiatives and objectives (i.e., internal, customer/market-based, supplier diversity, and community outreach);
- Spending levels and impact (i.e., internal programs, economic development/supplier diversity, target marketing, and advertising);
- Philanthropic and foundations (i.e., organizations, timeframe, and level of contributions);
- Recognition and awards (i.e., by identity group categories);
- Partnerships (e.g., alliances and joint-ventures); and
- Success stories (i.e., customers, markets, suppliers/economic development, community outreach, and partnerships).

Change Driver #4: Education and Training

Best-in-class organizations use diversity education and training for creating and maintaining a diverse, inclusive, and engaged workforce capable of providing culturally sensitive solutions to customers. Increasingly, organizations are extending their education and training efforts externally to ensure productive relationships with a diverse pool of suppliers and customers.

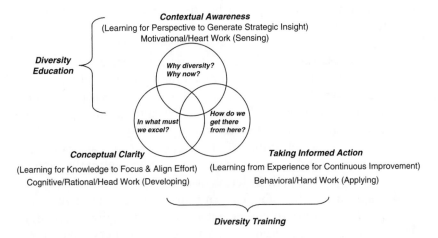

FIGURE 7.1 Learning to Leverage Diversity: Education and Training Cycle

Building on the Leadership Framework presented in Chapter 1, we position the process of learning to leverage diversity as a form of human performance that draws on both education and training (Figure 7.1). Use this learning cycle to guide your design and implementation of education and training interventions. The general structure of the learning cycle contains *motivational* (i.e., the emotional connection, affect), *cognitive* (the thinking connection), and *behavioral* (i.e., the action connection) elements. The capacity to leverage diversity is developed by continuously repeating the cycle, which over time builds a distinctive personal and organizational capacity to perform at increasing levels of effectiveness (Earley and Ang, 2003; Thomas and Inkson, 2003).

The education and training cycle is based on the assumption that learning is an iterative change process. You begin by diagnosing the situation (or the "context"). Next you determine the vital few things that must be done to respond effectively to situations involving diversity (or "content"). This is followed with experiments and action strategies (or "conduct"). Finally, you reflect on the results and outcomes of your actions to expand your thinking and behavioral repertoire in order to productively address situations involving diversity in the future (or "renewal").

The work of John Dewey (1938) on learning, and by Kurt Lewin (1946) on the social change process, guide our thinking on the diversity learning and change process applied to Change Driver #4. The cycle frames learning as a holistic process consisting of four essential components:

- Awareness (i.e., a reflection of how aware we are of our own attitudes and beliefs regarding culturally diverse others);
- Knowledge (i.e., a reflection of how much we actually know about the dynamics of diversity and cultural interactions, the needs and wants of diverse others);
- Skill (i.e., a reflection of how adept we are at translating awareness and knowledge into productive, culturally competent responses both in terms of thinking and behaving); and
- Application (i.e., the capacity to continuously invent and produce culturally competent responses in daily interactions with diverse colleagues, customers, suppliers, and other organizational stakeholders).

Dewey (1938) noted that the attribution and related meaning of knowledge cannot simply be a personal, unique, and private enterprise; learning to leverage diversity is a function of the interaction between each individual and their personal engagement with diverse others. Kurt Lewin (1946), credited as one of the fathers of organizational development, also expressed this connection between individual and systems level learning in his, now famous, theoretical formulation, $B = f(P, E)$, which indicates that behavior is a function of individual attributes and environmental factors. The implications of these seminal insights to learning to leverage diversity are clear.

Learning to leverage diversity occurs at multiple levels inside and outside of the organization — individual, group, and system level (i.e., organizational and societal). Each of these levels of learning emphasizes the important connection between learning and the environment (or context). Educational interventions enhance the strategic learning capabilities of *contextual awareness* (or the "why" of diversity) and *conceptual clarity* (or the "what" of diversity). Training interventions contribute to the strategic learning capabilities of *conceptual clarity* (or the "what" to inform the "how"), and *taking informed action* (or the "how") to leverage diversity during daily interactions with peers, employees, clients, suppliers, and other key organizational stakeholders.

While organizations can put infrastructures in place to deliver educational and training programs to respond to diversity, much of the learning related to cultural diversity occurs as a result of experience and action rather than learning from formal workshops or e-learning modules. Opportunities to learn to leverage diversity take place around the clock, during work and in all aspects of our lives. Learning apart from work through workshops and other formal approaches provides a foundation for deeper development. Informal forms of learning such as personal reading and interaction with peers and coaches can also support building a foundation for developing a deep capability to leverage diversity. Yet, the most powerful learning will be embedded in the work of interacting with diverse team members, subordinates, bosses, board members, customers, suppliers, and community stakeholders.

Education and training interventions are generally segmented by target population to maximize effectiveness. That is, while the core content is similar, education and training interventions are customized to meet the specific needs of different organizational audiences including top executives; managers and supervisors; individual contributors; full-time, part-time, temporary, and contingent employees; external clients and vendors. Blended delivery systems for learning that include some combination of face-to-face sessions and technology allow for both interaction and self-paced instruction.

Diversity education has two primary aims: (1) to motivate through increased awareness and (2) to provide the content needed to focus and align individual, group, and organizational efforts toward the achievement of diversity objectives. Diversity educational interventions targeted to motivate are further delineated into external factors; awareness of organizational specific diversity strategies, policies, and requirements; and personal awareness of one's own motives and responses to various forms of diversity.

Lewin (1946) described the change process as *unfreezing* (from the current state), *movement* (toward a desired, future state) and *refreezing* (institutionalizing the change). It follows that a critical first step in any change process is to answer the questions: *Why change? Why Now?* Sample diversity educational components designed to expand the contextual awareness needed to clarify the motivation for diversity change process by external, organizational, and personal factors are listed in Table 7.2.

It is the interplay between systematic re-examination of external and organizational factors, combined with systematic assessment of

TABLE 7.2 Diversity Awareness Education (Sensing)

Component	Description
External factors	■ The history of the diversity movement (see "Four Waves of Change" — Table 2.1) ■ World population projections (explore current and future workforce implications) ■ Labor force demographics (focused on inborn and experienced-based characteristics) ■ Market demographics (by inborn, experience and personal style characteristics) ■ National, state and local legal requirements (employment law and other government regulations) ■ Other mega trends (e.g., globalization, technological advances, shift from industrial to knowledge economy and related power shifts, margin squeeze and industry consolidation) ■ Diversity best-practice-organizations/research (e.g., Fortune's Best 50 Companies for Minorities and Women; Gay Financial Network's 50 Most Gay-Friendly Companies in American; Working Mother Magazine's 100 Best Companies for Working Mothers; U.S. Department of Labors Opportunity Award; DiversityInc.'s Top 50 Companies for Diversity, and the Catalyst Award)
Organization factors	■ Organization specific rationale for diversity and vision (including historical commitment to inclusion and diversity-related milestones) ■ Components of organization's diversity strategy (i.e., leadership structure and behaviors, objectives, initiatives, action plans, communication program, individual's role and expectations, accountability, and reporting system) ■ Success stories (internal successes related to teamwork, innovation and productivity; business examples and community-based examples) ■ Current status (i.e., financial commitment and other resources, cultural audit findings, inclusion/climate survey results, engagement index, customer satisfaction, various discrimination claims and results, external recognition and awards) ■ Resources to support movement toward leveraging diversity (e.g., education, training, internal expertise/contacts, and external contacts) ■ Organization specific workforce demographic (by inborn, experience-based, organizational level and function) ■ Employment procedures for supervisors (i.e., staffing, performance management, development, promotions, compensation) ■ Organization specific anti-discrimination policies (e.g., EEO/AA Plans, sexual harassment, etc.) ■ Complaint resolution procedures (e.g., internal and external mediation)
Personal factors	■ Personal responses to inborn, experience-based, style and organizational diversity factors ■ Origins of one's cultural programming (influence of diversity related factors i.e., assumptions about equality and fairness; stereotypes, prejudice and the "isms;" discrimination, power and oppression; dealing with conflict across differences, etc.) ■ Assessment results (e.g., Intercultural Sensitivity Inventory, Emotional Competence Inventory-360 from diverse observers and Racial Identity Assessment)

one's self as a diverse and cultural being that triggers the motivation for diversity-related change. In the context of diversity, we understand that for many successful people in the organization the status quo has worked for them. To commit to the diversity learning and change process in the midst of competing priorities, people need a clear personal and organizational reason to change due to dissatisfaction or discomfort with the current state of affairs regarding diversity.

The other side of the motivational coin is to paint a clear and shared vision of a positive future with regard to diversity, one that is better than the current state. It is this dynamic tension created by the gap between the current realty and a desired future that stimulates a strong motivation to engage in the diversity learning and change process. The basic aim of diversity awareness educational strategies is to provide: (1) information from diverse perspectives inside and outside of the organization, (2) opportunity for self assessment work, and (3) space for focused developmental planning.

Once a broad awareness of external, organizational, and personal factors has been established to trigger individual and collective motivation for change, the next educational task is to the address the question: *Where must we excel to effectively leverage diversity across the organization to spark performance breakthroughs?* Here educational strategies place an emphasis on learning for knowledge, and then combining this knowledge with skill-based training to take informed action when applying the learning to real-world situations. As such, the strategic learning capability of creating conceptual clarity serves as a transition from thinking and talking about diversity, to taking informed action in service of leveraging diversity while doing the work of the organization.

During this phase of the learning cycle diversity champions, advocates, and change agents refine strategic choices related to diversity, align the organization by ensuring people focus on a "vital few" priorities, and either have skills or develop skills to enact their plans. This phase of the education and training cycle places an emphasis on the "know what" and the "know how" to create movement from the organization's current state, toward a desired future state. An example of diversity educational and training components designed to create the conceptual clarity needed to transform words to deeds for one organization are listed in Table 7.3.

To complete the first pass through the diversity learning cycle we must apply what we have learned in a real-world context; that is,

TABLE 7.3 Knowledge-Based Education and Supporting Skills (Developing)

Priority (know "what" or "words" related to "talking-the-talk")	Supporting Skills (know "how" or "deeds" that demonstrate one is "walking-the-talk")
Accountability for results	■ Translate organizational diversity objectives into SMART objectives for self and area of responsibility ■ Link diversity objectives to other operational objectives in area of responsibility ■ Ensure role clarity and reduce role conflict by delegating specific diversity objectives to each direct report or work groups (including clear performance targets) ■ Establish work group procedures to communicate expectations, monitor and report progress (e.g., planning, problem solving and decision making, meeting management and dealing with conflict; performance coaching and counseling) ■ Provide explicit rewards for goal attainment and exercise direct sanctions for lack of performance
Supporting programs	■ Diagnose support (e.g., training, resources, etc.) needed to implement diversity strategy ■ Secure necessary support and evaluate effectiveness
Executive parity/balanced workforce	■ Gather, analyze, and maintain external and internal ability use to inform executive parity (representation at the top levels) and balanced workforce objectives ■ Apply strategies for attracting, developing, and retaining a diverse workgroup
Inclusive culture and climate	■ Ability to effectively connect with, engage and deploy a culturally diverse workforce ■ Move beyond compliance to build collaborative and trusting relationships with all employees
Productivity, growth and organizational effectiveness	■ Understand under what conditions diverse groups outperform or under perform homogeneous workgroup and applies insight in forming teams and assignments ■ Make best use of the unique talents of diverse employees to drive performance

taking informed action to leverage diversity. The learning strategies and tactics used during this phase of the cycle are less formal and rely heavily on learning while doing the work. Examples include applying diversity-general strategies on the job and reflecting on the level of congruence between intentions and outcomes; engaging in broadening assignments where one has the opportunity to apply current functional knowledge in a different work context; experimenting with new diversity behaviors and skills during meetings, while working to solve problems and making decisions with diverse others; and seeking out situations where one's success is dependent on effectively interacting with diverse others such as professional or industry associates.

We suggest that organizations encourage people to begin with education and training interventions that are sequenced with an emphasis on, the so-called diversity-general work to provide a solid foundation for the developmentally advanced diversity-specific work. As we pointed out in Table 2.2, advanced diversity topics for education and training include market diversity, gender communication, generational diversity, and dealing with the various "isms" (e.g., racism, sexism, ageism). While the content varies, the learning cycle of combing education and training focused on *sensing* (i.e., awareness), *developing* (i.e., thinking and action planning), and *performing* (i.e., taking informed action) is the same. The story that follows is an example of the diversity learning and change process in action.

PUTTING DIVERSITY TO WORK ACROSS THE GLOBAL
(STORY SHARED BY AN INTERNAL DIVERSITY LEADER)

Situation

In the U.S., we are used to dealing with the Wal-Marts and shipping by rail, car, truck, or other acceptable modes of transportation. You go to a place like South Africa and Kenya and grocery stores and the distribution system is very different. So the concept of rail car shipments does not translate very well in many places on the continent of Africa, particularly in the interior where transportation as we understand it is just not there. From a historical perspective, all the roadways in Africa were structured to take the wealth out of the ground, take it to the ships, and send them to the imperial powers. So you have a situation whereby the normal distribution modes that were used to in the Western world are not there.

Talking to the senior executive in South Africa, our aim was to frame this differently. We were really dealing with opportunities. We had a business opportunity, simply a different way of doing things. Now, the business landscape in South Africa at that time was two or three big wholesalers [that] controlled access to the trade. So we talked about ways to reach our objective, which was to take advantage of market opportunities in the new, emerging South Africa.

Strategy

Our main strategy was to develop a minority supply development and distribution process. We've been involved in not only minority supply development, but also setting up a funding arm for this process. So we helped some truckers and Black townships get into business. In time, as a result of this strategy, we were able to work around the big wholesalers that customarily would have dominated our access to this emerging market. We built long-term, trusting relationships with local small businesses, which allowed us to help to actually transform the way business was done in that part of the world. If we would have remained within the boundaries of our comfortable way of doing things this business and cultural transformation would not have been possible. Coming to understand a different business and cultural context, working with people in the townships to explore what was possible that provided benefits for them and our company, and then learning as we went about the business of executing our plan, is what made this a market diversity success story. There was not a road map; we drew it during our journey.

Outcomes

After a while, funny things started to happen. When people were delivering our products in Black townships and there were Black drivers, the quality of our service went up. Shrinkage went down and a variety of other business options opened up for both our company and our partners. That was the opportunity based on understanding people and devising a strategy that combined the needs of the business and the needs of the people. Our senior executive in South Africa was promoted and the region continues to grow.
— Corporate VP, Global Diversity and HR Center of Expertise
Fortune 100 Consumer Products Company

Clearly, learning to leverage diversity requires energy, direct engagement, and a long-term commitment. The return on diversity education and training investments is enhanced when the learning system is characterized by *repetition* (i.e., repeated messages and opportunity for practice), *duration* (i.e., there is adequate time during each learning unit for comprehension), *intensity* (i.e., that each learning unit provides sufficient challenge and support), and *frequency* (i.e., conditions for applying learning in real-world context and completing reinforcement education and training as needed).

Continue to Gain Buy-In. Model the Way. Lead as You Learn

Express the "what" and "why" of leveraging diversity with simplicity, clarity, and sincerity. Provide general direction while empowering individuals with the discretion to act (or the "how" of diversity) through personal and intentional accountability. Commit to relying on the collective insights of all in the organization to co-create an equitable, high-performance work culture. During implementation, leaders often must combine both rewards of performance and consequences for lack of progress toward diversity aims.

Reinforce your leadership pledge to leverage diversity often and continue to call for absolute commitment of making diversity a way of operating. Model the way by taking action and making business decisions daily that are consistent with the organization's vision of diversity. Remember, the collective behavior of the organization's senior leaders communicates what is truly valued with respect to diversity.

Action speaks louder than words, and leaders acting — walking the talk — is the way to leverage diversity across the organization. Be present at the front lines to identify opportunities to "coach in the moment" by restating commitments, sharing observations, emphasizing what is possible, highlighting what is getting in the way, making suggestions, testing reactions, and calling people to action. Gain new insights from each strategy as it is implemented and take the new learning to modify the strategy where needed. Continue to refine the organization's diversity story, monitor progress, communicate successes, and highlight what is yet to be done.

References

Beckhard, R., and Harris, R. T. *Organizational Transitions: Managing complex change*, 2nd Reading, MA: Addison-Wesley Publishing Company, 1987.

Corporate Leadership Council. *Fact Brief: Developing, Communicating, and Measuring Diversity Initiatives*. Washington, DC: The Corporate Executive Board, 2003.

Dewey, J. *Experience and Education*. New York, NY: Collier Books, 1938.

Earley, P. C., and Ang, S. *Cultural Intelligence: Individual Interactions Across Cultures*. Stanford, CA: Stanford Business Books, 2003.

Kotter, J. P. *Leading Change: An Action Plan From the World's Foremost Expert on Business Leadership*. Boston, MA: Harvard Business School Press, 1996.

Lewin, K. "Action Research and Minority Problems'." *Journal of Social Issues* 2(4) (1946): 34–46.

Maltbia, T. E. (2001). "The Journey of Becoming A Diversity Practitioner: The connection between experience, learning and competence." Unpublished Dissertation, UMI Dissertation Services, Ann Arbor, MI.

Nadler, D. A. *Champions of Change: How CEOs and Their Companies are Mastering the Skills of Radical Change*. San Francisco, CA: Joseey-Bass Publishers, 1998.

Nutt, P. C., and Backoff, R. W. "Facilitating Transformational Change." *The Journal of Applied Behavioral Science* 33(4) (1997): 490–508.

Senge, P. *The Fifth Discipline: The Art and Practice of the Learning Organization*. New York: Doubleday, 1990.

Thomas, D. C., and Inkson, K. *Cultural Intelligence: People Skills for Global Leadership*. San Francisco, CA: Berrett-Koehler Publishers, 2003.

Walton, M. S. *Generating Buy-In: Mastering the Language of Leadership*. New York, NY: American Management Association (AMACOM), 2004.

Wheeler, M. (2001). *The Diversity Executive: Tasks, Competences, and Strategies for Effective Leadership* (Research Report No. 1300). New York: The Conference Board.

Wilson, T. *Diversity at Work: The Business Case for Equity*. New York, NY: Wiley, 1996.

8

Diversity Measurement and Evaluation

The future doesn't just happen — people create it through their action, or actions, today.

— *The World Futurist Society*

Measurement and evaluation are crucial to assuring that the future you envision becomes a reality. And, systems alignment insures that people systems, structures and processes, organizational culture, measurement, and rewards are in line with your business and diversity priorities, values, and vision. What we know is that leveraging diversity is not a spectator sport — especially at the implementation stage when everyone in every system must get involved and take action. As a leader, it is up to you to set the example. If you allow any part of your organization to opt out of the change process, you might as well abort your launch here because you will not reach your desired state.

A crucial factor in moving from planning to the implementation of diversity strategies is systems alignment across the organization. Systems alignment begins with data. As we discussed in Chapter 6, comprehensive, evidence-based diagnostic work, the key to the strategic learning capability, *contextual awareness*, is an essential part of building future diversity initiatives. You should make the effort and take the time to build your diversity strategy on a solid foundation — one that is data based and reflects your current reality. This data drives your initiatives and provides the baseline for determining if you are heading in the right direction.

Leadership Practice 8

*Lead From the Future to Leverage
Diversity Today.*

To lead from the future you need to create a compelling goal that draws people out of their comfort zone. And then, begin to act as if you are already there. Everyone in the organization needs to be clear that "business-as-usual" will not realize the aims of a compelling diversity vision. Be certain to actively scout out, recognize, and reward those in the organization who have the courage to join you in the future today. In this chapter, we focus on our eighth leadership practice.

In this chapter, we guide you into the future with two change drivers:

- Use measurement and evaluation (i.e., Change Driver #5) and
- Systems alignment (i.e., Change Driver #6).

Together, these two change drivers allow leaders and others in the organization to be laser beam focused and future oriented by using metrics to monitor progress and alignment to ensure collaboration and coordination across systems.

Measurement and Evaluation

If the language of business is ultimately money, then its alphabet is numbers. A number of participants in our study confirm the essential role of measurement as a critical success factor for leveraging diversity in organizations. For example, one of our diversity champions expressed a simple, yet common belief, "what gets measured gets paid attention to, and what gets paid attention to gets done." Plain and simply, measurement is the way all other critical aspects of business effectiveness are determined. As one of our internal diversity leaders noted "no metrics, no movement." Diversity must not be treated differently or held to a lower standard. Measurement is critical to assessing the effectiveness and related outcomes associated with diversity work, and understanding the impact of learning and change.

Generating a Fact-Based Rationale

To effectively leverage diversity your efforts must begin with an extensive data collection effort — one that you cannot short-change. There are two predictable outcomes that might occur as a result of taking shortcuts in this up-front and ongoing data collection and analysis work. One scenario is that you engage in activity, expend time energy and other value resources, and at the end of the day, generate very few measurable results. The second scenario is far worse. In this case, you find your organization is the victim of a well-publicized lawsuit as a result of employment discrimination, even though you established diversity programs and processes.

To be certain that your diversity program is not simply window dressing you need reliable data. You do not want to find yourself in a situation where your good intentions and hard work are not addressing the issues most important to leveraging diversity directly. In such cases the result likely will be that your diversity programs unintentionaly raise awareness of the inequities within your organization among your minority employees. Measurement helps you target your initiatives and provides the data to show the results of your efforts.

In the United States, fair employment practices including hiring practices, promotions, treatment, and an overall work environment free from discrimination is the law. A comprehensive diversity discovery process should trigger early warning signs of potential legal exposure, which allows organizational leaders to be proactive in taking informed and corrective action. In addition to meeting compliance requirements, the results of the diversity discovery process generally have a number of desired outcomes consistent with any strategic organizational diagnostic process including:

- Clearly identified diversity-related issue tensions and opportunities to leverage diversity;
- Catalogued set of research-based best practice alternatives for addressing issue tensions and leveraging diversity;
- Organization-specific rationale for leveraging diversity grounded in facts, trends, and strategic requirements; and
- Starting set of strategic priorities related to diversity with preliminary success indicators and measures.

TABLE 8.1 Rationale for Leveraging Cultural Diversity

• Legal compliance • Avoidance of lawsuits • Changing labor force demographics • Internal workforce demographics • Reduce cost associated with turnover, training, absenteeism, and lost productivity	• Recruitment and retention of talent • Enhanced teamwork • Workforce utilization • Creativity and innovation • Improved productivity, efficiency, quality and profitability	• Competitive advantage • Globalization • Diverse markets/ customers • Customer and competitor diversity initiatives • Community relations

Source: Authors' adaptation of concepts in J. P. Fernandez's, *The diversity advantage* (1993); T. Wilson's, *Diversity at work* (1996, pp. 29–38); and E. E. Hubbard's, *The Diversity Scorecard* (2004, pp. 7–24).

As we have stated before, the outcome of the strategic learning capability of contextual awareness is that the diversity discovery process reveals organizational specific factors that when combined, clearly and succinctly establish the overall rationale for investing time and other resources to engage in a cultural change process needed to leverage diversity. The culmination of trends converging from the historical profile, internal cultural audit, external scan, and the start of the employment systems review process will generate a fact-based rationale, or business case for diversity. Table 8.1 augments Table 2.4 by listing some of the major reasons organizations state for launching an initiative with the aim of leveraging cultural diversity.

Many diversity practitioners go to great lengths to separate diversity from Affirmative Action (AA) and Equal Employment Opportunity (EEO) regulations. While we agree that diversity and AA/EEO are not the same, given the legal reality in the United States we see them as part of a comprehensive talent management process. At a very basic level, strengthened people practices triggered by a focus on effective AA/EEO has generally resulted in policy and improvements in management practices that have a positive impact on the effective utilization of the entire workforce.

Work Climate Matters

Warner Burke, Professor of Psychology and Education at Teachers College, Columbia University and noted organizational development expert, makes important distinctions between culture and climate in organizations (see Table 4.5 for definitions from others). He defines culture as "the way we do things around here and the manner in which norms and values are communicated" (Burke, 2002, p. 205). Accordingly, this view of culture positions organizational culture change and related transformations as the work of leadership in congruence with the organization's mission and strategy.

Organizational climate, however, represents the "collective perceptions of members within the same work unit" (Burke, 2002, p. 207). This distinction is important because it highlights the influence individual managers have in shaping a work climate that reinforces the value of diversity, thus attracts and retains talent. Senior executives are accountable for ensuring the organization's vision, mission, strategy and systems include a focus on leveraging diversity. It is the day-to-day transactional work of front-line managers to ensure that their actions and practices reinforce and reflect a true valuing and effective utilization of diverse talent.

Cost

The cost associated with not attending to diversity and maintaining a productive work climate goes beyond the threat of employment legal settlements. The fact is "climate" affects individual and organizational performance. If any segment of your workforce is not fully engaged in the business of generating results because on feeling, or actually being excluded, the productivity of the organization suffers, which has a bottom line impact. In addition, a climate that is not diversity friendly has a negative impact on factors such as morale, work quality, customer service, absenteeism, retention, and co-worker relationships. The work climate has a direct impact as to whether employees turn on, turn off, or turnover. Employees who turn off, that is, they remain with the organization yet do the minimum to get by, represent a major hidden cost to organizations in terms of productivity and lost opportunity.

Given high recruitment and retention costs, unwanted turnover negatively impacts the organization's bottom line. A widely accepted calculation of replacement costs is at least 1.5 times a given employee's annual salary, with the replacement costs for women and people of color exceeding this ratio given the typically longer time-to-fill rate. Some examples of retention costs include $116,340 for a chief engineer earning an annual salary of $77,560, $110,000 for a government services underwriter, and $52,065 for a store manager earning $34,710 a year (Hubbard, 2004, p. 13). Increasingly, dissatisfied employees use the so-called Law of Two Feet, that is they go to organizations that truly value employees as a source of human capital.

Data from the Center for Women's Business Research (http://www.womensbusinessresearch.org) shows that talented employees in general and women in particular, leave organizations when their skills and abilities are not utilized, as well as, when they do not perceive equity reward and recognition for their contribution. Such employees seek more compatible situations by either starting their own companies, as evidenced by the nearly 10.4 million women- and equally-owned firms who employ 12.8 million people and generate 1.9 trillion in sales.

The War for Talent

Work climate not only impacts an organization's ability to retain talent, but also impacts its reputation for being a "great place to work," which influences its ability to attract talent. A year-long study conducted by the management consulting firm of McKinsey & Co. noted that the most important organizational asset then and in the future would be talent. They defined talent as "smart, sophisticated businesspeople that are technologically literate, globally astute and operationally agile" (Smart Company, August 1998). In short, they believed that people would truly become an organization's most valuable resource and major source of competitive advantage in the 21st century.

In 2007, McKinsey & Co. consultants, Lowell Bryan and Claudia Joyce in their book *Mobilizing Minds*, proposed that 20th-century companies must be redesigned for the 21st-century and the emphasis of this redesign is on the workforce. They suggested that "By remaking them to mobilize the mind power of their 21st-century workforces, these companies will be able to tap into the presently underutilized talents, knowledge, relationships, and skills of their employees, which will open up to them not only new opportunities but also vast sources of new wealth" (p. 1). One idea they proposed is the development of talent markets that "mobilized mind power by getting the right talent to the right job" (p. 65).

If you agree that "getting the right talent to the right job" is a strategic priority, you will want to make finding, hiring, and retaining talent one of your "vital few" critical success factors — factors related directly to, "what must go well" to win the competitive race and realize your intentions related to leveraging diversity for business success. Identifying critical success factors is a primary focus of strategic learning capability conceptual clarity.

Becoming a Great Place to Work

There are a number of resources available to help organizations understand the key factors associated with creating and sustaining a productive work climate that leverages diversity. We have found two in our work with organizations to be of value. Founded in 1991 The Great Place to Work Institute, a global research and organizational consulting firm with offices in 29 countries, in collaboration with FORTUNE Magazine annually produces The 100 Best Companies to Work For list. This list has always attracted significant attention from organizations seeking to be recognized for their accomplishments, and from people looking for great places to work.

To choose the 100 Best Companies to Work For, FORTUNE and the Great Place to Work Institute conduct the most extensive employee survey in corporate America. According to the Internet home of FORTUNE http://money.cnn.com, for the 2007 list more than 105,000 employees from 446 companies responded to a 57-question survey. Two-thirds of a company's score was based on the survey, which was sent to a minimum of 400 randomly selected employees from each company and asked about things such as attitudes toward management, job satisfaction, and camaraderie. The remaining third of the score came from an evaluation of each company's responses to the institute's Culture Audit, which included detailed questions about demographic makeup, pay, and benefits programs, and open-ended questions about the company's people-management philosophy, internal communications, opportunities, compensation practices, and diversity programs.

After evaluations were completed, if news about a company came to light that significantly damaged employees' faith in management, it could be excluded from the list. After 20 years of research The Great Place to Work Institute has found that a great workplace is measured by the quality of the three, interconnected relationships that exist there:

- The relationship between employees and management,
- The relationship between employees and their jobs/company, and
- The relationship between employee and other employees.

Data shows that being a great workplace pays off. Using various profitability indicators, a financial analysis conducted by the Russell Investment Group, using various profitability indicators illustrates that the publicly traded 100 Best Companies to Work For on FORTUNE's list have consistently outperformed major stock indices over various time periods. For example, over a 5 year time period the 100 Best Companies had an average annual return to shareholders of nearly 30 percent compared to an annual average of roughly 19 percent for all Russell 3000 companies (The Great Place to Work Institute, 2005).

Work Climate Assessments

The Great Place to Work Institute has three tools organizations can use to conduct various climate assessments within their specific workplace. The Trust Index measures employee's perceptions of the quality of their workplace relationships; The Trust Audit, a technique that can be included as part of a cultural audit using focus groups for an in-depth analysis of trust within an organization; and The Action Planning System that guides managers through the process of reviewing their Trust Index Employee Survey results, choosing focus areas, and taking action.

The Gallup Organization provides another useful tool for assessing work climate factors that contribute to organizational effectiveness, The Gallup Q12 (www.gallupconsulting.com). Gallup's research has identified 12 questions that measure employee engagement and links to important organizational outcomes such as retention, productivity, profitability, customer engagement, and safety. Table 8.2 lists the 12 factors measured in the Gallup's Q12 employee engagement tool.

Similar to The Great Place to Work Institute's survey, this tool looks at factors such as clear expectations, resources, recognition, involvement, support, performance feedback, and relationships at

TABLE 8.2 Employee Engagement Factors

1. Compelling mission and purpose	5. Utilization of talent	9. Personal development
2. Clear expectations	6. Value input/opinions	10. Co-worker relationships
3. Appropriate resources	7. Performance feedback	11. Caring/trusting supervisor
4. Quality work product	8. Recognition	12. Opportunities for learning and growth

Source: Authors' adaptation of concepts in M. Buckingham and C. Coffman's, *First, Break All The Rules: What the World's Greatest Managers Do Differently* (1999, pp. 25–41).

work. Using this tool provides organizations with both internal benchmarks as well as the ability to compare organizational results to Gallup's database, which includes over 4.5 million employees, nearly 423,000 workgroups, 332 organizations in 12 major industries, in 7 regions around the world made up of 112 countries. One advantage of the Gallup tool is how it links to performance metrics critical to a given organization such as productivity, retention, customer service, and so on. Gallup has a suite of related assessment tools that can be combined to generate comprehensive insights in terms of customer engagement and employee inclusion.

Regardless of the specific set of tools and protocols used to assess work climate, research reveals that organizations that strive to enhance the work environment yield results. A variety of studies tracking the nation's best employers realized a number of benefits such as:

- More qualified job applications for open positions (i.e., the first step in waging the war for talent);
- Lower turnover rates (i.e., the second step of waging the war for talent);
- Reductions in health care costs and absenteeism (i.e., indicators of organizational health);
- Higher levels of customer satisfaction and customer loyalty;
- Greater levels of creativity, risk taking, and innovation (i.e., predictors of competitive advantage); and
- Higher productivity levels and profitability (i.e., indicators of market leadership).

Changing Demographics

In addition to culture there are other important factors for you to consider when you are determining your strategic choices including the myriad of changing demographic trends (see Cetron and Davies, 2003). For example, you will discover in reviewing a number of demographic and educational attainment trends that in the next 10–15 years there will be 15 percent fewer Americans in the 35–45 year-old range (prime development and productivity stage) than there are today. Further, based on current estimates, the U.S. economy is expected to grow at the rate of 3–4 percent annually. The projected impact is that the demand for talent between the ages of 35 and 45 will increase by approximately 25 percent, while the supply could decline by as much as 15 percent. These data combined with the fact that according to Hudson Institute's Workforce 2020 study minorities will account for roughly a third of total new entrants during the early part of the 21st century suggest that the talent pool today and in the future continues to diversify. Minorities are expected to represent over 30 percent of the workplace by the year 2020 (i.e., 14 percent Hispanic, 11 percent Black, and 6 percent Asian).

There is also a gender shift in the workplace both in terms of labor participation and the proportion of women of total new entrants. Women now account for nearly 46.3 percent of the total labor force and 50.6 percent of managerial and professional specialty positions (Catalyst, 2006). Women are expected to account for half of the total workforce by the year 2020. Catalyst, a non-profit organization based in New York City is an excellent source for data related to women in the workplace. The committee of 200, a professional organization for women entrepreneurs and corporate leaders, is another great source for data on women in the workplace.

Based on educational attainment trends, women continue to make significant strives in preparing themselves for careers in the New Economy. Women currently hold 55 percent of the bachelor's degrees, 53 percent of all master's degrees, and nearly 40 percent of doctorates. Similar shifts are occurring in educational attainment for various minority groups. These data provide growing evidence that organizations need to attract and leverage a diversity of talent as a source of competitive advantage.

Keeping in mind the strategic learning capabilities of contextual awareness and conceptual clarity, it is important for organizations to monitor the demographic trends in disciplines critical to implementing their strategy. These will help them take informed action (the third strategic learning capability) to ensure recruitment and retention practices reflect the reality of the emerging talent pool. The projections summarized in this section suggest that women and minorities will represent a significant proportion of the available talent pool and organizational work climates must reflect these new realities.

Customer Satisfaction

Just as attracting and retaining talent is a key to organizational success, so is attracting and retaining customers. Heskett, Jones, Loveman, Sasser, and Schlesinger's article entitled "Putting the Service-Profit Chain to Work" in the February 2005 *Harvard Business Review On Point Enhanced Edition* is a great source for understanding the relationship between employee satisfaction and commitment, superior customer value and satisfaction, and customer loyalty and organizational effectiveness. Further, drawing on expectancy theory, diversity consultant Trevor Wilson (1996) makes connections between the employee and customer satisfaction chain and equity employment systems (Figure 8.1).

The employee equity–customer chain purports a positive relationship between leadership practices focused on equitable employment practices, outcomes related to employee satisfaction and engagement, employee loyalty and commitment, productivity and customer value. These factors in turn contribute to customer loyalty and commitment, which in turn contribute to overall organizational effectiveness. In today's service-oriented and global economy, high-performing leaders focus on the factors that drive service quality, mainly ensuring an ongoing investment in people; providing technology support to front-line employees; focusing on attracting and retaining diverse talent; and rewarding talent by making a link between compensation and performance.

The first connection in Figure 8.1 between an equitable employment system and employee satisfaction was established in our earlier discussion on organizational work climate. Leaders are accountable for creating a culture that designs and executes equitable employee systems for all employees, at all levels of the organization. The main aim of equitable employment systems is to attain talent and retain employees who contribute while, weeding out non-producers. General Electric is an example of a company that employs this practice consistently identifying what they call their "C Player," the bottom fourth of the organization and taking corrective action,

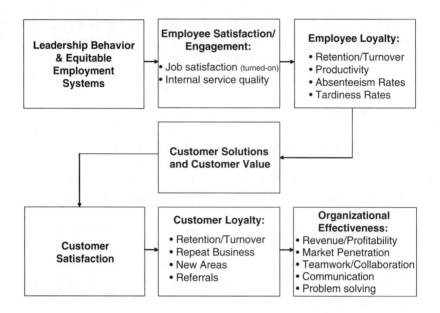

FIGURE 8.1 Organizational Rationale for Equity (The Employee Equity–Customer Chain).

including termination where necessary. Keeping non-producers on the payroll drains time and financial resources.

Satisfied, engaged employees are intrinsically rewarded when they have the autonomy and capacity to act in service of achieving results for internal clients and external customers. Internal service quality is measured by the "feelings employees have toward their jobs, their colleagues and their companies" (Heskett et al., 1994, p. 168); it is the way in which people serve each other inside the organization.

The next critical link in the model is the focus on retaining highly productive employees who generate customer value, either directly or indirectly. This leads to customer satisfaction, loyalty, retention, repeat and expanded sales, and potential customer referrals. Satisfied, engaged, and loyal employees are more productive than their moderate to dissatisfied counterparts. Satisfied, highly engaged employees focus on understanding the expectations of their internal clients and external customer base. They then strive to exceed expectations by co-creating solutions to their problems and generating ideas to help leverage opportunities.

Loyal employees are long-term employees. Because of their longevity, they build a critical knowledge base about customer needs. They then use this knowledge to solve problems on behalf of customers, and to generate innovative solutions. Employee satisfaction drives employee loyalty and ultimately customer loyalty. Studies show dissatisfied employees represent a potential turnover rate three times higher than that for satisfied employees. Low employee turnover is closely linked to high customer satisfaction.

Over time customer satisfaction leads to customer loyalty as measured by repeat business from the existing customer base, opportunities to expand and explore new ventures, and service offerings with the existing base of business and new customer referrals. Savvy organizational leaders know that it takes more time, money, and effort to attract new customers than retain or grow the business with existing customers. The bottom line benefit of understanding the employee equity–customer chain is the realization that keeping loyal customers as a foundation for business growth, while seeking to add targeted new customers, drives profitability. Edward E. Hubbard's (2004) book, *The Diversity Scorecard*, is an excellence resource for developing a measurement system to track linkages between employee satisfaction/engagement, customer satisfaction, and organizational effectiveness.

Market Demographics

We cannot leave the discussion of customer satisfaction without examining the impact of changing market demographics on the employee equity–customer chain. America has become a multicultural marketplace and similar trends exist in many places around the globe. The landscape of our emerging multicultural marketplace can be categorized along the lines of various primary and secondary dimensions of diversity such as gender, race, sexual orientation, religion, and age. The following overview characterizes the terrain of U.S. multicultural markets (Diversity Best Practices, 2004) and highlights the importance of developing intercultural competence to meet the changing needs of diverse markets. Smart organizations learn the lifestyle preferences and spending habits of various identity groups and devise targeted solutions to meet their needs and wants.

Gender

First, women wield significant purchasing power across a number of market segments ranging from buying homes to purchasing sports and fitness equipment. For example, women purchase or directly influence the purchase of 91 percent of all new homes based on 2003 data. Single women made up 21 percent of home buying transactions. They comprise more than 60 percent of online new home shoppers. Markets need to understand that women often make decisions for the entire family. For example, while women only account for 20 percent of all golfers, they buy 50 percent of all golf products with the exception of clubs. Women also spent more on technology in 2003 than men accounting for roughly $55 billion of the nearly $96 total spent on consumer electronics.

Race

In addition to gender diversity, race is increasingly becoming a significant factor in U.S. multicultural markets. According to data in from the Selig Center for Economic Growth, the combined buying power of African-Americans, Asians, and Native Americans will be $1.8 trillion — nearly quadruple its 1990 level of $454 billion — which amounts to a gain of $1.3 trillion or 289 percent. The combined buying power of these three minority racial groups will account for 14.3 percent of the nation's total buying power in 2111, up from 10.6 percent in 1990.

The Selig Center projects buying power of African-Americans will rise from $799 billion in 2006 to $1.1 trillion in 2011. Nationally African-Americans will account for almost nine cents out of every dollar spent. Five major markets accounted for over 37 percent of African-American buying power in 2003: New York, California, Texas, Georgia, and Florida. Based on 2003 U.S. Census Bureau data 55 percent of the Black population is concentrated in the South, 18 percent live in both the Northeast and Midwestern part of the country and 9 percent live in the West. In 2003, there were 823,000 Black owned businesses in the United States that employed 718,300 people and generated $71.2 billion in revenues. Not only are smart organizations including minority vendor programs as part of comprehensive diversity strategies, many make a concerted effort to provide goods and services to these concerns as well.

The Selig Center projects that Hispanic buying power will rise from $798 billion in 2006 to nearly $1.2 trillion in 2011 and will account for 9.5 percent of all U.S. buying power. California accounts for 27 percent of Hispanic buying power. In 2006 the five states with the largest Hispanic market shares included New Mexico (29.6 percent), Texas (19.5 percent), California (17.4 percent), Arizona (15.2 percent), Florida (14.6 percent), and Nevada (13.8 percent). The U.S. Census 2000 showed that more than one person in eight is Hispanic and the Hispanic population continues to grow faster than the non-Hispanic population. By 2011, practically one person out of every six living in the United States will be of Hispanic origin.

Asian-American's buying power is also growing rapidly and is expected to reach $622 billion in 2011 compared to $427 billion 5 years prior (Selig Center, 2006). Compared to the general U.S. population, as a group, Asian-American's tend to live in metropolitan areas (95 percent), are highly educated (51 percent of men and 44 percent of women have at least a bachelor's degree compared to 32 percent of white men and 27 percent of white women), and proportionally fair well in the managerial and professional ranks in organizations (41 percent of Asian-American men in the civil workforce and 37 percent of the women). In 2006, the states with the largest Asian consumer markets were California ($140.5 billion), New York ($41.5 billion), New Jersey ($26.8 billion), Texas $25.9 billion), and Hawaii ($20.4 billion).

Gay, Lesbian, Bisexual, and Transgender (GLBT) Population

According to Business Week, the Gay, Lesbian, Bisexual and Transgender (GLBT) population purchasing power reached $485 billion in 2003 and is quickly gaining the attention of astute markers. According to the 2000 U.S. Census data, 1 out of 10 individuals in the United States is gay, with gay and lesbian families totaling 304,148. GLBT couples are slightly more educated than the overall U.S. adult population with more than 35 percent of people living with same-sex partners holding a college degree in 2000 (compared to 28 percent), purchasing power reached $485 billion in 2003 and is quickly gaining the attention of astute markers. There is evidence that the nation's top 500 companies are working to expand policies to meet the needs of GLBT people, with 70 percent offering domestic partner benefits and a major (95 percent) having explicit policies barring discrimination based on sexual orientation.

Business Ownership

The growth of minority entrepreneurs and small business owners represent emerging opportunities for diverse talent, in additional to having a significant impact on the U.S economy. According to the National Women's Business Council, as of 2006 there are an estimated 10.4 million privately held businesses in which a woman or women own at least 50 percent of the company. Of them, 7.7 million are majority owned. Nearly half of all privately held U.S. firms are at least 50 percent owned by women. These women-owned firms employ 12.8 million people and generate $1.9 trillion in sales. Majority women-owned firms employ 7.1 million workers and generate $1.1 trillion in sales. An estimated one in five women-owned firms is owned by a woman or women of color. As of 2006 there are an estimated 2.1 million privately held firms that are majority owned by women of color.

Minority-owned businesses contributed over $1.4 trillion in sales revenue to the economy in 2002 and emerging at a rate of 6 million new businesses each year. According to the 2000 U.S. Census, Hispanics owned 1.4 million business (or 39.5 percent of the total minority-owned businesses), Asian-Americans owned 913,000 (or 30 percent), African-Americans owned 823,500 (or 27.1 percent), and Native Americans owned 200,000 businesses (or 6.5 percent).

In addition to race and gender, the GLBT population compared to the overall U.S. population is more likely to be self-employed (12 percent compared to 6 percent overall).

While not an extensive treatment, these data demonstrate how important it is for organizational leaders to recognize the changing demographic profile of both the available talent pool and consumer markets. A productive diversity climate yields limitless potential, while over time a poor climate will impact long-term business results as far reaching as customer satisfaction and customer loyalty, which in turn spirals into strategic performance areas such as cost management, profits, and ultimately shareholder value. The Leveraging Diversity Scorecard displayed in Figure 8.2 (Wheeler, 1996;

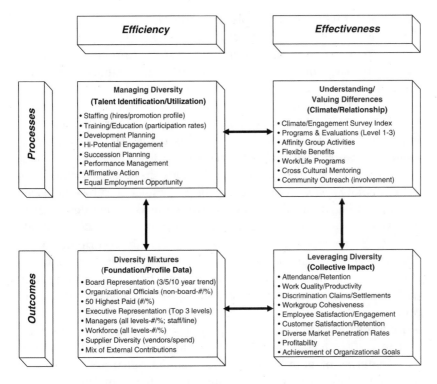

FIGURE 8.2 The Leveraging Diversity Scorecard.

Hubbard, 2004) provides a comprehensive dashboard for monitoring many of the factors we have discussed. The dashboard aligns core *processes* and related *outcomes* with *efficiency* and *effectiveness*.

Change Driver #6: Ensure Systems Alignment

Systems alignment ensures that the core factors that drive behavior in a given organization are congruent with the overall enterprise strategy and supporting diversity strategies, including: (1) *measurement and rewards* (i.e., strategy and performance planning, compensation, succession planning, and promotions); (2) *culture* (i.e., shared organizational core values and beliefs, leadership practices), (3) *structure and work processes* (i.e., organization and work design, decision processes, and information systems), and

(4) *people practices* (i.e., people first, competencies and motivation, development, selection, mentoring and coaching).

High-performing organizations align systems to reinforce strategic focus; diversity must be treated in the same manner. This is a leadership challenge, yet without clear systems alignment and line-of-sight accountability, no strategy, no matter how brilliant will succeed. During your initial, and periodic, diversity discovery process it is imperative that you identify a set of potential strategic priorities related to diversity with related success indicators and measures. Once these strategic choices related to diversity have been defined, an accountability system to track and generate results must be established or you can be certain little progress will be made. The integration of diversity within the organization's planning and accountability systems is the factor that will most significantly contribute to the effective implementation of diversity initiatives. Yet, in our work with clients, we begin early to lay the foundation for insuring that measurement of success is an end result of the diversity discovery process.

Building on the factors displayed in Figure 8.2, Table 8.3 demonstrates that diversity interventions and related measures vary in terms of both process and intended outcomes on the one hand, and their focus on compliance and integration on the other. While linked later in the learning and change process, diversity metrics are most effective when tied to performance, compensation, and other organizational reward systems — in short, systems alignment. Edward E. Hubbard's (2004) book, *"The Diversity Scorecard,"* is an excellent resource for clear and explicit strategies and tactics for evaluating the impact of diversity on organizational performance.

Structuring and Aligning Change Interventions

Strategies for measuring the impact of diversity work are dependent, in part, on the intentions of both diversity practitioners and their client. Expanding the diversity mixtures in organizations requires a variety of change interventions, a focus on the full utilization of a diverse workforce, and striving to enhance the work climate. Further, the approach and criteria used to assess the effectiveness of a given

TABLE 8.3 Measuring Effectiveness and Impact of Divesity Initatives

Diversity Mixture (Parity Focused)	Valuing Differences (Climate Focused)	Managing Diversity (Utilization Focused)	Leveraging Diversity (Impact Focused)
■ Workforce mix (i.e., representation) in Comparison with National Demographics) ■ Offer/Acceptance Ratio (AA goals and targets) ■ Employee retention by focal area of diversity (e.g., race, gender, ability, education and level, function, etc.) ■ Recruitment and training costs ■ Turnover costs ■ Strategic staffing (i.e., key roles)	■ Organizational cultural and work climate survey results ■ Degree of multilingualism ■ Leadership behavior/ management practices ■ Degree of flexible work arrangement (i.e., part-time, job sharing, etc.) ■ Utilization of work-life balance benefits and initiatives (e.g., cafeteria benefits, domestic partner, etc.) ■ Employee networks ■ Multicultural events ■ Number of bias related employee complaints/ lawsuits ■ Number of diversity-related programs (e.g., mentoring, flextime, etc.)	■ Promotions (Mix) ■ Movement/career paths (Mix of line/staff, decision making/support) ■ Representation considerations during organizational structural changes (i.e., cutbacks, down-sizing, hiring freezes, etc.) ■ Representation consideration in succession plans ■ Applying diversity management skills to key HR processes (i.e., staffing, compensation, performance management, etc.)	■ Customer satisfaction rates ■ Customer retention ■ Successful penetration of diverse market segments ■ Success/failure in foreign cultures and markets ■ Corporate/public image ■ Representation of vendor/suppliers ■ Employment brand ■ Community relations ■ Overall organizational effectiveness (i.e., ROI, Market Position, Quality, etc.) ■ Full economy/ global competitiveness

Source: Authors' adaptation of concepts in J. P. Fernandez, *The diversity advantage* (1993); T. Wilson's, *Diversity at work* (1996, pp. 29–38); E. E. Hubbard's, *The Diversity Scorecard* (2004, pp.7–24); M. Wheeler's, Diversity: Making the business case, *Business Week* (1996, December 9); and A. Carnevale and S. C. Stone's, *The American mosaic* (1995).

intervention, or set of interventions, vary by intentions and related learning objectives (i.e., creating awareness and knowledge; building skills and capability; applying learning real-world situations; or a combination of the three). Table 8.3 provides a listing of sample metrics organized by our accountability framework.

Opening Doors

The first set of measures evaluates an organization's activities, geared toward building a diverse workforce or acknowledging the diversity that exists. This set of measures place an emphasis on striving to achieve a level of parity compared to external and internal benchmarks, e.g., availability, current and projected in key disciplines critical to organizational strategy — in other words, *opening doors*. Measures related to this first area focus on demographics and representation.

Opening Minds

The second set of measures relates to initiatives that aim to create or prepare the environment for diversity; to recognize, understand, and potentially value differences — in other words, *opening minds*. Measurements related to this second area are grounded in aspects of organizational culture, diversity training, and educational programmatic measures, including climate survey results and program evaluation data.

Opening Systems

The third set of measures relates to how management practices align with the values of diversity — in other words, *opening systems*. System metrics range from new hire distribution by primary dimensions of diversity (e.g., race, gender, and age) to demographic profiles of retained and terminated employees during a re-organization. Finally, leveraging diversity metrics monitor the collective impact of the various diversity process elements of a company's diversity strategy, including internal factors such as employee satisfaction rates and external factors such as customer satisfaction and retention.

The combined use of these three sets of measures to guide your diversity change process provides you with the tools to insure alignment as you pave your way into the future. This chapter ends as it began with an emphasis on the importance of measurement and evaluation to your final outcomes — that is, making certain, as much as possible, the future you envision becomes a reality. And, we stress again that systems alignment depends on measurement and evaluation to ensure your organizational systems, structures, and processes are in line with your business and diversity priorities, values and vision.

References

Buckingham, M., and Coffman, C. *First, Break All the Rules: What the World's Greatest Managers do Differently.* New York, NY: Simon & Schuster, 1999.

Burke, W. W. *Organization Change: Theory and Practice.* Thousand Oaks, CA: Sage, 2002, pp. 201–216.

Carnevale, A., and Stone, S. C. *The American Mosaic.* New York, NY: McGraw-Hill, 1995.

Cetron, M. J., and Davies, O. *Trends Shaping the Future: Economic, Societal and Environmental Trends.* Bethesda, MD: The Futurist, 2003, January–February, pp. 27–42.

Diversity Best Practices and Business Women's Network. *Wow! Facts 2004 U.S. Multicultural and Global Market: A resource for women and diversity facts.* Washington, DC, 2004, pp. 15–16; 103–271.

Fernandez, J. P. *The Diversity Advantage.* New York, NY: Lexington Books, 1993.

Heskett, J. L., Jones, T. O., Loveman, G. W., Sasser, W. E., and Schlesinger, L. A. *Putting the Service-Profit Chain to Work.* Boston, MA: Harvard Business Review, 1994, March–April, pp. 164–174.

Hubbard, E. E. *The Diversity Scorecard: Evaluating the Impact of Diversity on Organizational Performance.* Boston, MA: Elsevier, Butterworth Heinemann, 2004.

Wheeler, M. L. *Corporate Practices in Diversity Measurement: A research report.* New York, NY: The Conference Board, 1996, pp. 15–28.

Wilson, T. *Diversity at work: The Business Case for Equity.* New York, NY: Wiley, 1996, pp. 432–438.

III

HUMAN INTERACTION: LEVERAGING DIVERSITY AT ITS CORE

Part III suggests a number of human interaction practices and a framework for engaging in productive conversations. The ability to perform leadership and management tasks such as integrating diversity into business systems depends on your ability to deal with conflict head-on. Because we know that all conversations do not go down smoothly and some end up, or even begin, as difficult conversations, we present strategies for addressing conflict and disagreements. When individuals with diverse perspectives work together conflict results.

To effectively leverage diversity you will need to accept and plan for the resistance and conflict that evolve as a result of this challenging process. We want you to be prepared and we suggest ways that you can use the issue tensions that emerge to engage in productive conversations with far-reaching results. Because leveraging diversity requires you lead a complex, learning and change process, we suggest you surround the effort with a vast array of talent. Therefore, we end Part III with a thorough overview of the help that is available to you during your journey.

9

The Art of Human Interaction

Diversity represents one of the most powerful paradoxes for us. We would not be able to live without it, and often it seems as though we won't be able to live with it.

It is troublesome and difficult because we are more comfortable with sameness. We are socialized to look for our similarities. Yet it is our differences that provide us with our individuality and the unique perspectives and talents we bring to any collaborative effort.

— Linda Ellinor and Glenna Gerard

To develop your strategic story, communicate your vision, gain understanding and generated buy-in, you will need face-to-face engagements — human interaction at its core. Leveraging diversity is not a solo activity accomplished via the Internet! Showing your heartfelt commitment to leverage diversity is a necessary foundation for building the bridge from the "way we are" to the "way we aspire to become." Your ability to call to action, ask for collective courage, open minds, and make commitments depends on skillful human interaction.

As we near the book's end, we offer a number of human interaction practices and a framework for engaging in productive conversations — the cornerstone of positive human-to-human engagement. If you are a leader who works continuously on your capacity to communicate effectively, this framework may fit nicely with your current way of operating. For those of you who regularly find yourself in situations where you feel you are misunderstood, this framework provides a roadmap for productive conversations that can help you improve your daily interactions.

In our work with organizations we find this framework for productive conversations enhances the ability to perform leadership and management tasks such as integrating diversity into business planning processes, strategy development, and performance coaching. Leaders we work with also find it improves problem solving, decision-making, and conflict resolution. We share these insights related to the ninth leadership practice:

Leadership Practice 9

Practice the Art and Science of Effective Human Interactions.

As a leader you likely have memories of conversations involving various dimensions of diversity that took a wrong turn because you hurt someone's feelings or pushed a "hot button." Or, you have been in meetings when a member of your leadership team told an ethnic joke and all eyes turned to you to see how you handle the situation. Or perhaps you were planning to talk with one of the VPs about rumors concerning their involvement in an office affair, but before you had the conversation a sexual harassment lawsuit was on your desk. Situations like these, when diversity influences the effectiveness of interactions, are difficult to handle yet can and often do impact bottom line results, the human interaction skills outlined in this chapter really matter.

For example, misunderstandings, conflicts, and other tensions cause meetings to last longer and create rework. Long meetings and rework create more tension. Tension lowers morale. Low morale increases water cooler conversations and gripe sessions. Gripe sessions decrease productivity. All of this equates to time. Time equates to work-hours. Work-hours equate to dollars paid in salaries. Lost salary or lost productivity, as a result of one unproductive meeting, has a tremendous impact on the bottom line. In contrast, the next story tells about a company that is committed to minimizing bottom line losses caused by negative interactions.

DIFFERENCES AROUND THE TABLE
(ADVICE FROM AN INTERNAL DIVERSITY LEADER)

I believe that when there is harmony in a group we can have results that increase exponentially. And when we have division, it takes us twice as long to go half the distance. So we think we can only get better if everybody is represented and if we have everybody's ideas on the table. In other words, not just one person's culture trying to drive this whole process. And I'm saying not just what my beliefs are, but this is what the chairman will tell you, as will the president. We have seen the value of having the differences around the strategy table.

We believe diverse teams outperform homogeneous teams, and that we get a better product, or provide better customer service, if our inside profile matches the marketplace. Because the marketplace happens to be very diverse along many dimensions, our leadership, our employee base, and our thinking needs to be very diverse so that we can figure out how to reach and appeal to the various groups. We believe that diversity is the way to go. It appeals to all of America, and increasingly, the world!

— Chief Diversity Officer
Major U.S. Based Restaurant Group

At a basic level communication is simply talk, a very natural state of affairs, an art that we refine overtime. For many of us, interacting well with others is thought of as something we learn to do informally, as we go about our daily activities. Early in life we learn social cues from our families and others important to us, about the appropriate way to interact with our siblings, other relatives, friends, and members of our community. This socialization process continues when we go to school, where we learn acceptable behaviors from our teachers and other authority figures. We are taught how to behave in a variety of situations. These rules of engagement are grounded in values, attitudes, and beliefs, and are generally understood within a specific group or cultural context. We also learn how to communicate as part of our formal education (i.e., rules of grammar, in both written and spoken forms).

Recent advances in the neurosciences, emotional and social intelligence, intercultural communications, and communication

TABLE 9.1 Books on Conversations (Since 2000)

Title	Year
Difficult Conversations: How to Discuss What Matters Most	2000
You Just Don't Understand: Men and Women in Conversation	2001
Crucial Conversations Tools for Talking When the Stakes are High	2002
Corporate Conversations: A Guide to Crafting Effective and Appropriate Internal Communications	2003
Fierce Conversations: Achieving Success at Work and in Life One Conversation at a Time	2004
The World Cafe: Shaping Our Futures Through Conversations That Matter	2005
Naked Conversations: How Blogs are Changing the Way Businesses Talk with Customers	2006
Compelling Conversations: Connecting Leadership to Student Achievement	2007

theory provide exciting insights about the way we make meaning, and how this impacts the way we relate to each other. Since 2000 there have been literately 1,000s of new books focused on helping people enhance their conversational capabilities to achieve personal and organizational goals (see Table 9.1).

Anatomy of Productive Conversations across Differences: A Primer

An interaction is any exchange between two or more people. The exchange may be verbal, as in a conversation, or non-verbal, as in trading shrugs or glances during a meeting or trading e-mails over a period of time. The most basic parts of an interaction are the *"who,"* *"what"* and *"how"* of the exchange. Other elements to consider include:

- The reason for the interaction.
- How the message one receives matches the message another sends.
- The urgency of the message.
- The tone of the message.
- Each party's physical and emotional response to the message.

The pattern of the interaction: its beginning, middle, and end, its high and low points and its points of contention and agreement, are

TABLE 9.2 Three Phases of Productive Conversations

Phase	Description
Engaging (Beginning/opening)	Effectively aligns expectations between all parities involved in the interaction, clarifies general needs and wants, while setting the stage for a productive interaction with other(s).
Progressing (Advancing purpose)	Moves you and others closer to realizing intentions, promoting understanding, making a decision or building commitment to action while enhancing the relationship.
Disengaging (Setting the stage for informed future action)	Clarifies accomplishments, key learning, agreements, unfinished business and next steps. Leaves the door open for future, productive interactions.

also important factors. An effective interaction is one in which all of these factors come together and have the desired impact of creating a productive exchange that moves us toward our intentions and desired results. Table 9.2 briefly describes each of the three major phases of the conversation process.

It is important for leaders to be fully engaged during conversations. It is the combined force of head, hand, and heart work that promotes diversity's two guiding principles of (1) respect for the individual and (2) integrity through authentic leadership. To succeed at diversity, you must imbed these principles in your core values and demonstrate them in every human interaction occurring in your organization on a daily basis.

One consumer goods company understood the need to do so, and as a result of their efforts was recognized for its world-class diversity initiatives receiving both the Catalyst Award and Opportunity 2000 Award. "We are committed to serving consumers and achieving leadership results through principle-based decisions and actions. Our corporate tradition is rooted in the principles of personal integrity, respect for the individual, and doing what's right for the long term. C&F (pseudonym) is its people and the core values by which they live," their VP of Global Diversity told us.

Having a respect for the dignity of the individual governs the way you communicate with, see, and experience others. This essential value acts as a springboard to compassion, equity, and stewardship. As each of us challenges our traditional ways of thinking about leadership, we begin to discover our connection to the world around us. As Einstein said, we "widen our circle of compassion to embrace our varied human experiences and the whole of nature in its beauty." Respect for the individual serves as the antidote to the often unintentional acts of prejudice and discrimination in the workplace.

Having integrity reinforces the value of respect for the individual. Webster defines integrity as "completeness, wholeness or an unimpaired condition." At its core, integrity means being consistent in what you say and what you do. *Do your actions match your words? Do the audios match the visuals?* This is the first element of integrity. *Do your actions match your values?* This is the second element of integrity. Authentic leaders work to ensure that their actions and decisions are congruent with their values. The story below speaks to the importance to diversity and authentic leadership.

DO YOUR ACTIONS MATCH YOUR VALUES?
(ADVICE FROM AN INTERNAL DIVERSITY LEADER)

You have to operate in an environment of ethics. You have to be very ethical in your operation because of the work that you're doing. If you're at all viewed as working without ethics or morals, then your whole diversity initiative dies. It dies, because of all the things that you profess this work to be, don't align with your actions. So you have to have high ethical and moral standards. You're just not forgiven if you tell an ethnic joke, if you say something that demonstrates homophobia. You're just not forgiven.

— Director, Diversity, EEO & Work-life
Fortune 50 Insurance Provider

The human interaction practices described in the remainder of this chapter provide a basis for you to become more aware of the consistency between what you communicate to others by word and what they observe in your actions. Figure 9.1 depicts a framework for crafting productive conversations across differences, in ways that deepen understanding, provide a foundation for effective communication, and contribute to building solid personal and professional relationships. We describe the components of this three-phase process in the balance of this chapter.

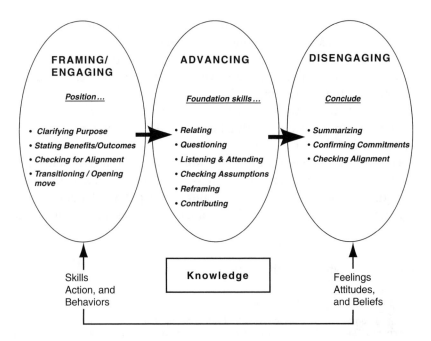

FIGURE 9.1 The Anatomy of Productive Conversations across Differences.

Phase I: Engaging

Engagement is one of the most critical aspects of human interaction because it sets the stage for what follows. Unfortunately, it is also the aspect that is the easiest to short-change. Given time pressure and deadlines, it is all too tempting to *jump right into* a conversation without explicit preparation or framing, both of which are necessary for effective communication to occur. Productive conversations require preparation and forethought, in addition to being fully present during the course of the entire interaction.

While interacting with others, you should focus not only on your own needs, but also on the needs of others. Engagement prepares us and frames an interaction, making clear its scope in terms of the desired results and the process for getting there. Engagement is an active process involving four key elements: clarifying purpose, stating the benefits of engaging in the conversation (including desired outcomes), checking for alignment with regards to the expectations of the various parities, and making an explicit transition to the advancing phase of the process with an opening move. Table 9.3 summarizes the core elements involved in launching a conversation in ways that engage the "whole person" (i.e., head, hand, and heart): (1) clarifying purpose, (2) stating benefits, (3) checking for alignment, and (4) transitioning.

To begin a conversation it is important to clearly state the purpose of the interaction and then ask others if they have anything to add. The next step is to talk about the potential benefits for engaging in the interaction. The leader continues the engagement

TABLE 9.3 Whole Person Engagement (Head, Hand, and Heart Work)

Element	Description
Clarifying purpose (Intentions/Outcomes)	Begin conversation with a clearly stated purpose of the interaction and then ask others if they have anything to add. An example of a purpose statement might be: "I'd like to explore potential objectives to guide next year's diversity strategies. Does anyone have anything they would like to add to frame our agenda today?"
Stating benefits (For self/others/value proposition)	Next, talk about the benefits of the interaction. Articulating benefits often requires providing space for everyone involved in the interaction to state their needs and/or wants, either from the interaction itself or the commitments that may result from the interaction. Continuing with the previous example, the person leading the conversation might say, "I want to hear from each of you as we begin to develop our objectives. Your input now, and commitment later, to the final action plan is important to successful implementation."
Checking for alignment (Congruence of expectations)	Checking for alignment involves summarizing the key needs and wants, restating the purpose of the interaction while integrating the perspectives of others, and asking a series of questions. The questions are simple, but play a major function in setting the stage for productive conversations. For example... "Shall we begin?"
Transitioning (Opening moves)	Here you transition to the body of the conversation with an opening move. A useful approach is generally to pose a series of questions that allow people to share information, facts, opinions, and other perspectives related to the presenting problem, challenge, or opportunity. For example... "A place to start might be to review our accomplishments to date regarding this year's diversity strategy as a basis for thinking about what to keep doing, stop doing, and start doing in the future. Who would like to begin?"

process by providing space for everyone involved in the interaction to state their needs and/or wants, either from the interaction
itself or the commitments that may result from the interaction.
Here it is important to let everyone know "there will be no back-
and-forth conversation until each of you has had a chance to speak
at least once." This ensures that everyone has an opportunity to
speak.

It is also important to separate positions from needs and wants.
Positions are demands people make or a stance they are taking
(or the "what"). Needs or wants represent the underlying reasons
people are taking a given stance (the "why"). If the leader has
taken the time prior to the conversation to think about their own
needs and wants, they can model the process. While enacting this
component of the engagement process remind participants that the
aim is to understand everyone's starting point in terms of needs and
wants, not to address them or start to problem solve.

Checking for alignment has three primary aims:

- Ensures everyone feels involved in the interaction.
- Brings to light any hesitations about participating.
- Finds out what others need and want from the exchange.

Checking for alignment involves summarizing the key needs and
wants, restating the purpose of the meeting while integrating the
perspectives of others, and asking a series of questions. It is critical
to listen carefully to the responses provided to assess the degree and
nature of alignment achieved during the opening engagement. The
questions are usually as simple as those listed below, but play a
major function in setting the stage for productive conversations:

- "Does that sound okay to you?" To everyone?
- "Does that approach make sense?"
- "What do you need from the conversation?"
- "Shall we continue?"

Achieving alignment helps everyone feel more committed to
accomplishing the purpose of the interaction. Sometimes you will
need to change or expand your agenda to include other parties'
agendas as well. By doing so, you send the message that you are
interested in others' opinions and that it matters to you that

everyone is *on board*. Being approachable increases the likelihood future conversations will be productive. The engaging phase concludes by making an explicit transition to the body of the conversation, signaling that the engagement will proceed.

Phase II: Advancing

Advancing is often the most intense, yet when done well, can be the most rewarding part of an interaction. During this phase different opinions surface, perspectives are transformed, synergy is stimulated and the seeds to cooperation are planted. Communicating effectively across difference requires whole person engagement, including our *thinking* (i.e., head work, cognition), our *behavior* (i.e., hand work), and our *feeling* (i.e., heart work). Yet, human interaction is fundamentally a relational process.

Daniel Goleman's (1996, 2006) *New York Times* Best Seller, *Emotional Intelligence: Why It Can Matter More than IQ,* highlights how success in today's global and complex business environment requires more than cognitive intelligence. The Emotional Intelligence Consortium is an excellent resource for viewing the growing body of evidence that supports the business case for social and emotional intelligence (www.eiconsortium.org).

Goleman (1998) positions the idea of leveraging diversity as a social competence that determines how we handle relationships, specifically one's capacity to cultivate opportunities with different kinds of people (p. 27). Extensive research conducted by the Center of Creative Leadership (McCall et al., 1988; Lombardo and Eichinger, 2002) identified three factors that can significantly stall and/or derail executives: (1) trouble interacting with others, (2) difficulty navigating change, and (3) trouble delivering results. The first two factors are associated with social and emotional intelligence.

Drawing on emerging insights from *neuroscience* (e.g., Restak, 2006; Pink, 2006), *social network analysis* (e.g., Gladwell, 2002; Scott, 2000), and *social intelligence* and *cultural intelligence* (e.g., Goleman, 2006; Thomas and Inkson, 2003; Mayer et al., 2004), we describe six fundamental communication skills that facilitate movement through the progressing phase of productive conversations to advance the agreed upon purposes of the interaction, these include: (1) relating, (2) questioning, (3) listening, (4) checking assumptions, (5) reframing, and (6) contributing. Each fundamental communication consists of two or more components.

There is nothing new about these skills, as successful leaders you use them everyday. We review them here as a primer. Learning to apply them in new and different ways, particularly during intercultural interactions, has the power to transform your understanding of others and situations in unexpected yet productive ways. Throughout this discussion, we make connections between the six fundamental communication skills and the eight social intelligence competencies described by Goleman (2006) as being essential for effective human interaction, or what he calls Social Intelligence. Specifically, he identifies four social awareness competencies (i.e., primal empathy, attunement, empathic accuracy, and social cognition) and four social facility competencies (i.e., synchrony, self-presentation, influence, and concern). Table 9.4 presents brief descriptions of each social–emotional competency.

Relating

There are over 6.7 billion people in the world from a myriad of different cultures. Given radical advances in information technology, electronic communication, and transportation, it can truly be said that we live in a global village (Thomas and Inkson, 2003). The extent to which we are able to leverage such global access, in large part depends on how we respond to cultural differences. Cultural intelligence (or CQ), incorporates the capabilities embedded in cognitive intelligence (or IQ) and emotional intelligence (EQ, the ability to handle emotions during interactions, our own and those of others).

Leaders with a high CQ capacity breathe energy, commitment, and motivation into organizations. This contributes to employee engagement, customer satisfaction, and organizational effectiveness as we discussed in Chapter 8. Low CQ work climates are likely to respond to cultural differences in a less than optimal manner. Behaviors that trigger tension, misunderstanding and conflict between people, drain the overall effectiveness of the organization. While the six communication skills presented here appear across cultures (i.e., cultural-general capabilities or *etic*), the way they show up are unique to each

TABLE 9.4 Descriptions of Goleman's Social/Emotional Competencies

Social awareness cluster — refers to a spectrum that runs from instantaneously sensing another's inner state, to understanding her feelings and thought, to "getting" complicated social situations	
Primal empathy	Feeling with others; sensing non-verbal emotional signals; the ready ability to sense the emotions of another (i.e., a low-road capacity that occurs — or fails to occur — the rapid and automatic reading of non-verbal cues). Intuitive, gut-level.
Attunement	Listening with full receptivity; attuning to a person; full sustained presence that facilitates rapport; seek to understand others (meaning beyond words and our point of view).
Empathic accuracy	Builds on primal empathy by adding an explicit understanding of another person's thoughts, feelings, and intentions (i.e., brings low road together with high road circuitry in the neo-cortex).
Social cognition	Knowing how the social world works in a variety of situations (recognizing the operative norms of a given situation-context) and the capacity to find solutions to social dilemmas (e.g., making new friends when moving to a new city).
Social facility cluster — simply sensing how another feels, or knowing what they think or intend, does not guarantee fruitful interactions. Social facility builds on social awareness to allow smooth, effective interactions. The spectrum of social facility includes	
Synchrony	Interacting smoothly at the non-verbal level, getting "in synch" with another person by observing and responding to cues without thinking about it (also a low road capacity).
Self-presentation	Presenting ourselves effectively in ways that make a desired impression; charisma is one aspect of self-presentation; ability to control & mask emotions as needed (linked to emotional self management).
Influence	Constructively shaping the outcome of social interactions by using tact and combing self-control, with empathy and a keen understanding of the social context; putting others at ease.
Concern	Caring about others' needs and acting accordingly with compassion.

Source: Daniel Goleman's, *Social Intelligence: The New Science of Human Relationships* (2006, pp. 84–100).

cultural group (i.e., cultural-specific capabilities or *emic*). Table 9.5 highlights the importance of relating, an essential element for building rapport.

Two components are at play when relating effectively: (1) making a personal connection, and (2) encouraging others to contribute to the conversation and stayed engaged. Relating well with diverse others requires using your social intelligence. Establishing deep connections with others requires going beyond the spoken word to what

TABLE 9.5 Advancing: Relating

Element	Component Descriptions
Relating ⇩	*Connecting*: Strive to establish a connection with others early in the process by starting with "small talk" and trying to find areas of mutual interests and common experiences. Continue to build the relationship throughout the conversation. Flex your style by using compatible speaking patterns, gestures, and body language. Connecting requires a focus on non-verbal forms of communication, in addition to the words being expressed.
SQ Competency Primal empathy Synchrony Concern	*Encouraging*: Keep others actively involved in the conversation. Prompt others to talk and to stay engaged. Reinforce by giving short verbal (e.g., "I see," "ah," "I hear you," "okay"), non-verbal signals (e.g., nods, smiling, or leaning forward to share concern) to others, using supportive questions (e.g., "say more about that"), and paraphrasing.

Daniel Goleman (2006) calls *primal empathy*, that human capacity to instantaneously sense another's inner emotional state. Research shows that the ability to respond in this way is triggered by the brain's neural circuitry, which operates beneath our awareness, automatically, effortlessly, and with immense speed. Goleman calls this the brain's *Low Road*. Paul Ekman, the world's most famous face reader, identifies seven universal facial expressions based on extensive cross-cultural studies and neuropsychological research. Table 9.6 summarizes the seven "universal" facial expressions that reflect one's emotions.

Ekman's book, *Emotions Revealed* (Ekman, 2003), provides useful insights for reading and understanding other's emotions and learning how to respond accurately. He developed the MicroExpression Training Tools (METT) and Subtle Expression Training Tools (SETT) to provide self-instructional training for improving one's ability to recognize facial expressions of emotion. These tools improve one's ability to recognize *micro*-expressions, that are so brief lasting less than a quarter of a second, occurring involuntarily, yet can reveal emotions not deliberately expressed (www.paulekman.com).

Additionally the tools increase your awareness of *subtle*-expressions involving minor movement in parts of the face that signal the beginning of an emotion. Recognizing micro-expressions and subtle-expressions are useful for connecting during any human interaction, and is crucial when establishing a personal bond with culturally diverse others.

TABLE 9.6 Ekman's 7 Universal Facial Expressions

Expression	Description
Anger	A strong emotion; a feeling that is oriented toward some real or supposed grievance; the emotional aspect of aggression; mild forms of anger are typically described as "distaste," "displeasure," or "irritation;" while "rage" refers to an extreme degree of anger associated with a loss of calmness or discipline (in the case of human conduct).
Disgust	An emotion that is typically associated with things that are perceived as unclear, inedible, or infectious; something revolting (often related to taste, smell, touch, or even observation).
Fear	A defensive, survival advantage; usually a response to a particular stimulus; serious fear grows out of the discernment of some formidable impending peril; trifling fear is that which arises from being confronted with harm of inconsiderable dimensions, or, at any rate of whose happening there is only a slender likelihood; related emotional states include worry, anxiety, terror, horror, dread; results from distrust in an interpersonal context.
Joy	Feelings of happiness and satisfaction; well-being, delight, health, safety, contentment, and love; often associated with the presence of favorable circumstances such as a supportive family life, a loving marriage, and economic stability.
Sadness	A state of unhappiness, or to a relatively minor downturn in mood that may last only a few hours or days; generally situational and reactive, and associated with grief, loss, or a major social transition (e.g., moving, marriage, divorce, the break-up of a significant relationship, death, graduation, or job loss are instances that might trigger a depressed mood).
Surprise	A feeling of shock due to something perceived as unexpected; could be pleasant or unpleasant; there is also non-emotional, intellectual surprise.
Contempt	Lack of respect accompanied by a feeling of intense dislike; open disrespect for a person or thing; it is related to feelings of resentment and bitterness; willful disobedience to or disrespect for the authority.

Questioning and Listening

Relating provides the foundation needed to establish trust and engage in the process of sharing and exchanging information, knowledge, and generating insight. The fundamental communication skills of questioning and listening are two sides of the same coin, both are essential to effectively combining *inquiry* (i.e., creating a shared pool of knowledge) with *advocacy* (i.e., presenting a point-of-view). Questioning is the key to inquiry and discovery. The three types of questions: (1) open-ended questions, (2) closed-ended questions, and (3) four-level questions are presented in Table 9.7.

Open-ended forms of questioning are productive early on to establish a foundation for discovery and insight. As the conversation

TABLE 9.7 Advancing: Questioning and Listening

Element	Component Descriptions
Questioning ⇩ SQ Competency Attunement Empathic accuracy Social cognition	*Open-ended*: require more than a yes or no answer; generally take the form of "what, why, and how," and are useful early in the progressing stage of the conversation to surface what is known about a given situation from multiple perspectives. Use open probes to help get a balanced picture to any situation (both problems and opportunity), people tend to focus on the problems leaving opportunities unexplored. *Closed-ended*: intention is to generate a focused response either "yes" or "no" as in the case of "Can you support this decision?" or "What do we know for a fact about this potential hire?" This form of questioning is effective for checking for alignment and understanding or checking the facts. *Four-level*: *objective* (externally focused on gathering data, facts, and opinions); *reflective* (internally focused on surfacing feelings, impressions and perspectives); *interpretative* (focused on identifying patterns, themes, and lessons learned/meaning); and *decisional* (focused on exploring options, consequences, and payoffs; making commitments).
Listening ⇩ SQ Competency Attunement Concern	*Gathering* and *Synthesizing data*: Listening is an active communication process that requires attention, concentration, and a willingness to step away from your own opinion and actively hear the opinion of others; being present, being "here" and nowhere else. *Attentive listening*: Allows leaders to hear what people are really saying and not saying. Deep listening combined with empathy facilitates understanding others, to gain access to the meaning behind their words. Listen not only for facts but also opinions and feelings such as hopes, fears, passion, concern, and excitement; confirm what you have heard to make progress and understanding explicit.

continues, closed-ended questions are useful to confirm understanding and alignment. When we are present during our questioning a degree of moving, operating, and working together is achieved that results in a form of synchronized attunement with others. Questioning combined with listening allows us to transform primal forms of empathy to empathic accuracy, knowing not only what others are saying, but also responding by being present and attending to others on multiple levels (verbal and non-verbal).

The two components associated with listening include: (1) gathering and synthesizing data, and (2) attentive listening. Questioning and listening is the key to effective human interaction across difference. Figure 9.2 displays the progressive and developmental nature of moving from data to strategic insight. *Objective*

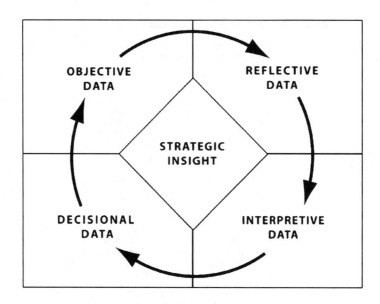

FIGURE 9.2 Progressive Questioning and Listening.

questions seek to gather externally focused data and facts about a person or situation based on our senses (or learning from the outside-in); *reflective questions* are internally focused to surface feelings, reactions, and draw on prior experience with external factors (or learning from the inside-out).

Interpretive questions stimulate people to engage in a meaning making process. Through critical thinking we identify the patterns, themes, and lessons learned embedded in the data that came from the external and internal questions. *Decisional questions* combine the insights before taking informed action. In conversation, people tend to focus on interpretative and decisional data, yet given the importance of context, it is important to ensure that objective and subjective data are available for people to join together in collaborative forms of interpretation to take informed action across differences. Table 9.8 lists sample questions based on the Objective, Reflective, Interpretative and Decisional (ORID) framework (Spencer, 1989) and the Experiential Learning Cycle (Kolb, 1984).

The ORID framework can be used to employ active listening by understanding the speaker's starting point to inform both follow-up questions and contextually appropriate responses. Listening occurs on three levels: (1) *self-talk* (i.e., being aware of one's own internal

TABLE 9.8 Sample ORID Questions

Question Form	Sample Questions
Objective What's happening? (external focused) ⇩ Concrete experience	■ What is the history of diversity within our organization? ■ What is the demographic portrait of our workforce by employee status (i.e., union and non-union) and level (i.e., entry to executive)?
Reflective How do you/I respond? (internal focused) ⇩ Reflective observation	■ What prior experiences with difference can help prepare me/us for diversity leadership? ■ What are some examples of "highs" and "lows" while interacting for diverse others?
Interpretative What does it mean? (relationship & possibility focused) ⇩ Abstract conceptualization	■ What have we learned from our diversity work so far? What stands out? Why? ■ What happens if we don't learn to better leverage diversity?
Decisional Now what? (action focused) ⇩ Active experimentation	■ What are our next steps regarding diversity? How should you/we respond? ■ What are our diversity priorities? What needs to happen first? ■ What resources (i.e., people, financial, etc.) can be used?

voice), (2) *other-talk* (i.e., hearing what people say and observing what they do and do not say), and (3) *meta-communication* (i.e., focus on the meaning that is being created between people). When taken together, the effective use of progressive questioning and listening leads to strategic insight. This is one of the major benefits of leveraging cultural diversity when people know how to interact productively across differences.

Reflecting on the Strategic Learning Model presented in Chapter 1, the strategic learning capability of *contextual awareness* is achieved through the use of objective and reflective questioning and listening. *Conceptual clarity* is achieved when reflective questioning and listening are combined with interpretation. *Taking informed action* is the focus when combining interpretative and decisional questioning and listening. So far, we have introduced three of the six fundamental communication skills to show how relating, questioning, and listening combine to form what we call the "success pyramid" of human interaction.

The success pyramid (i.e., relating, questioning, and listening) is the result of the process of social cognition where people effectively

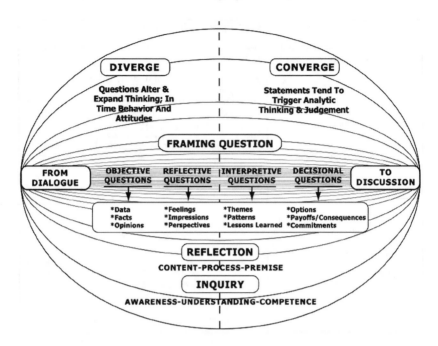

FIGURE 9.3 Divergent and Convergent Forms of Communication.

encode, store, retrieve, and apply various sources of information to social situations and interactions. Figure 9.3 (Ellinor and Gerard, 1998) displays two forms of interactions present during effective communication: (1) dialogue and (2) discussion.

The intention of dialogue is to open up the conversation with objective and reflective questioning and listening (or divergent, non-linear forms of communication). The intention of discussion is to make decisions to guide informed action once there is a shared pool of knowledge grounded in a clear interpretation of the situation (or convergent, linear, and structured forms of communication). Reflection is at the core of productive learning and change.

The questioning and listening cycle can be completed through instrumental learning (i.e., problem solving and decision making informed by current worldview), or more transformative form of learning (i.e., critically testing and expanding assumptions). Jack Mezirow (2000), the father of transformative learning theory, notes that instrumental forms of learning are appropriate when faced with operational challenges, where our current repertoire of knowledge and skills are sufficient to address the situations at hand. He explains that transformative forms of learning are appropriate when current ways of knowing are no match for specific adaptive challenges characteristic of contemporary life.

When we operate in the zone of more instrumental forms of learning we often use *content reflection* (or a focus on "what" questions) and process reflection (or a focus on "how" questions), what Chris Argyris, Professor of Education and Organizational Behavior at Harvard Business School, calls single-loop learning. Transformative forms of learning require that we critically examine the very premises, our belief systems, worldview and mental models used to frame problems and related actions strategies, or premise reflection (a focus on "why" questions). These more transformative forms of reflection relate to what Chris Argyris calls double-loop learning.

Checking Assumptions and Reframing

In our human interaction framework, reflection is enhanced during conversation through the elements of checking assumptions and reframing. Table 9.9 outlines the components of checking assumptions (i.e., testing for accuracy, exploring blind-spots) and reframing (framing and transforming). The dynamic interplay between exploring externally and internally focused data, feelings, and experiences has the potential for generating a shared pool of knowledge. This happens best when individuals, who come to the interaction with diverse perspectives, are invited to consider the value, meaning, or significance of a situation. This is the focus of the human interaction skills of checking assumptions and reframing. The insights that emerge from interpreting situations from multiple perspectives provide a solid platform for expanding thinking and capacity to respond appropriately to cultural diversity.

Checking the accuracy of one's assumptions helps us to become more aware of the nature and sources of hot buttons and blind-spots. Hot buttons are triggered when others: (1) challenge your sense of competence, (2) do not appreciate the value you bring to the situation, (3) communicate in ways that irritate you, (4) act in ways that you find condescending, (5) share unsolicited advice, (6) are

TABLE 9.9 Advancing: Checking Assumptions & Reframing

Element	Component Descriptions
Checking assumptions (Your own/those of others to stay on track) ⇩ *SQ Competency* Empathic accuracy Social cognition	*Testing for accuracy.* Check your assumptions throughout the conversation by restating the key messages you have heard, including inferences you are making about others (or what they are saying) and checking for alignment by watching for non-verbal signals or asking directly. *Exploring blind-spots.* Be mindful of your mindset during conversations and examine the potential mindsets of others; work to surface dysfunctional ways of thinking (others & your own); be intentional about the time you spend in "judger" vs. "learner."
Reframing (Realigning/Expanding) ⇩ *SQ Competency* Attunement Concern Empathic accuracy Social cognition Synchrony	*Framing.* Individual's (or group's) initial perception of the situation (i.e., problem, challenge, or opportunity), person, or object based on current mental models and past understanding (including prior experiences). *Transforming.* Results from the process of transforming initial perceptions into a modified, new or expanded understanding or frame as a result of dialogue with others with different perspectives, research, additional information, or other forms of focused discovery and inquiry; reframing is often the result of experimenting, crossing boundaries & integrating perspectives.

quick to judge you, and (7) in general, behave in ways that you experience as disrespectful. These hot buttons are often amplified when triggered in situations involving diversity.

A metaphorical tool created by Joseph Luft and Harry Ingham (1955), the Johari Window, demonstrates that many people are blind to such hot buttons. The mindsets that we employ to make sense of our experiences with diverse others have a major influence on our capacity to productively leverage difference and the outcomes we realize. In her book, *The Art of the Question*, Marilee C. Goldberg (1997), forwards two such mindsets: learner and judger. She clearly describes how each mindset influences the way we think, feel, behave, and relate to others, and ultimately the outcomes we experience.

Each of us are unique mixtures of the learner self and judger self. Goldberg points out that virtually everything we think and do is generated by the questions we ask. The point is not that the "learner" mindset is good and the "judger" mindset is bad. Yet, understanding the conditions where each is most useful to realize our intentions is empowering.

Learner Mindset

When we operate from a learner mindset, we are accepting of ourselves and others. We engage in various situations from a place of genuine curiosity and exploration. We are empathic, flexible, and seeking possibilities. Such a mindset is useful during the early stages of any human interaction; when we are presented with adaptive challenges; and in situations where the innovation and creativity that can be tapped for diverse perspectives is critical. When we engage in objective and reflective forms of questioning it is helpful to do so from a learner mindset.

Judger Mindset

When we operate from the judger mindset the focus is on convergence and contraction, often informed by proven approaches that are ideal in situations characterized by operational challenges, competition, emergencies, or crises. For many of us, the judger mindset is the default, based on automatic and reactive thinking. It is important to recognize that the "self-talk" associated with the judger mindset can be emotionally heavy (e.g., problem-focused, irrational, blaming, and defensive), and when left unattended, can result in a toxic work climate. On the other hand the self-talk associated with the learner mindset consist of positive emotional tones (e.g., solution-seeking, possibilities, acceptance, and inquiry). It is the combination of learner and judger mindset that provides us with full access to the range of our humanity.

Finally we have used the "ladder of inference" tool displayed in Figure 9.4 (Argyris, 1993) as a framework to help people surface, and productively work with, assumptions that often go unstated. This tool can be applied in conversations. For example, when contributing to a conversation you intentionally "walk-up the ladder" to make explicit the data that support your values, beliefs, and actions. Also, as you listen to others, when necessary, you can gently guide them

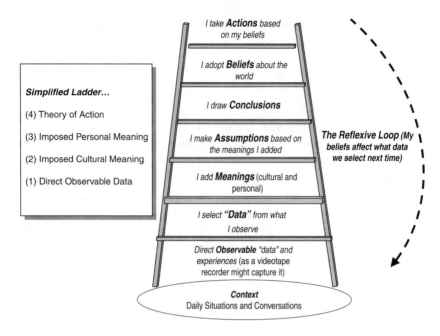

FIGURE 9.4 The Ladder of Inference.

down the ladder asking questions to surface unstated beliefs, values, and relevant data.

Contributing

The sixth and final fundamental communication skill is contributing. High performing leaders build on the information and insights generated from applying the fundamental communication skills to create a positive image of themselves, their ideas, and their organizations. We present the contributing skill last because sharing our opinions and viewpoints come natural to most of us, yet the essence of effective communication is knowing not only how to share one's perspective, but knowing when doing so will have the most impact. The two essential components of the contributing skill include providing information and doing so in a focused, clear, and concise manner (see Table 9.10).

TABLE 9.10 Advancing: Contributing

Element	Component Descriptions
Contributing (Sharing) ⇩ *SQ Competency* Self-presentation Influence	*Providing*. Share information and your point of view or opinion. Strive to advocate your position or point of view in a way that creates a positive image of you; state the benefits related to your point of view, reveal the reasoning or support for your perspective; invite others to respond to your viewpoint and asking if others can help you identify any potential unintended consequences of your position. *Focusing*. Speak in a clear and concise manner by using "headlines" and "captions" early in your delivery of a point. Go into detail after (1) you have invited others to test or respond to your point of view and the information you are sharing and (2) you understand the context and the intentions of others. Show excitement and a strong conviction for your point of view, while demonstrating that you value the input of others.

Early in the advancing stage the parties should use data, information, perceptions, feelings, prior experiences, and opinions to frame the situation. An important dimension of framing the situation is exploring the gap between how people perceive things are (i.e., the current state) and things should be (i.e., the desired state). Fundamentally, needs revolve around increasing or decreasing something (e.g., sales, profits, customer complaints, employment claims, or unwanted turnover) along quantitative, qualitative and time dimensions.

Once needs have been clarified, it is important to determine priorities amongst the needs identified by exploring consequences and payoffs associated with each need. The payoffs focus on the benefits associated with addressing the needs as well as the consequences of not taking action to resolve various needs. Common consequences include cost, productivity, quality, reliability, and personal and political impact. Exploring consequences serves to create a sense of urgency and energy to focus action to address needs, while exploring payoffs serves as a bridge to a desired future state. Later during the advancing stage the nature of contributing moves from problem identification to generating solutions by exploring options. This should be an interactive process where you share options and encourage others to do the same, thus co-creating a pool of options.

Phase III: Disengaging

Disengaging is the capstone of any interaction. When done well, it completes the interaction and contributes to a sense of both progress and closure for all who are involved. During the disengaging stage outstanding issues are identified and discussed. Disengaging gives closure to the conversation (Table 9.11).

Summarizing

If your conversation has gone well, summarizing wraps it up with three questions:

- What were the key points?
- Where did we agree or disagree?
- And, what has been left unresolved?

TABLE 9.11 Disengaging

Element	Description
Summarizing (Reviewing)	Summarizing helps to make the transition from the body of the conversation to bringing it to its conclusion by highlighting the major insights and learning that emerged from the interaction. This is a time to recap the key points covered during the conversation including areas of agreement. It's also useful to celebrate what went well during the interaction. If the interaction needs to be continued at a later date, it is useful to review and summarize whatever was accomplished and to set a time for the next conversation.
Confirming commitments	Building on the summary to capture the action steps and other commitments made by each party in the conversation, it is important that commitments are explicit, and have clear success indicators or measures. Confirming commitments is a process of responsibility charting: who owns each task, who needs to support each task, and who needs to approve various commitments, and the timeframe for completion.
Checking final alignment (Level of congruence)	The main purpose of summarizing and confirming commitments is to set the stage to check for final alignment. Just as it is important to check for alignment at the beginning of an interaction, so that all involved parties can agree on what will occur, it is equally important for everyone to walk away agreeing on what has just occurred.

Confirming Commitments

The key to organizational effectiveness is ensuring the right mix between strategy formulation and execution. Research on leadership effectiveness reveals that gaining commitment is a natural outcome of productive conversations. By applying the fundamental communication skills outlined in this chapter, you will increasingly earn the right to ask for commitment from others. The basic process is to confirm the areas of agreement that emerged during the conversation and ask each party a simple, direct request to implement their commitments. Specifically, ensure commitment by asking the following question:

- What commitments were made during our conversation today?
- Who is accountable for ensuring each commitment is realized?
- How will we know that each commitment is successfully accomplished?
- When will each commitment go into affect?

Checking Final Alignment

This component brings the conversation to a close. Checking alignment should be clear and direct and include questions like the following:

- Did my summary match your experience of the meeting?
- Was there anything I left out of the summary?
- What other things did we talk about?
- Can you commit to working with me on those next steps?

Again, when the various phases, elements, and components of productive conversations are employed as described in this chapter, checking for final alignment will feel like a formality. Objections that emerge as the conversation is coming to a close indicate there is unfinished business from earlier in the exchange.

We close this chapter with the following advice, from an internal diversity leader, which provides a potent segue to the next chapter. In Chapter Ten we present a process model for applying human interaction skills to address conflict in ways that facilitate individual and organizational transformation related to diversity.

CREATING TWO-WAY DIALOGUE
(ADVICE FROM AN INTERNAL DIVERSITY LEADER)

One skill or an attribute that is really important is empathy. If you want to create effective relationships, you have to be able to understand each other. So opening channels, creating two way dialogs, being able to drive to closure, and at the same time being able to slow down to let people have time to be heard — that's really important. Sometimes the process is as important as the outcome.

— Director of Workforce Effectiveness
Large U.S. Based Commercial Bank

References

Argyris, C. *Knowledge for Action: A Guide to Overcoming Barriers to Organizational Change.* San Francisco, CA: Jossey-Bass Publishers, 1993.

Ekman, P. *Emotions Revealed: Recognizing Faces and Feelings to Improve Communication and Emotional life.* New York: Henry Holt and Company, 2003.

Ellinor, L., and Gerard, G. *Dialogue: Rediscover the Transforming Power of Conversation.* New York: Wiley, 1998.

Gladwell, M. *The Tipping Point: How Little Things Can Make a Big Difference.* New York: Little, Brown & Company, 2002.

Goldberg, M. C. *The Art of the Question: A Guide to Short-Term Question-Centered Therapy.* Hoboken, NJ: Wiley, 1997.

Goleman, D. *Emotional Intelligence: Why It can Matter More than IQ.* New York: Bantam Books, 1996.

Goleman, D. *Social Intelligence: The New Science of Human Relationships.* New York: Bantam Books, 2006.

Goleman, D. *Working with Emotional Intelligence.* New York: Bantam Books, 1998.

Kolb, D. *Experiential Learning: Experience as the Source of Learning and Development.* Englewood Cliffs, NJ: Prentice-Hall, 1984.

Lombardo, M. M., and Eichinger, R. W. *The Leadership Machine: Architecture to Develop Leaders for the Future.* Lominger Limited, Inc, 2002.

Luft, J., and Ingham, H. *The Johari Window, a Graphic Model of Interpersonal Awareness, Proceedings of the Western Training Laboratory in Group Development.* Los Angeles: UCLA, 1995.

Mayer, J., Salovey, P., and Caruso, D. "Emotional Intelligence: Theory, Findings, and Implications." *Psychological Inquiry* 15(3), 197–215.

McCall, M. W., Lombardo, M. M., and Morrison, A. M. *The Lessons of Experience: How Successful Executives Develop on the Job.* New York: The Free Press, 1988.

Mezirow, J. *Learning as Transformation: Critical Perspectives on a Theory in Progress.* San Francisco, CA: Jossey-Bass, 2000.

Pink, D. H. *A Whole New Mind: Why Right-Brainers Will Rule the Future.* New York: Riverhead Books, 2006.

Restak, R. *The Naked Brain: How the Emerging Neurosociety is Changing How we Live, Work, and Love.* New York: Harmony Books, 2006.

Scott, J. *Social Network Analysis: A Handbook*, 2nd ed. Thousand Oaks, CA: Sage, 2000.

Spencer, L. *Winning through Participation.* Dubuque, IA: Kendall Hunt Publishing Company, 1989.

Thomas, D. C., and Inkson, K. *Cultural Intelligence: People Skills for Global Business.* San Francisco, CA: Berrett-Koehler Publishers, 2003.

10

Addressing Conflict Head On

Getting real about diversity means having a dialogue about diversity's challenges and promise that rings true to the whole picture, rather than an airy notion of how we'd like things to be.

It means we will speak our truth, but know it is only one of many that make up the reality in which we swim.

— *Dr. George F. Simons, Co-Author, Cultural Diversity Sourcebook*

Thinking about diversity is easy. Doing the work is hard. Conflict results naturally when individuals with diverse perspectives work together. This is especially true when the group is working in pursuit of stretch goals to drive innovation and push the organization to grow. Ignoring this reality will not make it go away. For this reason we highlight the tenth leadership practice in this chapter:

Leadership Practice 10

Be Prepared to Address Misunderstanding, Resistance, and Conflict Head On.

Effective leadership means looking for creative ways to address differences and conflict head on. You must surface undiscussables by demanding straight talk (i.e., bringing water cooler conversations into strategic conversations). You must help build the organization's muscle to identify and work through differences. You must encourage difficult conversations to harness breakdowns (unmet promises to customers, to each other). In today's global context, handling disagreement productively requires uncovering the root causes of diversity-related breakdowns and responding with honesty and intention, while being mindful of the gap that often exists between intentions and impact. The capability to engage in productive conversations around difficult issues is a critical global leadership competency.

We all know that our conversations influence the quality of our relationships with others, and ultimately impact the results we realize at work. Yet how many times have you left a meeting thinking you had a good fix on what was said, only to find out later how wrong you were? With this in mind, the following story presents the upside of learning to communicate effectively:

WORKING TOGETHER IN A SYNERGISTIC WAY
(ADVICE FROM AN EXTERNAL DIVERSITY EXPERT)

When we talk about cultural diversity, I think we are talking about that aspect of diversity that has to do with people defining different types of behaviors, that are influenced by differences in values and beliefs, in the context of two or more cultures interacting. These often result in the various kinds of misunderstandings that are referred to as the downside of diversity.

But, on the up side, the kind of productivity and creativity, and general synthesis that can occur from having this hybridization going on, or having this interaction going where you are not amalgamating. You are not ... there's not a melting pot. These are people maintaining their differences but working together in a synergistic way.

Then we need to say, what happens given that we've got people who are culturally diverse coming in face-to-face contact and interacting with one another? What's the down side of that? How can we minimize the damage? What's the up side of it? How can we maximize the benefits?

— Co-Director
West Coast Based Intercultural Institute

One way leaders prepare themselves to productively address the misunderstandings, resistance, and conflict associated with diversity is by applying the Strategic Learning Model introduced in Chapter 1. In this model we first highlight the importance of clarifying contextual factors that trigger the diversity-based conflict. Next, we outline a number of cultural prototypes (versus stereotypes) and identify the vital few focus areas that would be useful for harnessing cultural-based breakdowns (or content). Finally, we describe how the human interaction skills outlined in the previous chapter can be used to reduce, if not resolve diversity-based conflict (or conduct, taking informed action).

Clarifying Contextual Factors Triggering Conflict in Organizations

Surfacing constructive contention is the key to building a capacity to identify and work through the variety of different opinions that are the result of different worldviews. We find out what needs to be changed in ourselves and in our organizations by surfacing tension and being open to a myriad of perspectives, while challenging our own point of view. When clarifying the contextual factors that trigger conflict in organization it is important to understand the nature of the phenomenon. Conflict in general and the tension that often occurs during intercultural interactions in particular, is natural — neither positive nor negative, good or bad — it just is.

Many of us are conditioned to view conflict, in any context, as bad. Many of us are acculturated to see conflict as something to be avoided, that is, we hold a "judger" mindset. If diversity is to be leveraged, this way of thinking needs to be transformed to a "learner" mindset where disagreement and conflict are viewed as opportunities for learning. When we approach conflict from the perspective of a learner mindset we can leverage conflict or disagreement as a motivator for discovery, expanded insight, and creativity. Differing perspectives are a part of life. The question is: *What do you do with conflict and disagreement when they occur?* Learning, collaboration, and growth are the goals of handling conflict productively, not winning and losing. Similarly, resistance can be reframed as a source of energy because a person who defends what they care about is involved and engaged.

It is also important to acknowledge that conflict is often a dynamic process that operates within each of us. As we interact with diverse others with different values and belief systems, many of our taken-for-granted assumptions about how organizations and life works are challenged. At its core, conflict is a perceived or actual incompatibility of goals, available resources, interests, and values; all amplified during cross-cultural interactions. Some sources of conflict in organizations are a reflection of conflict in patterns of behaviors and priorities, or issue tensions. Other sources of conflict reflect personal hot buttons.

Organizational Issue Tensions

Issue tensions are competing concerns that highlight conflicting interests and values amongst key organizational stakeholders (Nutt and Backoff, 1997, p. 493). Throughout the diversity learning and change process it is critical for senior leaders and others in the organization work to uncover issue tensions. When explicitly identified and productively addressed, these prompt divergent thinking and possibility thinking, both important for generating creative solutions. Table 10.1 presents descriptions of several issue tensions likely to surface in organizations, as well as related guiding questions to surface insights.

These four categories of issue tensions provide a useful contextual frame to use during the diversity discovery and assessment initiatives outlined in Chapter 6, and throughout the entire diversity learning and change process. Typically, the four categories listed in Table 10.1 are interconnected and dynamic in practice. For example, when equity and transition issue tensions are combined the guiding question at the root of the conflict is "*Who is effected by the change and how?*"

Issue tensions that combine transition and productivity concerns are rooted in the need to meet demands (e.g., from customers) during the change. Issue tensions related to preservation and productivity are triggered when change squeezes a stressed system steeped in tradition. Preservation and equity issues tensions emerge when fairness clashes with tradition. Dealing with inertia during change initiatives is often indicative of an issue tension involving preservation and transition. And lastly, productivity and equity issue tensions entail reconciling cost cutting with human commitments.

Personal Hot Buttons

Issue tensions provide a useful way to gain strategic insight regarding organizational, diversity-related factors that have the potential to trigger conflict at the group and systems level. In

TABLE 10.1 Identifying Issue Tensions

Category	Description	Sample Guiding Questions
Equity	Human resource needs that suggest equity concerns; concern with fair treatment related to opportunities for growth, development, contribution, and reward.	■ Whose interest will be served by a given change, people practice, policy, or procedure?
Preservation	The human and cultural need to maintain tradition; key stakeholders often desire to maintain the status quo during times of change; a focus on preserving the culture and related practices.	■ How will a given change impact the way we do things around here? Which identity groups serve to gain and lose as a result of the change? Which groups will not be impacted?
Productivity	Concern with the need to maintain or optimize output levels during times of change and adaptation; a focus on effectiveness and efficiency.	■ How do we diagnose the situation to determine the best course of action? Understand the impact of various stakeholder and/or identity groups? ■ What measures or indicators should/will be used to evaluate performance?
Transition	Concern with the "how" to manage proposed changes intended to respond to opportunities or environmental flux; focus on planning and clarifying expectations; understanding the new "rules of the game"	■ How do we effectively plan for this change? ■ What needs to be in place for us to succeed?

Source: Authors' adaptation of Paul C. Nutt and Robert W. Backoff's, *Facilitating Transformational Change* (1997, pp. 490–507).

addition, each of us has personal hot buttons, things that "set you off." These influence your emotional state. Spend a moment to complete the reflective prompts and questions in Table 10.2. Answer the questions to gain access to your hot buttons and their impact on your capacity to respond to conflict in intercultural situations.

Hot buttons are triggered when people:

- Challenge your competence or seem surprised by your intelligence/capabilities.
- Do not acknowledge your contributions, yet seem to pay attention to similar contributions made by others.
- Do not show you basic respect and dignity.

TABLE 10.2 Tool: Identifying Culturally Based Diversity Hot Buttons

Directions: Use the space below to generate a list of people and situations that trigger your emotional "hot buttons" and think about the implications for you. How do they impact your responses to intercultural resistance and conflict?	

Question/Reflective Prompt	Responses...
List a series of situations and/or things people do that "push your buttons," that is trigger negative reactions (e.g., fear, anger, shame, frustration, confrontation, or flight)? Write down your top five.	1. 2. 3. 4. 5.
Review your responses and consider the following question for each: *What is the impact or influence of people from other groups or cultures? Do they push your hot buttons?*	
As you examine your responses above: *In what ways do your cultural values and beliefs influence how you respond to hot buttons in general, and those that involve intercultural interactions in particular?*	

Insights: What are your major take a ways from this reflective activity. What did you learn?

- Act in ways that you find condescending.
- Provide you with unsolicited advice.

In her work, *Barriers to Equality* (1990), Mary Rowe of Harvard University describes a particular form of hot buttons, which she calls micro-inequities. These involve a subtle form of discrimination involving a perpetrator and a victim. Also referred to as micro-aggressions, these hot buttons are characterized by slight, verbal, or non-verbal personal assaults that are often ephemeral and covert. As such they result in hard-to-prove events embedded in a history of superiority and inferiority dynamics among identity group members, such as Whites and Blacks in the United States, or between men and women in certain male-dominated industries (Franklin, 1999).

Further, perpetrators are generally unaware that they commit micro-inequities. When confronted, their typical response is that of being "surprised," seeing the "other" as "overreacting" or being "highly sensitive," or at best, they say the perceived assault was unintentional. These situations are all too familiar to the victims who can readily innumerate a list of examples of these behaviors that are committed by others in the perpetrator's cultural, often racial identity group. When the reaction of the victim is that of anger, rage, or other intense forms of confrontation, it is generally because the current situation served as the trigger or tipping point resulting from the cumulative effect of experiencing literately 100s or even 1,000s of these slights daily.

Micro-inequities can induce disillusionment, self-doubt, guilt, confusion, and loss of hope because such experiences tend to eat at an individual's core and self-confidence over time, if they do not have productive coping strategies. Micro-inequities can take the form of comments the victim experiences as derogatory or insulting, for example a Black American being told by colleagues "you are a credit to your race," or the ever common statement "wow you are so articulate" made at the end of a presentation; or an Asian American being asked their country of origin (i.e., being a foreigner in your own land). These are rather subtle examples of what happens daily in our workplace and reflect the multiple realities that are experienced in any given organization based on identity group membership.

Micro-inequities come in a variety of behavioral forms. A common scene involves a woman making a recommendation during a meeting that is ignored or not acknowledged, and moments later the same idea is presented by a male colleague who receives a positive reaction from the group. What is the woman to do in this situation? How does she feel, and what options are available to her if this is a common occurrence? Other behavioral examples include people of color having difficulty haling taxis in urban areas; young men of color being followed by security guards in retail establishments or the racial profiling that occurs when they drive an expensive car in an "upscale" part of town and get stopped by the police for no apparent reason.

Because we know that issue tensions, hot buttons, and micro-inequities occur in social and workplace settings, the strategic learning capability of contextual awareness places an emphasis on looking for evidence of these patterns, especially when misunderstandings, resistance, or conflict surface during intercultural interactions. Responding productively to diversity-related breakdowns involves gathering and sharing information about issues, interests, and needs from multiple perspectives; and, acknowledging that reactions often extend beyond and reflect more than the present situation.

Diverse perspectives provide opportunities for enhanced learning because they often surface tension around issues. These tensions trigger learning. Ronald Heifetz (Flower, 1995) said, "If people don't engage across the divide of their differences, there is no learning ... people don't learn by looking in the mirror. They learn by talking with people who have different points of view." The conflict that results from asking people with different worldviews to tackle an issue is in essence the engine of adaptive diversity work.

When a breakdown occurs as a result of a diversity-based conflict, you have an opportunity to grow as you reflect on your approach, as well as others' approach, to conflict. Mitchell R. Hammer, Ph.D., President of Hammer Consulting LLC and noted intercultural communications expert, developed the *Intercultural Conflict Style Inventory* (ICSI). This inventory assesses culturally learned approaches to managing disputes or disagreements in terms of direct or indirect communication approaches and the emotionally expressiveness or restraint associated with one's response to conflict. Figure 10.1 displays Hammer's (2002, 2003) Intercultural Conflict Styles Model that reveals four general approaches, or styles to conflict based on four factors.

When thinking about how to apply the strategic learning capability of contextual awareness to situations having the potential for intercultural conflict, we find that we must examine three contextual factors: (1) the nature of conflict in general, (2) common issue tensions that emerge at the group and organizational level of the system, and (3) the importance of personal hot buttons as contextual factors related to intercultural conflict. A combination of these three factors helps you to situate and focus on the "where" in time and place and the "why" of the various factors that serves as triggers of intercultural conflict in organizations. We next apply the

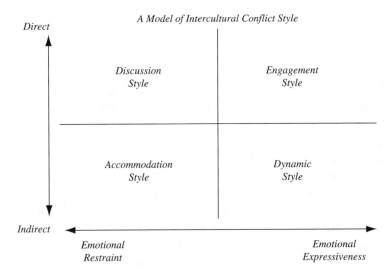

FIGURE 10.1 Intercultural Conflict Styles Model.

second strategic learning capability, conceptual clarity, to situations involving intercultural conflict.

Identifying the Vital Few Factors for Harnessing Diversity-Based Breakdowns

Applying the strategic learning capability of contextual awareness amplifies your ability to focus your attention on multiple perspectives when various intercultural conflicts emerge. The emphasis of conceptual clarity is to identify those vital few factors that must be in place to align your action strategies with the context. You do this so that diversity-based breakdowns can be effectively harnessed during intercultural interactions. Conceptual clarity focuses on: (1) determining the sources of the specific conflicts and (2) exploring relevant cultural prototypes needed to take informed action.

Determine the Source of the Conflict or the Breakdown

There are many sources of conflict in organizations from *organizational conflicts* (e.g., resource allocation), *informational conflicts* (e.g., access to information), *interest-based conflicts* (e.g., based on function or location), *interpersonal* (e.g., personality clashes within identity groups), or *cultural conflicts* (e.g., between identity groups based on differences in values, backgrounds, and beliefs systems). Taking informed action to harness breakdowns requires understanding the source of conflict and having an appropriate response. The strategic learning capability of conceptual clarity emphasizes working to understand the source of conflict prior to determining how to respond to it or not.

Figure 10.2 displays a tool from the field of organizational development for distinguishing between four sources of conflict that can occur in the absence of alignment (Rath & Strong Management Consultants, 1994). Unfortunately we often misdiagnose many situations involving conflicts as poor interpersonal or cultural relations, when often such conflicts are in part or completely related to a lack of goal alignment, role clarity, or unclear operating procedures related to problem solving, decision-making and communication. In the absence of clarity in these areas, it is easy for interpersonal and cultural factors to take center stage.

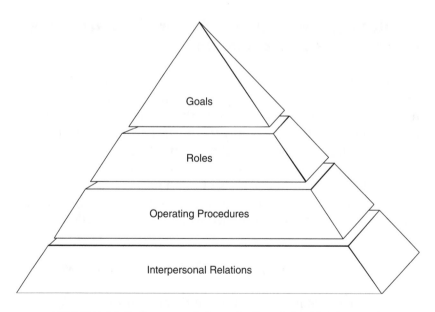

FIGURE 10.2 Sources of Organizational Conflict Pyramid.

Operating Procedures

When experiencing what is perceived as an interpersonal issue, particularly during intercultural interactions, it is helpful to "walk-up" the "sources of organizational conflict pyramid." That is, before assuming the person or people you are interacting with are uncooperative, rigid, or otherwise unhelpful, start by exploring the extent to which operating procedures related to problem solving, decision-making, methods of communication, and processes for dealing with disagreement are clear between parties. Is the conflict or misunderstanding a function of variations in access to relevant information, or the way available information is analyzed or interpreted? Or is the conflict embedded in other organizational factors such as allocation of resources and implementation of various policies? These are common sources of organizational conflict that are often misinterpreted as interpersonal or cultural in nature.

Roles

If your assessment determines that the conflict is not operational or procedural in nature, then move to the next level of the pyramid, that is role clarity and role conflict. Role clarity has to do with the scope of your work in terms of core responsibilities and tasks in relation to achieving one's personal and organizational goals. While role conflict is a boundary issue where the scope of one's role is not clearly differentiated from work performed by others. Asking good questions will help you to gain a high degree of conceptual clarity in these areas. The following questions are often useful in exploring role clarity:

- Are the roles of the parties involved clear or are they ambiguous?
- Does each party know what they can expect from the other?
- Does each party understand and accept their roles, or are some in need of renegotiation?

The following questions are often useful in examining potential role conflicts:

- Are there embedded conflicts in the way the roles among various parties are currently defined, such that meeting the expectations of one party violates the expectations of another?

- Are there other stakeholders (besides the involved parties) whose expectations create role conflicts for some of the parties? If so, what options might be explored to help resolve these situations?

Asking questions, or "Question thinking," can quickly resolve many role-based issues and related conflicts. Yet if left unattended, what start off as relatively minor role-based challenges can escalate to major interpersonal problems, especially when working across cultural boundaries.

Goals

Once you have determined that both operating procedures and roles are clear, then move to the top of the pyramid and confirm goal alignment. Goal clarity and alignment play a central role in organizational life and make a significant contribution to organizational effectiveness. In short, our work at the individual, team, and organizational levels is defined by our collective goals. Question thinking can help to ensure that goals are clear and people have in fact signed up for their individual goals in the context of broader organizational strategic priorities. The following are questions to help clarify goals:

- What are each party's goals (recall the SMART criteria)? What is to be accomplished by the goal?
- Will they/have they been given to each party? Or is each party to be involved in formulating their own goals?
- How are each party's goals connected to key strategic organizational priorities? How are each party's goals related to each other?
- What are the boundaries to each party's goals?
- Do all parties have a clear and common understanding of their individual and collective goals?
- To what degree has each party accepted and committed to their individual and collective goals?

This list may appear to be basic, yet it is surprising how many employees indicate a lack of clarity around expectations related to goals, roles, and "how things work around here," as evidenced by the results of the Gallup Organization's employment engagement research. Recall from Chapter 8 that of the 12 factors in the Gallup

Q12 assessment, "I know what is expected of me" was the most important factor associated with high performing individuals and teams.

It is possible that when you have completed your walk-up the "Sources of Organizational Conflict Pyramid" you will have confirmed that you were in fact dealing with an interpersonal conflict (e.g., personality clashes, emotional incompatibility, or communication difficulties) or culture-based conflict. In the next section we discuss a framework for enhancing intercultural communications and relations.

Explore Cultural Prototypes

Intercultural communications is a unique form of interpersonal interaction. In Chapter 1 we drew on insights from the field of organizational behavior to describe various individual differences that reflect personal dimensions of diversity. These include both *personality factors* (e.g., extraversion or agreeableness) and *personal style factors* (or preferences) such as learning style, decision-making, and approaches to problem solving. Clearly, there is considerable style variation within identity groups. Our focus here is to introduce you to tool to help you understand how a number of cultural factors combine to create a variety of cultural prototypes, illuminating how you and others approach conflict.

Figure 10.3 (Hofstede and Hofstede, 2005; Lewicki et al., 2005; Simons and Abramms, 1996; Thompson, 2005) displays nine "universal" cultural factors. When these are applied to various identity groups they result in a number of cultural prototypes. Prototypes provide a general map for understanding and constructing productive responses to local intercultural interactions, including conflict.

We intentionally position this cultural frame as "prototypes" vs. the stereotypes we discussed in Chapter 2. Stereotypes, when uniformly applied to a given identity group, can result in misunderstanding at best, and prejudice, discrimination, and other "isms" at their worse. A cultural prototype represents a typical profile for a given identity group. Prototypes can be used as a starting point when facing new cultural situations characterized by uncertainty and the unexpected, and as such the content of each should be based on observation and interaction prior to confirmation.

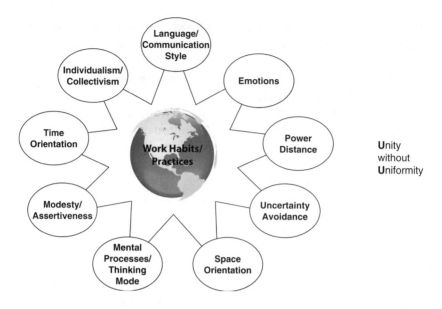

FIGURE 10.3 Cultural Factors and Prototypes.

Table 10.3 (Lewicki et al., 2005; and Thompson, 2005) is a tool that provides descriptions of nine cultural factors. Each of the factors contains two or more variations resulting in over 300 possible combinations of cultural prototypes, demonstrating the complexity of intercultural interaction. The tool serves as a resource for making you more aware of the influence of cultural programming on how you approach intercultural conflict, resistance, and other forms of disagreements. It can also be used as a planning tool when you anticipate interacting with culturally diverse others. There are a growing number of resources available that catalogue countries by these cultural factors. Geert Hofstede and Gert Jan Hofstede's (2005) book, *Cultures and Organizations Software of the Mind,* suggests several cultural factors including: (1) power distance (i.e., the degree of inequality in society), (2) the individualism (i.e., "I" focused) and collectivism (i.e., "we" focused) continuum, (3) gender roles (or the assertiveness-masculinity and modesty — femininity continuum, (4) uncertainty avoidance (i.e., tolerance of ambiguity), and (5) time orientation (i.e., past, present, and/or future).

Mitchell R. Hammer's, *Intercultural Conflict Style Inventory* (ICSI) – *Facilitator Manual,* provides country profiles based on the communication (direct and indirect) and emotion (expressed and

TABLE 10.3 Nine Cultural Dimensions

Guidelines for using this resource — Review the descriptions related to each of the nine cultural dimensions listed below. These can help you better understand the nature and origins of your cultural programming. Knowledge of these cultural variations can also enhance your observational skills, especially when you are interacting across cultures. They can serve as a basis for effectively adapting your thinking and behavior appropriately during cross-cultural interactions

Dimension: *Communication*

Direct communication pattern (low context) — To the point, potentially blunt communication approach; use of precise, explicit language to state needs, offers and related rationale; reliance on face-to-face (or other direct modes) resolution of disagreements; speaking one's mind including difference of opinion; persuasion through logic; substantive disagreement; in short the meaning is the "message." Prefer direct information exchange and direct questions	*Indirect communication pattern* (high context) — Diplomatic, more circular approach to communication; the meaning is often "outside" the verbal message (e.g., rely on prior experience or reputation); ambiguity and vagueness in language use; reliance on third parties for resolution of disagreements; use of discretion in voicing goals; might "talk around" disagreements; persuasion through face-work (i.e., protecting one's public honor); place a priority on preserving and repairing relationships

Dimension: *Emotions*

Emotional expressiveness — Overt, external display of emotions; visible display of feelings through nonverbal and expansive vocalization; relational trust demonstrated by the explicit display of feelings. View emotional information necessary for credibility	*Emotional restraint* — Often disguise display of public emotions; minimal display of feelings through non-verbal behavior; constrained vocalizations because of sensitivity to hurting the feelings of other party; relational trust through emotional maturity; emotional suppression necessary for credibility

Dimension: *Relational focus*

Individualism — "I" focus, driven by an individualistic motivational orientation; goal is to maximize own gain; source of identity is the "self" where people regard themselves as free agents and independent actors. In individualistic societies there is the belief that everyone should be treated alike, *universalism*	*Collectivism* — "We" or "team" focus, a very strong "group" orientation; goal is to maximize the welfare of the group or collective; source of identity is the group; individuals regard themselves as group members; place an emphasis on social relations. The distinction between "our group" and "other groups" is central, treating one's friends and family better than others is natural and ethical, or *particularism*

Dimension: *Power distance*

Small power distance (Egalitarians) — inequalities among people should be minimized; social relationships should be handled with care; there should be, to some extent, interdependence between less and more powerful people; people from various age groups are viewed as equals; decentralization is popular in	*Large power distance* (Hierarchists) — inequalities among people are expected, and to some extent desired; status should be balanced with restraint; less powerful people should be dependent; younger people are taught to be obedient as a basic sign of respect and lifelong virtue; authority figures are to take initiative and

TABLE 10.3 (*Continued*)

organizations with this cultural orientation; managers rely on their own experience; few levels; the use of power should be legitimate and follow criteria of good and bad; often regard best alternative to a negotiated agreement to be major source of bargaining power	control; centralization is popular in organizations with this cultural orientation; managers rely on superiors and on formal rules; might prevails over right; the powerful are right and good; regard social order to be important in resolving conflict

Dimension: *Uncertainty avoidance*

Low/weak uncertainty avoidance (Flexibility) — more risk taking, see uncertainty as a normal feature of life and each day is accepted as it comes; there is tolerance for ambiguity and chaos; aggression and emotions should not be shown; what is "different" is viewed with curiosity and as a potential resource; more changes in employment, shorter service; there should be no more rules than necessary; top management is concerned with strategy; time is a framework for orientation; generalists and common sense focused; and tolerance, even for extreme ideas	*High/strong uncertainty avoidance* (Need for order) — more risk avoiding, the uncertainty inherent in life is a continuous threat that must be controlled; aggression and emotions may at times, in proper situations be ventilated; fear of ambiguous situations; what is "different" is dangerous; fewer changes in employment; there is an emotional need for rules; top management is concerned with daily operations; time is money; there is a need for precision and formalization; expertise and technological solution focused; repression of extremism

Dimension: *Degree of assertiveness*

Assertive (Masculinity) — competitive and tough; focus on challenge, earnings, recognition, and advancement; management as decisive and aggressive; rewards are based on equity; resolution of conflicts expects the strongest to win; humanization of work by job content enrichment; control over	*Modesty* (Femininity) — collaborative and open; relationships and quality of life are important; management as intuitive and consensus seeking; rewards are equality and fair treatment; resolution of conflicts by compromise through dialogue; humanization of work by contact and cooperation

Dimension: *Time orientation*

Past — fixed; focus on history, stories, and ancestry is important; tight, punctuality and deadlines; respect for tradition	*Present* — short term; here-and-now focused; spontaneous; cyclical; seasons, events, rhythms of life and death; produce quick results	*Future* — more fluid; longer term; forward and possibility thinking, planning and imagining; respect for circumstances

Dimension: *Mental processes/Operating mode*

Doing — on the move, task-oriented; "don't just sit there, do something" *Deductive thinking* — a tendency to move from the general to the specific, from principles to action *Judger mindset* — reactive, more automatic thinking; either/or thinking; very focused and sometimes rigid; depends on positions; more statements and opinions; emphasis on the external, or outside-in	*Being* — content to relax; "don't just do something, demonstrate presence" *Inductive thinking* — a tendency to move from the specific to the general, from particulars to principles *Learner mindset* — responsive, more reflective and intentional thinking; both/ and thinking, often flexible and adaptive; questions assumptions; more questions and engaging from a position of curiosity; inside-out

TABLE 10.3 (*Continued*)

Dimension: *Space orientation*	
Public — comfortable with social space and require less personal distance between self and others, often engage in and comfortable with touching and other forms of public human contact	*Private* — prefer more intimate social interactions; require more personal space during social interaction, when people get too close during conversation one feels like the "other" is "in your face" and will back away

Your Personal "Cultural Profile"	
In the space provided below, for each of the nine cultural dimensions, list the factor that best reflects your cultural preferences in a majority of situations:	
Self	*Partner*
1.	
2.	
3.	
4.	
5.	
6.	
7.	
8.	
9.	
Insights:	

restrained) cultural factors. The tool presented in Table 10.3 draws heavily on the field of intercultural negotiations as a framework for understanding cultural factors to shape our worldview.

Taking Informed Action to Address Diversity-Based Conflict and Resistance

Much of the work related to crafting productive responses to diversity-based conflict and resistance is done by applying the two strategic learning capabilities of contextual awareness and conceptual clarity. If done well, taking informed action is a natural progression of this work. Here we outline how to operationalize the insights gained through contextual awareness and conceptual clarity. Taking informed action in the context of intercultural conflict involves: (1) applying the foundational communication skills outlined in Chapter 9 to implement your response in dialogue with diverse others and (2) aligning actions strategies with the nature of the resistance or source of conflict.

Apply Foundation Communication Skills

Figure 10.4 presents a process model for applying selected founda-tional communication skills to take informed action when crafting productive responses to culturally based conflicts involving diversity. The relating, questioning and listening skills are used in a cycle as a platform for clarifying the nature of the presenting conflict, resistance, or form of disagreement. The figure displays four common forms of disagreements. Each requires a different response or informed action.

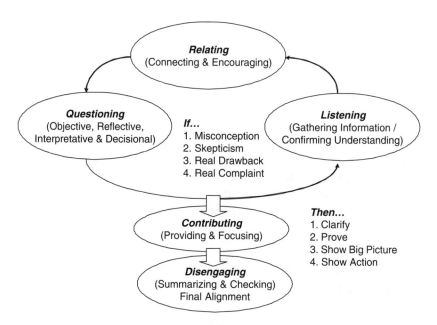

FIGURE 10.4 Process Model for Addressing Conflict and Disagreement.

TABLE 10.4 Aligning Actions with Context and Content
(Intentions and Outcomes)

If...	Then...
Misconception A person believes in a concept, or holds a point-of-view, which is objectively false or not totally accurate. Misconceptions are often a reflection of deeply ingrained mental models, the maps that we use to make sense of the world.	*Clarify* Fill-in the elements that may have been filtered out by others, as a result of different perspectives or assumptions, to reduce misunderstanding. In cross-cultural interactions this often involves closing the gap between ones "intentions" and the actual "impact" of one's actions or approach.
Skepticism When a person expresses doubt, caution, or a lack of confidence in a given claim or lacks confidence in the motives of others.	*Prove* Provide a compelling argument, that reflects rigor using approaches or evidence that others value or find trustworthy where possible (fact/data focused).
Real drawback When the person's resistance or objection is grounded in an actual disadvantage, shortcoming, or political issue.	*Show the big picture* Acknowledge the drawback and explore potential connections to larger goals or strategies, unintended consequences; reframe to focus on common aims.
Real complaint When a person expresses displeasure as a result of a gap in expectations, an agreed upon level of performance, or misalignment.	*Show action* Focus on potential actions or other strategies to remedy the situation in ways that are satisfactory to the other party and restores the relationship·

Once you confirm the nature of the conflict, then the figure suggests you progress to the contributing stage of the process model by applying the providing and focusing components of the contributing skill to co-create a resolution appropriate to the specific situation and context (see Table 10.4). It is at this point of the process that the insights gained from the strategic learning capability of contextual awareness are applied. These are combined with the focus and alignment that results from the learning capability of conceptual clarity and they all come together in an integrated way.

Align Action Strategy with Context and Content

When you apply the foundational communication skills in sequence they provide a foundation for aligning actions with the context and relevant content as listed in Table 10.4. We close the chapter by sharing a number of insights that have emerged from our work with clients in devising strategies to harness breakdowns.

First is acknowledging one of the most common errors in productively addressing conflict, the habit of using the same response without regard to the nature of the disagreement. By now, it is clear that there are many sources, forms, and responses to conflict. Yet, habits-of-mind are hard to change, even when doing so is in our best interest. It is estimated that if you use the same response regardless of the situation, you are likely to address conflict successfully roughly 20% of the time!

Second is recognizing that conflict is neither good nor bad, and certainly is a part of the package when you bring people with diverse perspectives together in the workplace. While it is counterintuitive for most, the approach outlined in this chapter suggests that you actually engage in situations involving conflict, not avoid them. You do this by encouraging others to talk about and clarify the nature of the disagreement or objection before you attempt to respond to it. A prerequisite to aligning actions with the cultural context and relevant content involves encouraging others to talk and express their views, needs, interests, and requirements. You listen and ask additional questions until you are confident that you know the nature and source of the "real" conflict. It is in the process of questioning and focused listening that people discover the common ground needed to bridge differences.

Third, the Process Model for Addressing Conflict and Disagreement presented in this chapter provides a framework to slow down and as William Ury, Author of *Getting Past No* suggests "go to the balcony" and look at the situations involving cultural-based conflict more objectively. The balcony is a metaphor for taking yourself off the dance floor in the middle of the conflict and placing yourself in a position where you can see what's going on more clearly. The developmental sequence of focusing on context and content before action is a strategy for slowing down the process, going to the balcony, and taking on a learner mindset to productively adapt to various intercultural interactions.

Fourth, harnessing breakdowns is a cultural discipline of surfacing misalignment in expectations. It is a discipline that requires identifying their source and clarifying related consequences of not productively addressing them and the payoffs for doing so. That is, it is important to make explicit the upside of gaining realignment and the downside of failure. We are skilled at either avoiding or dodging touchy issues at work. This has the unfortunate consequence of limiting our individual and collective learning capacity. The discipline of harnessing breakdowns requires an insistence on uncompromising straight talk, as well as committing to a set of new behaviors to prevent a repeated cycle of breakdowns.

Fifth, dealing with hot buttons, issue tensions, and other forms of intercultural conflict involve engaging in dialogue focused on: (1) reviewing what was "supposed to happen" or what each party "wanted to happen," (2) examining the gap in expectations by sharing perceptions of what "did happen," (3) determining what "needs to happen" to repair the breakdown while identifying common ground, and (4) committing to explicit behavioral change to restore alignment (in an existing relationship) or to create alignment (in a new relationship).

Lastly, understanding the distinction between two forms of conversation-dialogue and discussion – is important. Understanding the differences will help you follow the process model for productively addressing conflict and disagreement that we discussed earlier in this chapter. As outline in Table 10.5, this method requires an emphasis on the meaning-making process of dialogue on the front end and progressively moving toward discussion.

Because each conversational form is guided by very different intentions, these differences represent more than a matter of semantics. Further, the conversational tactics used for effective dialogue and discussion also differ. And importantly, each contributes to the nature of our relationships with others in different ways.

Our purpose in highlighting the distinctions between dialogue and discussion is not to suggest that one is better or more effective than the other. Rather, our aim is to recognize that most conversations include a mixture of these two ways of communicating, and being clear about the different intentions that guide each form is important for taking informed action and realizing our intentions. Having this awareness will help you diagnos the context, identify the conversational form being used at any moment, determine whether it is consistent with your intentions and shift where necessary to the form

TABLE 10.5 Productive Conversations: Two Forms

	Dialogue (Meaning Making)	Discussion (Persuading)
Form	Divergent conversation — an opening up, multiple perspectives, opinions and options	Convergent conversation — a narrowing down, one "best" perspective, opinion, option, or decision
Intention	Defining the nature of the problem, challenge or opportunity	Make a decision on the course of immediate or future action
Tactics	Working to see the whole among and connections between the parts, seeking to understand what others mean; inquiring into assumptions	Breaking issues/problems into parts; use of logic and reasoning, rational problem solving; justifying and defending assumptions
Nature of relationship	Collaborative, comparatively longer term; people focused	Competitive, comparatively short term; problem focused

Source: Authors adaptation from Linda Ellinor, and Glenna Gerard's, *Dialogue: Rediscover the Transforming Power of Conversation* (1998, pp. 20–25); Roy J. Lewicki, and David M. Saunders, Bruce Barry and John W. Minton's, *Essentials of Negotiation* (3rd ed., 2004, pp. 28–58).

that best aligns with the desired results you and others would like to achieve.

Dialogue

When we talk with each other in order to learn from one another and to reach common understanding, then dialogue is the preferred form of conversation. It is important to understand the conditions or factors that make this form of conversation effective, they include situations where:

- The problem is ill defined and multiple areas of specialization are needed to frame the issue.
- The expertise needed to make an informed decision and take collective action is distributed amongst more than one individual.
- The level of acceptance by those needed to effectively implement the decision is high, if people responsible for implementing a decision do not agree with it, there are often problems with execution and quality.

Discussion

On the other hand, when the main intention of those engaged in the conversation is achieve a degree of closure, make a decision or reach agreement on one course of action, then discussion is often both an effective and efficient form of conversation. The conditions for this form include situations where:

- Decision maker(s) has relevant expertise and is familiar with the specific situation.
- The acceptance level from others not directly involved in making the decision is not critical to successful execution of the decision.
- Available time for decision-making is limited and responsiveness in delivering a solution that is roughly 80 percent technically correct is the priority.
- There is an emergency, there is no time to consult with others and explore multiple perspectives, even when doing so might lead to a technically better or more acceptable decision.

Our experience shows that if the purpose of a conversation is not clearly stated, people tend to operate in ways more consistent with discussion vs. dialogue. This is a result of our bias toward action and decisiveness in western cultures. Given the reality of globalization and the increased diversity of workplaces around the world, it makes sense to work toward achieving a level of balance between these two conversational forms to enhance understanding.

In addition, research on creativity and innovation indicates that wherever possible using more dialogic forms of conversation early during the interaction, problem solving or decision-making process opens things up. This provides access to a broader set of options and possibilities informed by various perspectives. It has the added effect of fostering understanding, building commitment, and enhancing relationships. It is also true that organizations need to generate results, and so the ability to integrate different perspectives into an agreed-upon solution and set of actions is crucial for effective execution. Gaining access to all available talent in an organization is in part due to one's ability to productively address conflict and other forms of disagreement. In the final chapter of this part of the book we share what we have learned about key considerations when leaders are looking to secure advice and support for cultural diversity initiatives.

References

Ellinor, L., and Gerard, G. *Dialogue: Rediscover the Transforming Power of Conversation.* New York: Wiley, 1998.

Flower, J. "A Conversation with Ronald Heifetz: Leadership without Easy Answers." *The Healthcare Forum Journal* 38(4) (1995).

Franklin, A. J. "Invisibility Syndrome and Racial Identity Development in Psychotherapy and Counseling African American Men." *Counseling Psychologist* 27(6) (1999): 761–793.

Hammer, M. R. The Intercultural Conflict Style (ICS) Inventory (Self published psychometric instrument), 2002.

Hammer, M. R. *The Intercultural Conflict Style Inventory: Facilitator's manual.* North Potomac, MD: Hammer Consulting Group, 2003.

Hammer, M. R. "The Intercultural Conflict Style Inventory: A Conceptual Framework and Measure of Intercultural Conflict Resolution Approaches." *International Journal of Intercultural Relations* 29 (2005): 675–695.

Hofstede, G., and Hofstede, G. J. *Cultures and Organizations Software of the Mind: Intercultural Cooperation and Its Importance for Survival.* New York: McGraw-Hill, 2005.

Lewicki, R. J., Saunders, D. M., Barry, B., and Minton, J. W. *Essentials of Negotiation*, 3rd ed. Boston, MA: McGraw Hill/Irwin, 2004, pp. 405–445.

Lewicki, R. J., Saunders, D. M., Barry, B., and Minton, J. W. *Negotiation*, 5th ed. Boston, MA: McGraw Hill/Irwin, 2005.

Nutt, P. C., and Backoff, R. W. "Facilitating Transformational Change." *The Journal of Applied Behavioral Science* 33(4) (1997): 490–508.

Rath & Strong Management Consultants. *Facilitation Skills Workshop*, Lexington, MA, 1994.

Rowe, M. P. "Barriers to Equality: The Power of Subtle Discrimination to Maintain Unequal Opportunity." *Employee Responsibilities and Rights Journal* 3(2) (1990): 153–163.

Simons, F., and Abramms, B. *Cultural Diversity Sourcebook: The Questions of Diversity.* Amherst, MA: ODT Inc, 1996.

Thompson L. L. *The Mind and Heart of the Negotiator*, 3rd ed. Upper Saddle River, NJ: Pearson, Prentice Hall, 2005, pp. 242–262.

11

Finding Help in All the Right Places

All worthwhile helping frameworks, models, or processes ultimately help clients ask and answer for themselves four fundamental questions: (1) What's going on? (2) What do I need or want that I don't have now? (3) What do I have to do to get what I need or want? and (4) How do I get results?

— *Gerard Egan, The Skillful Helper*

Leading to leverage diversity will require that you gather the most able minds from inside and outside your organization and probe for a diversity of perspectives and experiences (e.g., customers, suppliers, researchers, and other cutting edge thinkers). Remember that in today's competitive business environment organizations become more vulnerable as their leadership becomes more homogeneous.

Leveraging diversity is a complex, learning and change process requiring a vast array of talent. Leaders cannot tackle this job alone, nor do most want to. Often CEOs and other senior leaders state their commitment to diversity, and understandably they do not know what to do. The easiest route is to turn to a newly appointed internal diversity practitioner, or an external diversity expert, and suggest: "just tell us what to do and we'll do it." However, this is a mistake.

Leveraging diversity entails a major cultural shift across the organization. Crane (2002) suggests, "As a successful cultural-change initiative unfolds, it should be obvious to every member of the culture that leaders embrace the change. Senior leaders must share full accountability for the success of the initiative, even if the change effort includes the use of outside consultants" (p. 205).

225

If leveraging diversity is to be seen in the organization as a vital leadership responsibility, then senior leaders must be seen as diversity champions. This happens when they approach diversity as they would any other organizational imperative. If the typical course of action is for senior leaders to actively engage in the definition of strategic initiatives, they need to do the same with this strategic initiative. Any departure from the normal mode of operation determines how others will perceive a leader's level of commitment. Like other major strategic initiatives, leveraging diversity requires a "walks the talk" effort. That said, you will need to find and use trusted advisors and experts to help make your organization's efforts to leverage cultural diversity a success, the leadership practice of focus of this chapter.

Leadership Practice 11

Consult Prudent, Capable and Trusted Advisors.

Internal diversity leaders and external diversity experts are generally hired to serve as advisors, coaches, and mentors to the CEO and other senior executives. The learning and change associated with the cultural transformation characteristic of the current wave of the diversity movement requires that the senior leaders have the support of an advisor who serves in the role of executive "diversity" coach. The coach's job is to serve the leader in a supportive role while challenging the leader to explore their own assumptions, values, and actions as they relate to diversity, as well as illuminating a way for the leader to imagine a new and different future. This sort of relationship was viewed as a critical aid in our research for helping the leader develop, implement, and sustain the deep and far-reaching changes needed for personal and organizational transformation. A trusting relationship between the leader and their diversity coach provides the foundation for igniting the personal courage needed to tackle the multiple challenges that will emerge during the various stages of this cultural transformation.

Because the cultural transformation is an ongoing process, senior leaders will need the support of an executive diversity coach for at least the first year or two of the diversity initiative so that they can sustain their commitment and effectively model the new cultural behaviors. It is foolish to spend massive resources on window dressing — leveraging diversity takes deep personal change followed by behaviors demonstrating new values, beliefs, and expectations. To make these changes leaders need ongoing dialog and feedback from experienced diversity coaches, who will help them uncover their assumptions, expand their beliefs systems, and reflect on their actions. If leaders do not change in a demonstrable way, the culture will not change and any efforts to leverage diversity will be wasted.

In addition to serving as an executive diversity coach, both external and internal advisors help their clients drive various diversity initiatives as a comprehensive change process by (Lewin, 1958; Lippitt and Lippitt 1986; Schein, 2004):

- Defining the desired and current state with regard to an organization's ability to productively attract, value, manage, and leverage diverse to talent.
- Accurately accessing the distance between these two states through a process of critical thinking and diagnostic work; and
- Proposing, co-creating, and assisting in the implementation of cost-effective diversity interventions to close the gap.

A well-respected external diversity expert in our study viewed his role as an advisor and, more specifically, a strategist. He described five strategic considerations related to effectiveness in this work: (1) tying diversity work to specific business needs (e.g., market diversity or attracting diverse talent); (2) inviting input and co-creating interventions with those most affected by various changes; (3) eliciting the support of external stakeholders; (4) aligning diversity work with other organizational initiatives in place; and (5) keeping all stakeholders informed of the progress of all diversity initiatives and providing opportunities for ongoing input and feedback. Leaders, who successfully leverage diversity, use a variety of external and internal resources to help guide the diversity learning process and related cultural transformation. Both external and diversity practitioners provide three broad areas of assistance as displayed in Table 11.1.

Approach Drives Results

When looking to engage an external diversity expert or select an internal diversity practitioner, it is important to understand that these "experts" often see themselves filling different roles. How they

TABLE 11.1 Three Broad Areas of Assistance

Component	Description
Climate setting	Working to help clients create productive learning and work climates through surfacing the various experiences including identifying motives, interests, and needs to provide a safe space for exploring multiple realities.
Diagnostic work	Designing and developing diversity interventions, including upfront and on-going diagnostic and assessment work to understand the strategic context needed to focus and take informed action.
Implementation	Providing a mix of support and challenge in leading the diversity change process to trigger new levels of learning and making necessary adjustments in the moment to take informed action to leverage diversity for high performance.

FIGURE 11.1 Diversity Practitioner Role Identities.

view themselves influences the approach they take and the results they get. Generally, they identify with one (or a combination) of the six roles displayed in Figure 11.1.

Recognizing the importance of the preferred ways different diversity practitioners engaged in this work should be an important consideration when selecting both internal and external diversity professionals to support you in your leadership role. The important point to remember is that none of these six profiles are innately better than the other. Yet, given the influence that role identity has on how various diversity practitioner approach their work, understanding these tendencies is helpful in assisting organizational leaders to determine the form of support they need during different legs of the journey. Regardless of the role identity different diversity practitioners take on, our research reveals that there are three broad areas of assistance leaders need as they work to leverage diversity in organizations (Egan, 2002; see Table 11.1).

Table 11.2 provides brief descriptions of the six diversity practitioner role identities. Some organizations start the diversity journey by identifying an internal person to guide the leadership team in devising a diversity strategy and related initiatives. Others begin by getting advice from diversity experts outside of the organization, including consulting forms, research institutes with a focus on workplace diversity.

Other organizations seek assistance from civil rights groups such as the National Association for the Advancement of Colored People (NAACP), Leadership Conference on Civil Rights (LCCR), National Asian Pacific American Legal Consortium and the Gay and Lesbian Alliance Against Defamation (GLAAD). However, an internal expert noted "Civil rights groups can help but they can't solve issues embedded in your corporate culture ... it really starts with the CEO and other senior leaders, the chief architects of corporate culture."

Securing Help from Internal Sources

Internal diversity professionals have a unique challenge when compared to their external counterparts. Serving as advisors and strategists they provide diversity-related guidance to senior leaders and other key organizational stakeholders. Additionally, they often are responsible for managing a department and in some cases are responsible for other human resource functions such as employment, learning and development, and succession planning.

Some internal diversity leaders are business partners and still others act as change agents and take part in the actual implementation of various diversity interventions. In fact, the business partner role seems

TABLE 11.2 Diversity Practitioner Role Identity Factors

Role Identity Factor	Description
Advisor	Primary identification with providing strategic support and guidance to key organizational stakeholders (board of directors, leaders, line managers, and associates) regarding diversity matters; responsibilities include engaging in self-directed learning activities necessary to become an "expert" or taught leader in the field of workplace diversity; supporting organizational leaders devise overall enterprise and unit specific strategies and action plans to realize diversity related objectives; being a "cultural architect," and writing (mainly externals), representing the company (internals) or speaking about diversity to promote conceptual clarity about the meaning of diversity and how to realize its promise (both externals and internals).
Educator	Primary identification with teaching others about the "why," "what," and "how" of leveraging diversity; responsibilities include planning and/or directing diversity education programs including program design and development (or identification in the case of some internals), teaching, facilitating, and creating marketing and communication programs and materials as vehicles for learning using a wide of media (e.g., e-learning, newsletters, videos, lunch discussions, forums, etc.). Learning strategies include diversity awareness and skill building, as well as, reinforcement tools to drive learning transfer to the works of the organization.
Researcher	Primary identification with building and expanding what is known about effective diversity practice in organizations; responsibilities include conducting primary and exploratory research; diagnostic work including diversity/cultural audits and aligning these efforts with other assessment work in the organization; best practice benchmarking; measurement and evaluation tool development and activities.
Business partner	Primary identification with linking diversity with business strategy, for internals this includes striving to be a full member of the management team and integrating diversity into the core strategic planning, implementation and measurement processes in real time; responsibilities include aligning diversity with critical business issues, knowledge and skill transfer, building internal capability to leverage diversity by identifying and coaching diversity leaders/change agents.
Change agent	Primary identification with actually taking part in the execution of diversity programs and processes as individual contributors; core responsibility is the execution of designed diversity initiatives ranging from recruitment to learning and development; ensuring a tight connection between diversity-related intentions (or objectives) and outcomes (or results).
Manager	Primary identification with running the diversity function which includes supervising others, including direct reports, to assist in the design and implementation of various diversity processes; responsibilities include creating a vision for the function, establishing performance objectives and measures, ongoing coaching and counseling, rewarding the achievement of diversity related outcomes.

to be an emerging one, yet also seems to be associated with achieving measurable diversity-related results quickly, when compared to other internal diversity practitioners. In short, when an internal diversity practitioner is a strategic business partner in the full sense of the word, they have a seat at the executive decision-making table and often reports directly to the CEO or another very senior executive. One of our internal diversity leaders highlights the importance of situating the role in the organization for maximum success.

DIVERSITY PRACTITIONERS AS BUSINESS PARTNERS
(ADVICE FROM AN INTERNAL DIVERSITY LEADER)

In negotiating my role, I felt it important to report directly to the Chairman of the organization to lead this turnaround. I am a full member of the officer core. My peers are the presidents of our companies and the executive vice presidents of each of the staff groups. We are all at the strategy table. I am responsible for working with my colleagues to set a strategic vision for diversity. I then make sure that there's ownership of the strategy throughout the organization.

I coach and consult executives across the organization, because there are many crises related to diversity issues in the company, particularly in the beginning. I help my colleagues develop practical approaches to overcome barriers and effectively implement their diversity strategies. I run interference to ensure that groups can interact with the appropriate people to address various issues.

I can't execute the diversity strategy alone because it's multi-faceted. Everybody at the executive level has a piece of it. I can help people do what they need to do, and I will set the overall goal of what we need to achieve related to our diversity objectives and then make sure everybody owns a part of that, and then try to help people achieve it. But they need to be the drivers of it. This positioning of diversity enables me to focus on representing the company externally on diversity issues while internally integrating diversity into the strategic direction of the company.

— Chief Diversity Officer
Large U.S. Based Restaurant Group

Most internal diversity leaders across the U.S. are positioned at the director or manager levels. There are some who hold the title of Vice President, yet the title of Senior Vice President or some title that reflects being a direct report of the CEO is still rare, yet a growing trend. Is this is a reflection of the level of commitment to diversity held by Corporate America? Rightly or not, organizational title and reporting relationship sends a strong signal both internally and externally as to the importance placed on workplace diversity. Many senior leaders today proclaim a commitment to diversity and yet they position the diversity role two, three, and even four levels down in the organization. We invite you to think about where you have positioned or intend to situate the internal diversity role in your organization.

What is important to remember from the descriptions listed in Table 11.2 is that the way a person views themselves greatly affects their approach to diversity work and the results they achieve. In all cases, internal diversity leaders in best-in-class organizations focus on striving to position diversity as a strategic imperative and place a premium on execution to generate results. The advice from two of our internal diversity leaders presented on the following page capture the essence of the importance of getting things done.

It is important for senior executive sponsors to note that diversity research in best practice organizations demonstrates that the role of internal diversity leaders does, and should change over time (Table 11.3). Nevertheless, the trajectory outlined in the table, while proven to generate measurable and sustainable diversity results, is more the exception in organizations than the rule.

Securing Help from External Sources

Identifying the appropriate external resources to support diversity initiatives presents a real challenge to organizational leaders. The projected diversification of the workforce, as both women and minorities enter the workplace in greater proportions, has fueled the rapid proliferation of many, and often hastily prepared diversity practitioners whose objective is to help organizations achieve the purported promise of diversity. The reality is there are no barriers to entry, anyone who can convince an organization to secure their services can be a diversity consultant. There are many excellent external diversity experts available, buyer beware the quality varies greatly.

A FOCUS ON EXECUTION
(ADVICE FROM TWO INTERNAL DIVERSITY LEADERS)

I was hired because I'm known for getting results in terms of implementation, as opposed to just having the theoretical basis. That's what the CEO here wanted in a diversity person so he hired me. My role here is to frame diversity as a strategy for the successful integration of all our similarities and differences through processes that fully utilize everyone's capabilities and contribute to high performance and global leadership.

My responsibilities here include: (1) the whole recruitment and retention piece of how do you create an environment that can attract and retain the best talent anywhere (our people); (2) working with business leaders to figure out how do we ultimately maximize the human resources within the organization to make product and services and go after business opportunities anywhere in the world (our business) and (3) working with the senior leadership team to figure out how do you help create an environment where people work effectively together ... and have the ability to build relationships anywhere in the world (our markets)? We are not trying to create another 'United Nations' here; we are working to create a global mindset to support the business strategy.

— Director, Global Diversity
Fortune 1000 Metal Products Company

I was attracted to this organization because of the opportunity for growth and challenge. What brought me here was the challenge of turning things around and the leadership focus on the issues given the burning platform of the suit. I was with Johnson and Johnson, a very good company, prior to coming here. I left Digital Equipment Corporation to go to Johnson & Johnson. At J & J my role was more of an implementer of diversity programs, so it was not the strategist role I have here. I primarily worked to build and implement a lot of the work that an external consultant had done there. Here I'm involved in both the strategy and the implementation.

— Corporate Director, HR & Diversity
Fortune 40 Energy & Oil Company

TABLE 11.3 Defining the Internal Diversity Practitioner's Role

Role Maturity	Reporting Relationship and Focal Interventions
Lead Diversity Position: New role in the company or turnaround situation	Organizations that have only recently implemented the lead internal diversity practitioner role tend to have newly created or newly centralized diversity functions. At this early stage, organizations often elect to have this role report directly to the CEO, Executive Director, Provost, University President or some other very senior executive position as a means of gaining and displaying support for the diversity function. In a turnaround situation, this reporting relationship is essential to ensure the senior executive level focus and committed needed to generate measurable results quickly. In both start-up and turnaround diversity situations, progressive leaders understand for both internal and external purposes, it's best that the position be one of high rank, reporting directly to the senior most person in the organization so they know exactly what is going on at all times and the entire senior team has an ongoing opportunity to learn to integrate a diversity perspective in their daily operations. This reporting relationship also sends a powerful message internally that diversity is a senior officer role of the organization. Goals of the incumbent in this context focus on clearly defining the role and gaining support; devising a preliminary diversity strategy linked to strategic organizational priorities; the strategy should be grounded in a comprehensive situation analysis that is externally focused, internal cultural audit findings combined with diversity self-work for all senior executives to foster internalized leadership commitment. Systems work of executive level staffing and promotions, succession planning and creating clear consequences and payoffs for achieving diversity objectives. Here the diversity function is generally quite small (one to three people) to stay focused and strategic. This stage is foundation and results-focused at the top of the organization and generally takes 1–2 years to establish.
Established process	Here both the lead diversity role and function are established parts of the organization. As a result the lead diversity person's goals become more focused upon gaining buy-in from the entire organization on both the foundational work of diversity awareness and moving toward more "issue-specific" and developmentally sequenced diversity interventions such as addressing race-based tension, gender communication and relations, sexual orientation, cross-functional collaboration, vendor programs, and so on. The lead diversity person also continues to work with senior leaders to achieve executive parity. At this stage the lead diversity person begins to partner more with HR professionals to facilitate a cultural shift that incorporates a diversity perspective into the everyday operations of the organization. Every people practice (e.g., recruitment, training and development, performance management, etc.) must be examined and modified as necessary to be inclusive of various diversity perspectives and to see that management implements each practice in ways that promote equity.

TABLE 11.3 (*Continued*)

Role Maturity	Reporting Relationship and Focal Interventions
	A focus on comprehensive systems alignment at all levels of the organization is critical to sustain diversity progress and continuously raise the bar. Diversity must be linked to all people systems, organizational structure, work processes, measurement, reward systems and a broad-based cultural change effort. The diversity/issue specific and cultural integration stage takes between 2 to 4 years.
Long-term established process	At this stage, both the role and the diversity function have been established in the organization for some time. The integration of diversity goals and perspectives into all organizational units should be achieved to the extent that no one person or group is responsible for realizing diversity objectives. Rather, diversity is a part of everyone's job and the lead diversity person's role is to maintain these achievements and continue to support proactive initiatives. Here the reporting relationship is generally moved to the senior most HR person (3 years or more to achieve).

Despite the current reality, organizational leaders can take steps to ensure they identify appropriate external resources for their situation and the outcomes they hope to achieve through leveraging diversity. The first step is to be clear about your starting point (both personally and organizationally). The second step is to understand what's available and devise strategies for determining what resources will be a fit for your situation at various points in time. Here we provide some insights that might help get you started.

Some external diversity experts work almost exclusively with senior executives serving as advisor and educator. It is not unusual for their contracts to extend over 3 years. Most of these advisors have written a number of books about various aspects of diversity and have spent a great deal of their time developing educational materials, training current and future diversity practitioners, consulting and speaking at various conferences. Experts of this caliber are excellent education and training resources for organizations and can work effectively with people at all levels.

Other diversity experts approach their work from a research perspective and as a result are able to identify patterns across organizations and share their insights with broad audiences through their published research. They also conduct training programs for current or future diversity practitioners and are highly sought after keynote speakers for both organizations and conferences. This type of research-oriented expert is an excellent resource during the front-end diagnostic phase of the process because of their research capabilities in addition to providing education and training, generally to more senior audiences.

There is also a more general external diversity expert type. These are consultants who have transitioned from working inside of organizations to external consulting. They usually were in senior HR positions and have first hand experience working with diversity initiatives in the companies where they worked. An expert of this type said the following about their how they go about the business of helping their clients. Despite differences in role identity and approach, most external diversity practitioners self identify with the advisor and educator aspects of the role.

DIVERSITY PRACTITIONERS AS CHIEF DIVERSITY STRATEGISTS
(ADVICE FROM AN EXTERNAL DIVERSITY EXPERT)

My work involves consulting to executives, diversity leaders, and human resources professionals. With executives it primarily takes the form of briefings and one-on-one alignment sessions that focus on the "what," "why," and "how" of diversity.

My work with internal diversity professionals emphasizes professional development. This is more of a mindset than a competency, and says, "I care about your development and your success." I put in writing, "Part of what I will do is to help you develop the expertise needed to move the diversity process forward in this organization." So I'm not only there to support, to help, to challenge, but to make sure that you need fewer of my services, because you now know how to do what we did together yesterday.

One of the ways to drive that mindset that I use, if it's a company, I buy stock in the company, which forces me to think as a shareholder, and, as a shareholder, I don't want you wasting money on consultants who need to be doing this. But also, as a shareholder, I want you to do it right, and I have expertise to help you do it right, so I will appropriately use my expertise to help you do it right.

Whether internal or external, the role of the diversity practitioner is that of a strategist, with an emphasis on designing and implementing developmentally sequenced interventions which take into account differences in cultural styles and organizational patterns of behavior.

— Principle,
Organizational Effectiveness and Diversity Consulting Firm

TABLE 11.4 Selecting Diversity Resources: Planning Tool

Topic	Considerations
Definition of Diversity How do you define diversity? Why?	*Rationale:* This is a foundational question because the way a diversity professional defines diversity has in impact on how they approach the work. In other words exploring not only how they define diversity but why they define it in a given way provides valuable insights into their assumptions, what they will tend to focus on by way of intervention and by extension the range of possible outcomes. *Content:* Listen for the extent to which they define it broadly (i.e., inclusive of multiple dimensions such as age, race, gender, class, organizational role, culture, personal style, markets, globalization, etc.) or apply the narrow definition (i.e., EEO/AA and other legal requirements). Definition should capture both diversity's descriptive nature (i.e., the dimensions) and dynamic nature (i.e., diversity as a learning and change process, both its potential to be leveraged and its negative consequences when not managed such as various "isms," discrimination or other forms of injustice.
Critical Success Factors What are the "vital few" things that must be in place for diversity to be successful?	*Rationale:* An extension of the first question with a focus on uncovering the change levers a diversity professional believe are essential for designing, implementing, and monitoring diversity initiatives. *Content:* Senior leadership support and broad ownership; clear and focused approach to organizational change; clear vision for diversity grounded in a clear "business" case/rationale; assessment and research; alignment with key strategic organizational priorities and organizational systems (accountability, rewards, and policy); identification/ development of change agents; education and strategic learning strategies; supplier diversity; community outreach and foundation alignment; and monitoring/measure process. Gather practical examples of each.
Situation Analysis What is your approach to assessing the situation and deciding how to proceed?	*Rationale:* Diversity is a broad and complex area of organizational change work and as a result a clear, comprehensive, yet timely upfront assessment of the organization's performance cultural drivers is essential for establishing an approach that meets the unique needs of a given situation.

TABLE 11.4 (*Continued*)

Topic	Considerations
	Content: Listen for the extent to which the diversity professional has a systematic approach to needs assessment and best practice research; should include multiple methods that capture both quantitative data (i.e., numbers/facts) and qualitative data (i.e., perceptions and experiences); use of existing data and performance measures, survey and documentation; focus on cost effectiveness of approach, use of feedback and target outcomes/deliverables. Experience with the diversity discovery process described in Chapter 6 and best practices.
Gaining Commitment How will you secure support for the various diversity initiatives from leaders across the organization?	*Rationale*: Diversity often competes with other high priority organizational change initiatives, so diversity professional need to have clear strategies for keeping diversity on the leadership agenda. *Content*: Listen for direct experience in working with senior executives and success with keeping them actively engaged in leading the diversity learning and change process; sound approach for clarifying the diversity vision, business case and personal rationale; solicit specific examples of demonstrating this capability.
Making the Case How do you help leaders connect diversity to organizational effectiveness?	*Rationale*: This is the "why" of diversity work needed to sustain momentum over time, if there is no why, then the "what" and the "how" quickly lose focus. *Content*: Elements include the "war of talent" based on changing population demographics; target marketing and cross-functional teamwork; market placed demographics; leveraging diverse employee resource groups; employee engagement; and productivity and cost avoidance.
Education and Training What is the role of education and training in making diversity happen?	*Rationale*: Important to ensure the diversity professional takes a developmentally sequenced approach to learning and change. *Content*: Listen for how they launch the education & training process (e.g., begin by clarifying definitions of diversity and related concepts; the business case, self-awareness and self-management first, awareness of others & relationships with others second); how they design and roll-out

learning (i.e., awareness, skill building, application, based on needs assessments and ongoing feedback and measurement, customized vs. off the shelf; models and tools; head and hand work required, strive for heart work).

Human Resources Function Connection
How do you align diversity process work with HR function?

Rationale: There is a critical overlap between diversity and the people systems managed through the HR function, diversity professionals need a clear approach for forming partnerships with HR professionals.
Content: Listen for experience with making linkages from recruitment to retirement; use to eliminate potential barriers of HR systems reinforcing behaviors counter to diversity; linkages to succession planning, performance assessment and recognition and reward early in the process.

Dealing with Resistance/Backlash
How do you deal with and even work to avoid the potential for diversity related backlash or resistance?

Rationale: When progress is made with leveraging diversity resistance is often encouraged because it requires a very personal change in individuals in addition to the organization, anticipating, recognizing, and addressing various form of resistance is an additional critical success factor.
Content: Listen for a clear approach to, and understanding of, conflict and negotiations across differences; effective strategies include addressing style differences, separating the content of the disagreement from the people, sequencing of interventions developmentally to build cultural change muscle, choice of implementation and delivery change agents.

Measurement
What is your approach to helping clients monitor progress?

Rationale: The language of organizational effectiveness is numbers and outcomes. Diversity is not real if clear measures and expectations are not put in place, in short, no metrics, no movement. We get measures signals what's important to the organization, what we measured, gets done.
Content: A detailed treatment of measurement is covered in Chapter 8, Two classes of measures are needed: (1) process measures (which serve as early indicators such as employees perceptions on climate surveys) and (2) outcome measures (results achieved such as progress toward executive parity objectives, improved retention rates across primary dimensions of diversity, productivity gains, increases in share in target diverse markets).

TABLE 11.4 (*Continued*)

Topic	Considerations
Critical Skill Set What essential competencies will you bring to the diversity change and learning process?	*Rationale*: This is a nice way to pull all the previous areas of inquiry into an overall assessment that capture the diversity professional's assumptions about effective practice and the capabilities needed for both strategic planning and execution. *Content*: Listen for essential competencies in three broad categories and how each align with responses to the practitioner's overall approach to diversity: (1) *knowledge areas* (e.g., diversity best practices, history of diversity movement, theoretical grounding in social and racial identity theory, information processing & decision making theory and legal requirements such as AA/EEO, knowledge of individual, group and organizational change theories), (2) *skills* (i.e., change management, emotional intelligence and interpersonal skills, design and development of learning interventions, leadership and influence skills and research and diagnostic skills, diversity specific skills such as dealing with the "isms"), and (3) *personal attributes* (e.g., adaptability, courage and staying power, passion for social justice, pragmatic and results oriented, sense of humor, personal stress management, creditability & credentialed). Diversity professional often draw from a multi-disciplinary knowledge base that includes psychology, sociology, anthropology, applied organizational behavior (e.g., culture, leadership, power and authority, group dynamics), business administration and adult learning.

Prepare for the Conversation

Selecting internal and external sources to support you in your leadership of leveraging diversity for performance breakthrough is a crucial decision, one that requires preparation and thought. The Productive Conversation framework introduced in Chapter 9 is a useful tool in helping you prepare for these important conversations. How will you launch the conversation by engaging with potential resources? What is your purpose? What critical questions will you ask during the progressing phase of the conversation to advance your purpose to inform your selection decision? We conclude this chapter with Table 11.4 where we provide you with a list of 10 topic areas and considerations to prompt your thinking.

References

Crane, T. G. *The Heart of Coaching: Using Transformational Coaching to Create a High-Performance Culture.* San Diego, CA: FTA Press, 2002.

Egan, G. *The Skilled Helper: A Problem-Management and Opportunity-Development Approach to Helping.* Pacific Grove, CA: Thomson Learning, 2002.

Lewin, K. "Group Decision and Social Change." In E. E. Maccoby, T. M. Newcomb and E. L. Hartley (eds.). *Readings in Psychology.* New York, NY: Holt, Rinehart & Winston, 1958.

Lippitt, G., and Lippitt, R. *The Consulting Process in Action,* 2nd ed. San Diego, CA: Pfeiffer & Company, 1986.

Schein, E. H. *Organizational Culture and Leadership,* 3rd ed. San Francisco, CA: Jossey-Bass, 2004.

LEVERAGING DIVERSITY BEGINS AND ENDS WITH LEADERSHIP

Part IV concludes our journey together. Throughout this book, we positioned leveraging diversity as a cyclical process of learning and change. We suggested that this self-renewing cycle requires ongoing strategic learning and adaptation to respond to changes in the internal and external business environments. In our concluding chapter, we present two perspectives that we believe are vital to your success as you lead the process of transforming your organization into one that effectively leverages diversity.

12

A Leadership Mindset: Outside-In and Inside-Out

If you don't know where you are going, any road will take you there.

— Anonymous

Throughout the book we demonstrate that leading to leverage diversity is as much of a leadership mindset as it is a set of action strategies and tactics. As we conclude, we remind you that leveraging diversity requires ongoing engagement in a learning and change process to help you determine where you want to go and how to get there. We want to re-emphasize this is not a linear process. Rather, we have found it is a two-pronged cyclical process that combines outside-in and inside-out work. We close the book by focusing on the final leadership practice:

Leadership Practice 12

Lead from the Outside-In and the Inside-Out

Two Perspectives of Diversity Leadership: Outside-In and the Inside-Out

The essence of outside-in work is the development of strategic initiatives that respond to changes in the external environment, or outside of the organization. Inside-out work emphasizes individual learning and change initiatives, which insure a work environment conducive to performance breakthroughs. And most important, effectively leveraging diversity requires that outside-in efforts and inside-out efforts interact seamlessly. The outcome of the dynamic interplay between the two is a set of organizational and individual transformations that impact our way of thinking, behaving and over time, our very being—who we are as individuals and collectives.

One of our study participants, the Vice President, Global Diversity for a Fortune 50 consumer and personal products company based in the Midwestern United States, clearly understood the importance of combining outside-in and inside-out work. He spoke about the reasons behind his company's diversity initiatives saying, "Diversity, at the end of the day, internally, is about cornering the market on the top talent on the planet (*outside-in*).

We are still one of the companies that are committed to promotion from within. So basically it is our life-blood in terms of the inputs that we have. We have to be sure that individuals are groomed, developed and move up in a manner that would have a continuous leadership pipeline reflecting the input that we have (*inside-out*)."

The popular press and organizational change management literature (e.g., Beer and Nohria, 2000; Cameron and Quinn, 1999; Heifetz and Linsky, 2002) provide many examples to illustrate the high failure rate for most change management efforts. The evidence of large, complex organizations' capability to adapt to the constantly changing external environment is not encouraging. For example, two-thirds of the firms on the Fortune 500 list in 1970 no longer exist. Dun and Bradstreet reports that only 7 percent of the 9 million companies currently registered in the United States have been in existence for 50 years or more. These data show that longevity in corporations is the exception, not the rule.

Large-scale diversity change efforts are among the most difficult change initiatives facing Corporate America today. Many of these efforts spend little time or money on the initiatives and failure is predictable. Others spend millions of dollars and an extraordinary amount of time and still fail. The diversity experts in our study were all clear about one thing: When an organization is successful in its diversity change initiative, it is the dynamic outside-in and inside-out process that stands out as a critical success factor.

When comparing diversity leadership from the outside-in to diversity leadership from the inside-out, one sees several distinguishing factors ranging from the type of questions that guide action and decision-making, to the motivators for a given change, to the type of interventions that will yield a given set of outcomes or results. Table 12.1 illustrates that each has a different emphasis, is guided by different questions, and generates different outcomes.

It is the dynamic interplay between these two leadership perspectives (outside-in and inside-out) that holds the potential for the individual and organizational transformation needed to leverage diversity for performance breakthroughs and to sustain gains over time.

When diversity initiatives are driven by the outside-in perspective alone, as soon as the organizational leadership changes or turns its

TABLE 12.1 Two Perspectives of Diversity Leadership

	Outside-In	Inside-Out
Emphasis (Guiding Questions)	Organizational transformation • How do we radically change our patterned organizational responses to difference? • How do we unleash the power and potential of diversity to drive performance breakthroughs?	Individual transformation • How do I change my perspectives about difference? • How can I engage with others in ways that are more open and inclusive of multiple perspectives?
Motivation (The "Why")	Common external motivators • Changing workforce, consumer and market demographics • Globalization • Government regulation and legal action	Common internal motivators • Multi-cultural challenges in the workplace • Other cultural living experiences • Personal experiences with difference
Change Drivers (The "How")	Organizational culture and climate change	Critical thinking and reflection skills
Desired Result/ Outcome	Adaptive and responsive organizations Effective and efficient organizations	Individual commitment and meaningful work Continuous learning and renewal

Source: Authors' adaptation from Gregory M. Henderson's, "Transformative Learning as a Condition for Transformational Change in Organizations," in *Human Resource Development Review*, Elwood F. Holton III, ed. (2002, pp. 186–214); and Terrence E. Maltbia's, *The Journey of Becoming a Diversity Practitioner* (2001).

attention to other strategic priorities, the system often loses focus, bounces back, or has difficulty sustaining gains. As an internal diversity practitioner said, "One of the most difficult things about diversity is that it is a process—a process that takes time. And, it is extremely difficult to maintain and continue to do in the organization over years. Organizational changes are made, strategic direction changes and people change. You've got to be ready to go back to the same business sector when there is change in leadership, a new President, and not assume the new cat has the message." Although his message is clearly one of the warnings—the job is never done—he also makes it obvious that the strength of your diversity learning and change process depends on leadership and as leadership changes so does the leadership agenda.

Throughout this book we emphasized that leveraging diversity is a leadership challenge. As we close we want to leave you with the thought that leadership may change, but the challenge does not go away. To survive in the global economy, leveraging diversity is not an option. Rather it is an imperative.

References

Beer, M., and Nohria, N. "Cracking the Code of Change." *Harvard Business Review* (May–June)(2000): 133–141.

Cameron, K.S., and Quinn, R.E. "Diagnosing and Changing Organizational Culture." *Series on Organizational Development*. Upper Saddle River, NJ: Prentice Hall, 1999.

Heifetz, R. A., and Linsky, M. *Leadership on the Line: Staying alive through the dangers of leading*. Boston, MA: Harvard Business School Press, 2002, pp. 13–26

Henderson, G. M. "Transformative Learning as a Condition for Transformational Change in Organization." In F. H. Elwood, III (ed.). *Human Resource Development Review*. Thousand Oaks, CA: Sage, 2002, pp. 186–214.

Maltbia, T.E. "The Journey of Becoming A Diversity Practitioner: The connection between experience, learning and competence." Unpublished Dissertation, UMI Dissertation Services, Ann Arbor, MI, 2001.

Appendixes

Appendix A: External Case Profiles

Participant Information (Pseudonyms Used)		
Case Participant	**Title**	**Organizational Profile**
1. Meg Auerbach/ Susanne Barre	Partners	The consulting firm of Auerbach & Barre provides a range of services including organizational assessment and cultural change work; custom diversity training and train-the-trainer certification; facilitating diversity councils and a variety of human behavior-related services such as team building, conflict management, stress management, and change.
2. Vivian Barnes	Chief Executive Officer	Vivian Barnes is the founder, president, and CEO of Vivian Barnes Associates (VBA), an organization development consulting firm. Many companies may spend more than million dollars annually over the course of several years for Vivian's diversity process. VBA's core philosophy is the amelioration of oppression (i.e., racism, sexism, heterosexism, ageism, anti-Semitism, and other systemic forms of discrimination).

(Continued)

Participant Information (Pseudonyms Used)		
Case Participant	**Title**	**Organizational Profile**
3. Martin Cheever	Co-Director	The Intercultural Communication Institute (ICI), a private, non-profit foundation, was founded on the beliefs that education and training in the area of intercultural communication can improve competence in dealing with cultural difference and thereby minimize destructive conflict among national, ethnic, and other cultural groups.
4. Portia Fenster	President	Portia & Associates provides products and services in the areas of conflict management, coaching, organization change, strategic planning, and diversity training. EPA works with a variety of Fortune 500 companies in the utilities, publishing, food processing, financial services, and telecommunications fields as well as non-profit and government.
5. Paul Forbes	President	Forbes Productions has developed award-winning strategies in the field of diversity. The full line of services includes needs analysis work, gap analysis, benchmarking, strategic thinking, training, off-the-shelf tools, customizable materials, and product development based on client needs and offered in a variety of delivery systems.
6. Elizabeth Ford	Partner	Finch McNaughton, an international firm of management consultants, has provided innovative advice and assistance to organizations for over 60 years. The firm's mission is to help organizations improve business performance through people. Practice areas of focus

(*Continued*)

Participant Information (Pseudonyms Used)		
Case Participant	**Title**	**Organizational Profile**
		include diversity; total rewards, organization communication, workforce and organization research, and human resources outsourcing.
7. Kathryn Greggson	President	Greggson Associates, Inc. is a full-service consulting firm with broad experience and state-of-the-art expertise. As one of the oldest diversity concerns in the country, the firm has developed an integrated set of consulting and educational services including organization climate assessment; executive coaching and development; human resources planning; and design and implementation of diversity-related employee education.
8. Clarence Hardy	Principle	An independent consultant with a focus on organization effectiveness and diversity. Practice focuses on building internal capability around the management of diversity, including executive briefing sessions; working with human resources, diversity professionals, and diversity councils; needs assessment and measurement systems; and problem prevention and resolution.
9. Cara Hegal	Chief Executive Officer	Cultural Communication Concepts (CCC) deals with diversity and cross-cultural communication and has provided consultative services in the area of workplace diversity and cross-cultural communications in business. Services include training and speaking on diversity topics, and products range from books and training materials to videos.

(*Continued*)

Participant Information (Pseudonyms Used)		
Case Participant	**Title**	**Organizational Profile**
10. Saundra Creston/ Craig Graham	Chief Executive Officer Director of Research	The Metropolitan Diversity Institute was founded to address the economic imperative for managing diversity effectively in one of the most racially divided cities in the nation. Services include focus groups, assessments, and a full-scale diversity audit, all designed to assess the organization's climate for valuing diversity and creating a pluralistic environment.
11. Jonathan Paulson	President	Paulson Communication Consultants (PCC)'s core mission is preparing individuals and organizations to deal with social and cultural diversity in ways that value and respect differences, rather than, as has been the pattern, treating differences as a social factor that individuals had to repudiate or leave at the doorstep of the institution in order to better "fit in."
12. Theodore Stokes	Chief Executive Officer	T. Stokes Consulting and Training (TSCT) services and products provided by the TSCT include coaching on diversity strategy, education and awareness building, analysis and support for structural systems and process changes, training first-line supervisors, process consultation, integration of diversity with other change initiatives, organizational cultural analysis, public seminars, speakers bureaus, articles, books, and videos.

Appendix B: Internal Case Profiles

Participant Information		
Case Participant	**Title**	**Organizational Profile**
13. Lynn Blakely	Director, Workforce Effectiveness	Omnium Bank is the oldest commercial bank in the United States, and one of the largest bank holding companies in the country, offering a full range of banking and financial solutions to corporations and governments internationally. The Bank's President and Chief Operating Officer commented on diversity in an annual report *"We are deeply committed to building a diverse workforce, and are confident that we can and must effectively manage our diversity."*
14. Michael Calderon	Director, Global Diversity	Intercron operates in the metal products industry, with sales revenues approaching three billion. Intercron firmly believes that maintaining its quality reputation, progressive work environment, and international growth is directly related to achieving diversity in the workplace and hiring the best talent available. The role of diversity is to realize the strategy by achieving high performance through multicultural team building, problem solving, and performance excellence.
15. Phil Chalmers	Corporate Director, HR and Diversity	Essanta is a major producer, marketer, and distributor of crude oil, natural gas liquids and natural gas, high-quality fuels and lubricant products, transportation and distribution facilities, and alternate forms of energy for power and manufacturing. The company is committed to developing a

(Continued)

Participant Information		
Case Participant	**Title**	**Organizational Profile**
		world-class, diverse workforce, with explicit leadership development at all levels. The organization experienced a major setback with the well-publicized settlement of its highly publicized racial discrimination lawsuit. Since that time Essanta has been recognized externally for its progress. For example, an article in *Business Week* states, "Essanta is recognized as a 'model for ridding corporate corridors of discrimination.'"
16. Clifton Eubanks	Director, Diversity, EEO and Work-life	Transcorp Insurance Company is a publicly held personal lines insurance company with revenues of nearly 26 billion dollars. Internal surveys indicate that employees increasingly say the company is meeting their expectations for regular feedback and communication, meaningful work and learning opportunities, respectful interactions and recognition, and rewards. In a 1998 survey of 48 leading U.S. corporations, Transcorp employees responded with the highest overall job satisfaction rating of any company. One area of focus is workforce diversity where the company has received an impressive list of external recognition.
17. Alberta Feinstein	Corporate VP, Global Diversity	X-Star is a global producer of electronics and communication equipment, systems and components. Beginning in the late 1980s and building on the lessons learned from the

(*Continued*)

Participant Information		
Case Participant	**Title**	**Organizational Profile**
		company's pioneering work in quality, X-Star positioned diversity as a platform for attracting and deploying the talent needed to execute the company's strategy around the world. The company's diversity strategy has received coveted awards in recognition of exemplary workforce diversity practice. The company believes diversity is good for business, its revenues were 9.5 billion when it started its diversity journey; by the end of 1997, revenues had grown to 28.7 billion.
18. Ray Holmes	Corporate VP, Global Diversity and HR Center of Expertise	Cunningham and Flyte (C&F) is a major producer of family care, household care, and personal products, with net sales over 38 billion. The company's 110,000 employees produce over 300 products for more than 5 billion consumers in over 140 countries around the world. The Chairman & Chief Executive in an internal company document stated *"Our success as a global company is a direct result of our diverse and talented workforce. Our ability to develop new consumer insights and ideas and to execute in a superior way across the world is the best possible testimony to the power of diversity any organization could ever have."* The company has received an impressive list of external recognition for its diversity programs.
19. Gayle Robbins-Carson	Chief Diversity Officer	Franky's Restaurants is the Pastora Restaurant Group's only national chain. In addition to

(Continued)

Participant Information		
Case Participant	**Title**	**Organizational Profile**
		Franky's, the company is comprised of four other restaurant chains, including Carrow's, Coco's, El Pollo Loco, and City Range. In total, the company operates nearly 3,000 restaurants, with revenues exceeding 2 billion annually, and more than 100,000 employees. Franky's, with its troubled past [i.e., a 54 million-dollar class action discrimination settlement that made the national headlines], is an emerging success story in diversity. Since that time, Franky's and Pastora have received numerous awards for achieving one of the nation's most racially diverse workforces.
20. Carol Thompson	Director, Corporate Diversity	Bulwer-Kemp core businesses include mail, production mail, facsimile, copiers, business, and financial services. Bulwer-Kemp's long-standing history of social responsibility and valuing diversity dates back to the 1940s. The company's CEO states *"Bulwer-Kemp is nationally recognized for our innovative and resourceful leadership in promoting diversity. The most strategic way for us to realize our business objectives is to leverage our unique and diverse workforce. It is the talent and productivity of our people that will sustain our competitive leadership now and well into the 21st century."* The company has been recognized for its comprehensive and strategic approach to diversity.

Appendix C1: Definitions of Diversity (Expert Sample)

Definitions of Diversity: Expert Voices	
Diversity Experts	**Description**
Case #1: Meg Auerbach and Susanna Barre	The definition must be "all-inclusive," number one, because it needs to encompass everybody. From a practical perspective, but also realistically, none of us are so simple to be described by one or two dimensions or descriptors. (Susanna) I think an all-inclusive definition of diversity encompasses the complexity of human experience, identity, and identity formation. (Meg)
Case #2: Vivian Barnes	Diversity means simply heterogeneity, or the advent of people who were previously excluded from, in the context of the workplace, corporations. Prior to 1964, corporate America was homogeneous. After that, with the change of law and the demographic changes in the United States, the workforce became and has increasingly become more heterogeneous, i.e., diverse. That is simply what it means; it doesn't mean anything else. The concept of managing diversity, then, is an effort to ameliorate racism, sexism, and other forms of discrimination in organizations. The work of managing diversity is about helping people and organizations transform from cultures based on homogeneity to those characterized by heterogeneity. The concept of managing diversity is an effort to ameliorate racism, sexism, and other forms of discrimination in organizations. The work of managing diversity is about helping people and organizations transform from cultures based on homogeneity to those characterized by heterogeneity.
Case #3: Martin Cheever	Intercultural communication is, as we are defining it, diversity in cultural terms, which is not the only way to define diversity — but it's one powerful way. Here we are saying, 'What happens, given that we have got people who are culturally diverse coming in face to face or having interactional contact with one another? What's the down side of that? How can we minimize the damage? What's the up side of it? How can we maximize the benefits?' Cultural diversity refers to people defining different types of behaviors and values in the context of two or more cultures interacting.

(*Continued*)

Definitions of Diversity: Expert Voices	
Diversity Experts	**Description**
Case #4: Portia Fenster	I use a definition of diversity that is generally accepted in my circles, that is, "all the ways in which we are different."
Case #9: Cara Hegel	Diversity refers to that variety of abilities, races, personalities, genders, ages, ethnicities, and other types of human difference that contribute and pertain to the harmonious and productive functioning of a given organization.
Case #5: Paul Dobson Forbes	I believe diversity should be defined in the broadest possible way. Not only does diversity include differences of age, race, gender, physical ability, sexual orientation, religion, socioeconomic class, education, region of origin, language, and so forth, but also differences in life experience, such as position in family, personality, job function, rank within organizational hierarchy, and other such characteristics that go into forming an individual's perspective of the world. Within an organization, diversity encompasses every individual difference that affects a task or relationship. Diversity also has an impact on the products and services developed by its workforce, as well as on personal, interpersonal, and organizational activities.
Case #6: Elizabeth Ford	I use the broader definition of diversity, in the three tiers of primary, secondary and organizational levels of diversity. The primary ones [are] the ones that don't change, we're born with them or acquire them early on in life. The secondary ones relate to the choices we make, and the third one would be organizational. And the managing diversity concept, my definition of managing diversity is creating an environment that works for everyone, regardless of primary, secondary, or organizational differences. Diversity is about creating this inclusive environment
Case #7: Kathryn Greggson	I describe diversity as group-based differences, not just individual differences. While this is a distinction that other people in the field don't often make, it is the group-based differences that lead to more fractious interaction, conflicts, misunderstanding, and stereotyping. In fact, individual differences, if not effectively negotiated, may become stereotypes.
Case #8: Clarence Hardy	I define diversity as all the ways in which we differ. [It] has a dual focus on similarities and differences that include common factors of human intelligence and

(*Continued*)

Definitions of Diversity: Expert Voices	
Diversity Experts	**Description**
	cognitive processes. Personality styles such as those rooted in Jungian psychology are examples of this. Related key concepts include unity without uniformity, and relationship between the ideas of sameness, fairness, and effectiveness. Creativity and innovation are difficult to achieve without diversity. If we accept this idea, we must also accept that it is neither fair nor effective to treat everyone the same.
Case #10: Metropolitan Diversity Institute (Saundra Creston)	We define diversity as shared and unshared differences. To a large extent, what you find is people [or consultants] focused on the differences. And what you need to do, based on the research literature, is also focus on the similarities that people have, the commonalties, because our cognitive psychologists and cognitive theory show us that our minds automatically process information differences automatically.
Case #11: Jonathan Paulson	As a firm, we pretty much define diversity in ethnic terms, that is, the culture conflicts that develop from different national ethnic backgrounds. We're also sensitive to the minority experience of discrimination in others as shaping issues relative to trust. Anything that bears on the communication process is something that we would include in the scope of our interest in diversity. We recognize, however, that people define diversity in terms of age and sexual orientation and disability. And we certainly would agree that those are differences that matter in terms of social access. And insofar as our goal at one level is equity and inclusion, social equity, social inclusion, any group that ends up being disqualified for reasons of race, gender, ethnicity, but also age, disability, sexual orientation, would certainly qualify in our definition of diversity. But it's not an area of our expertise.
Case #12: Theodore Stokes	Diversity refers to the collective mixture, characterized by similarities and differences. We use the term "diversity" as we use the word "stew." In the workplace, diversity defined from the perspective of the manager is the process of creating and maintaining an environment that naturally enables all participants to contribute their full potential in pursuit of organizational and personal objectives.

Appendix C2: Definitions of Diversity (Internal Sample)

Definitions of Diversity: Voices from the Front Line	
Internal Diversity Leaders	**Description**
Case #13: Lynn Blakely	I define diversity quite broadly; that is, the human differences that exists. I recognize that, in the minds of many, there is a fine line between "all differences" and "what matters." I think the risk that we run is that we trivialize institutionalized differences like racism, and homophobia, and sexism, and things that affect an entire class of people. At the same time, I think there's a much broader range of differences that we need to pay attention to that form a person's point of view and the experiences and talent they bring into an organization.
Case #14: Michael Calderon	At Intercron, we defined diversity as "all the ways we are similar and different that effects our interaction and performance." Building on my work at Deluxe, and my current situation at Intercron, diversity is defined as "the successful integration of all our similarities and differences through processes which fully utilize everyone's capabilities, and result in high performance and global leadership."
Case #15: Phil Chalmers	What I've done over the years is to first build on the idea of valuing differences, and this foundation is very important. I have evolved to the point where I now understand the criticality of having an inclusive process that as an outcome gives you respect for the individual. This is a different way of looking at valuing differences. Because what I'm saying is that you've got to have inclusive processes. You've got to have the things that include people, whether it's your systems, organizational change work, whatever it is. It's got to be an inclusive process that has as one outcome respect for the individual. For me, focusing on this outcome transforms diversity to a broad and global concept. If you respect individuals, if you value individuals, and if you include individuals, no matter where you are in the world, for me, this is the behavioral outcome that we're trying to achieve here at Essanta.

(*Continued*)

Definitions of Diversity: Voices from the Front Line	
Internal Diversity Leaders	**Description**
Case #16: Clifton Eubanks	I define the concept of diversity broadly. I believe it important that the concept of diversity not be limited to ethnicity and gender. So, I define diversity as "all of the ways in which we are different." And then I apply this, being asking "How do we take those differences and leverage them in such a way as to create a product or service that is best in class?" At Transcorp, the focus is firmly on accepting differences. We've defined diversity as creating this environment of inclusiveness, where everybody feels that they are being valued.
Case #17: Alberta Feinstein	In a word, diversity is about "differences." This definition is simple and very broad-based, that is diversity, referring to "the differences that make each individual unique." While this broad and inclusive definition is my starting point, I immediately focus on the dimensions of race and gender, because in this country if you aren't talking race and gender, you're really not talking diversity. You're really asking people to act like they're thinking about some thing, which we know they're not thinking about. You're asking them not to hold any accountability for it. Because you know they're not going to do anything if they can say, "We're doing something around diversity." Doing "something" around diversity does not get results. So in this country, being clear about the desired outcomes associated with diversity work is critical.
Case #18: Ray Holmes	We [at Cunningham and Flyte] define diversity in the broadest sense. As we look at our 104,000 people around the world, I have a vision that each one of them can close their eyes and see themselves in the picture relative to if they bring their talents, skills, dreams, and ambitions into the workplace. We have the kind of environment, culture, and work processes that will enable them to actualize to the extent that they want to vis-à-vis improving their contribution and whatever goes along with that.

(Continued)

Definitions of Diversity: Voices from the Front Line	
Internal Diversity Leaders	**Description**
Case #19: Gayle Robbins-Carson	I know the politically correct answer is to define diversity all inclusively. But if we can get half the population to operate in productive collaborative relationships with the other half (that's the gender piece) and the other two-thirds of the population talking with the other one-third (that's the race piece); then I think everything else about diversity could be transferable to the other differences captured in the broader definition of diversity. And I believe this is the work, because I see all my years of being in this (i.e., diversity) business, it boils down to race and gender.
Case #20: Carol Thompson	Diversity is simply the differences between individuals … My own definition of diversity centers around and mirrors how much of the literature defines the concept, that is framing diversity in terms of individuals' differences such as age, race, gender, background, where people grew up, what their education level is. At Bulwer-Kemp, diversity is defined in terms of objective and subjective characteristics. Objective characteristics include age, race, gender, religious beliefs, ethnicity, family circumstance, sexual orientation, physical and mental abilities, and education. Subjective characteristics include values, ethics, standards, prejudices, thinking, perceptions, motives, politics, decision, and work style.

Appendix D: Sample Sources of Conducting Cultural Audits

Sample Sources for Conducting Cultural Audits	
Source	Description
Gallup Organization	*Q-12 and I-10 Surveys:* The Q-12 is a short, yet powerful survey tool designed to gain a snapshot of the level of employee engagement generally linked to core performance metrics; the I-10 questions focus on dimensions associated with workplace inclusion.
Gardenswartz & Rowe, Consultants	The Consulting team of Lee Gardenswartz and Anita Rowe has developed a number of excellent resources to start upfront diversity/cultural audit work and ongoing support for the diversity learning and change process. A sample of three sources are listed below
Emotional Intelligence and Diversity Institute	*The Global Diversity Desk Reference* — by Lee Gardenswartz and Anita Rowe, with Patricia Digh and Martin F. Bennett. Great source for grounding diversity from a global perspective that includes a very extensive treatment of the concept of culture. The book includes a tool for conducting a "global diversity strategy audit," and several tools to support the design and conduct of the "employee systems review" component of the diversity audit, specifically related to selection, training, and performance management. *Managing Diversity: A complete desk reference and planning guide* — by Lee Gardenswartz and Anita Rowe. This source contains a chapter focused on "conducting a diversity audit" along with several tools throughout the book to support both the upfront audit, ongoing diversity awareness and skill building and aligning people systems such as performance management. *The Emotional Intelligence and Diversity Institute* — Gardenswartz and Rowe, Co-Directors The institute offers a "train-the-trainer" process with supporting tools to assist leaders and their organizations understand the role emotional intelligence plays in interpersonal effectiveness in diverse environments. The process focuses on four

(Continued)

Sample Sources for Conducting Cultural Audits	
Source	**Description**
	capabilities: (1) affirmative introspection (i.e., knowing and accepting self), (2) self governance (i.e., gaining mastery over emotions), (3) intercultural literacy (i.e., understanding a range of human behavior and (4) social architecting (i.e., structuring a compelling and respectful environment).
ODT Inc.	*The Questions of Diversity: Reproducible Assessment Tools for Organizations and Individuals* — by Dr. George F. Simons and Dr. Bob Abramms. This tool kit contains content that can guide both upfront diagnostic work related to the cultural audit process, as well as, on-going diversity awareness and skills training. This source includes an excellent primer understanding the diagnostic process, strategies for assessing organizational commitment to diversity, and suggestions for helping manager's surface their personal rationale for leveraging diversity. In addition, the workbook includes suggestions for co-creating the "case for diversity," clarifying the meaning of diversity, and tactics for linking diversity strategies to other core organizational efforts.
American Institute for Managing Diversity (AIMD)	*A Guide to Cultural Audits: Analyzing Organizational Culture For Managing Diversity* — by John D. Hucheson and Terri W. Kruzan. Comprehensive workbook that includes (1) a description of the cultural audit process; (2) a sample interview guide for executives, (3) employee interview guides, (4) sample questionnaires, (5) focus group questions and guidelines, (6) data analysis and synthesize tools and procedures, (7) recommended reporting and presentation guidelines, and (8) strategies for using data to drive the diversity learning and change process.

Appendix E: Six Mega-Social Trends

Six Mega Social Trends Shaping the World of Work	
Trend	Description
Trend 1: World's population expected to double in the next 40 years	The world's population reached 6.30 billion at the turn of the century and is expected to grow by almost two billion by 2025 then continue approach 12 billion by 2040; 80 percent of the world's population will be in countries least capable of supporting further population growth (e.g., Niger, Yemen, Angola and Uganda); the United Nations estimates a slower rate of growth predicts the world population to stabilize by 2100 at about 11 billion.
Trend 2: Fertility rates in many industrialized counties will decline	The birth rates on most developed countries (e.g., U.S. and Europe) are expected to drop below the replacement level and hence significant declines in populations, excluding the effects of immigration. In other words the population in developed nations is expected to fall from 23 percent of the total world population in 1950 and about 14 percent in 2000 to only 10 percent in 2050; this trend is likely to drive an increase in U.S. immigration and other developed counties in the future.
Trend 3: People in developed countries are living longer	Beginning in the 20th century, every generation in the U.S. has lived 3 years longer than the previous one on average, largely due to the development of new pharmaceuticals, medical technologies and government health programs; life expected increased from an average of 68.9 years for those born between 1950–1955 to an average of 76.5 for those born between 1995–2000; populations; increasingly workers are challenged to take care of both infant children and elderly parents and relatives during their working years, placing new demands on work-life balance.
Trend 4: Emergence of hyper-urbanization	The impact of the three trends listed above is expected to result in eight countries: Bangladesh, China, India, Nigeria, Pakistan, the United States, Ethiopia, and the Democratic Republic of Congo, accounting for one-half of all world population growth through 2050. Already, up to one-half of the populations in the largest cities in the developing world are living in unplanned and illegal squatter colonies that are highly vulnerable to disease and natural disasters.

(Continued)

| Six Mega Social Trends Shaping the World of Work ||
Trend	Description
Trend 5: Knowledge-dependent global society	Technological innovation and information has, and is expected to continue to transform the way we communicate and the nature of work; today 83 percent of management jobs in the U.S. require knowledge workers with Europe and Japan experiencing a similar shift; information has joined what economists have traditionally called the three factors of production: land, labor, and capital; given that knowledge is increasingly perishable, some observers predict that not everyone will be able to engage in life long learning resulting in severe social inequities.
Trend 6: Reality of cultural diversity	Aided by the unifying effect of mass media, we are experiencing the emergence of a truly global society, yet its effects are subject to local interruptions and reversals; information technologies have transform the ability to communicate with people across the globe; global organizations transferring people from one region of the world to the next is relating in the transfer of regional attitudes and values; intermarriage also continues to mix cultures geographically, ethnically and socially; and sexual orientation is emerging as a new force in many parts of the developed world; at the same time in many countries there are strong negative reactions to these changes sometimes resulting in increased conflict and even violence.

Index

Page numbers in *italics* indicate material presented in figures and tables